MISREADING THE BILL OF RIGHTS: TOP TEN MYTHS CONCERNING YOUR RIGHTS AND LIBERTIES

Kirby Goidel, Craig Freeman, and Brian Smentkowski

PRAEGER

AN IMPRINT OF ABC-CLIO, LLC
Santa Barbara, California • Denver, Colorado • Oxford, England

Copyright © 2015 by Kirby Goidel, Craig Freeman, and Brian Smentkowski

All rights reserved. No part of this publication may be reproduced, stored in a retrieval system, or transmitted, in any form or by any means, electronic, mechanical, photocopying, recording, or otherwise, except for the inclusion of brief quotations in a review, without prior permission in writing from the publisher.

Library of Congress Cataloging-in-Publication Data

Goidel, Robert K., 1967–author

  Misreading the bill of rights : top ten myths concerning your rights and liberties / Kirby Goidel, Craig Freeman, and Brian Smentkowski

    pages cm

  Includes bibliographical references and index.

    ISBN 978–1–4408–3233–8 (hardback) — ISBN 978–1–4408–3234–5 (ebook) 1. United States. Constitution. 1st-10th Amendments. 2. Civil rights—United States. I. Freeman, Craig, author. II. Smentkowski, Brian, author. III. Title.

KF4749.G63   2015

342.7308′5—dc23   2014044281

ISBN: 978–1–4408–3233–8
EISBN: 978–1–4408–3234–5

19 18 17 16 15   1 2 3 4 5

This book is also available on the World Wide Web as an eBook.
Visit www.abc-clio.com for details.

Praeger
An Imprint of ABC-CLIO, LLC

ABC-CLIO, LLC
130 Cremona Drive, P.O. Box 1911
Santa Barbara, California 93116-1911

This book is printed on acid-free paper ∞

Manufactured in the United States of America

Contents

Acknowledgments — vii

Introduction: Individual Freedoms, the Myths That Define Us, and American Public Opinion — ix

1. The Bill of Rights and the Myth of Individual Freedom — 1
2. Equally and for Everyone? Protecting Citizens Against the Federal Government — 11
3. The Myth of Unlimited Free Speech: Limited Freedom of Expression the American Way — 25
4. The Myth of a Free and Independent Press — 47
5. The Myth of a Christian Nation — 71
6. The Establishment Clause: Misreading or Myth? — 91
7. The Right to Bear Arms and the Myth of Gun Ownership: Guarding Against Tyranny, Not Your Neighbor — 113
8. Procedural Due Process and the Myth of Constitutional Loopholes as Criminal Protection — 131
9. The Right to Privacy and the Myth of Government Surveillance: Why We Believe in Privacy but Let Government into Our Homes — 151
10. Protections Against Cruel and Unusual Punishment and the Myth That Killing Isn't Cruel (or Unusual) — 169

Conclusion: Bringing the Frog of Citizenship to a Slow Boil — 189

Appendix: The Bill of Rights — 207

List of Cases Cited 213

Bibliography 217

Index 231

MISREADING THE BILL OF RIGHTS

Acknowledgments

This work is dedicated to the generations of students who, despite our best efforts, remain convinced they know their rights. On a daily basis, they revealed the myths that define us and the challenges we face in providing a forum for exchanging error for truth.

The authors wish to acknowledge and express sincere gratitude to those who have guided and challenged us—our mentors, our colleagues, our students, and our families. We are especially grateful to our families who tolerated and occasionally indulged our rants about the Bill of Rights and the myths that define American politics.

Introduction: Individual Freedoms, the Myths That Define Us, and American Public Opinion

Never let the truth stand in the way of a good story.[1]

Defining Political Myth

We are defined by the stories we tell, by their resonance in a popular culture that shapes and reshapes their meaning to conform to our collective memory and to our need to define ourselves as a community and a people. George Washington may have never cut down the cherry tree, but the "truth" of his honesty and integrity gave the story resonance and life long after it was first told. Defined narrowly as a factual or accurate version of events or meanings, truth is almost always a secondary consideration in our popular conceptions of who we are and what we aspire to become. Our stories define us and give meaning to our lives.

We see this easily in the myths and mythologies that define other civilizations. The 12 labors of Hercules easily capture our imagination, as Hercules displays the integrity, strength, and character befitting a son of Zeus and sufficient to overcoming great challenges and defeating evil. We understand that Aesop's Fables are just that, stories to teach deeper truths about morality and behavioral norms in a civil society.

Myths are harder to recognize when we move closer to home and as they speak more directly and clearly to our personal and contemporary realities. Myths surrounding the American Founding, for example, often portray the Founding Fathers as Moses-like figures who climbed a mountain and returned with the Declaration of Independence, the Constitution, and the Bill of Rights on stone tablets, or, alternatively, as great freedom fighters who embraced and embodied an irrepressible democratic zeitgeist.[2] Pragmatism, negotiation, and politics are lost in a retelling that simplifies and glorifies the past as if what transpired was divinely inspired and not the work of fallible, self-interested, and imperfect human beings.

In this book, we attempt to pull the curtain back on one set of myths that have shaped and defined the American political culture, the myths surrounding the nature of our political rights and individual freedoms as expressed in and protected by the Bill of Rights. In doing so, our goal is to write a provocative but fair retelling of how Americans have come to understand their individual rights and freedoms, how that understanding is often based on ignorance and misperception, and how it has shaped and limited contemporary political debates and policy decisions.

We should note at the outset that we are agnostic on the role that myths play in society. Myths shape and define culture and serve an important role in creating and maintaining our collective identity. This is particularly true in the American context, where the very definition of American is rooted in acceptance of an American mythology.[3] To be "American" has nothing to do with one's origin of birth and everything to do with one's acceptance (or rejection) of an American political creed that stresses freedom, individualism, and the protection of individual rights. In this sense, myths also narrow the scope of political debate,[4] allow societies to overlook collective wrongdoing, and serve as the basis for discrimination and injustice. Myths about American equality, for example, have long sat uneasily beside a history of racial injustice and discrimination, and an implicit acceptance of economic inequality as a societal *virtue* that drives innovation and effort. Horatio Alger myths enshrine equality of opportunity and work ethic as if they were part of a natural and unending American landscape allowing upper- and middle-class citizens to downplay persistent poverty and racial discrimination as barriers to economic well-being. The reality that economic mobility is more limited in the United States than in other advanced democracies[5] hardly subtracts from the "truth" of this persistent, often implicit, but always impactful belief. True or not, in the United States we believe we pull ourselves up by our own bootstraps.

Our goal is not to dispel the myths surrounding the Bill of Rights but to shed light on how they came to be and why they persist so that we can think more carefully, clearly, and critically about their meaning and consequences. We begin with a simple definition: Myths are popular beliefs or stories used to describe an event or a history and/or to justify existing social and political institutions. While myths may be factually untrue, they often exist in a netherworld between factual truth and fiction, where truth is indeterminate or reflective of individual values. Even if we cannot determine whether the Founding Fathers were divinely inspired in creating the American political experiment, for example, we can acknowledge that this belief has played an important role in how Americans define themselves and their place in history and the world. Such myths are created and survive because they are credible; because they serve a useful political, economic, or social purpose; or because they provide a compelling narrative.[6] The usefulness of myth—and not its truth—is what makes it enduring.

It is perhaps worth clarifying that myths are not simply lies. If they were, they would be easily dispelled and forgotten as false and inaccurate. Nor are they statistical or historical evidence that can be weighed on a balance of truth against competing claims. If they were, we could easily discard them as failed hypothesis when they no longer conformed to the best available data. Instead, they are rooted in narrative structures, their power reflected in an underlying "truth" revealed through a compelling story line and characters with cultural resonance. When they conform to our collective ideology as defined by the American political creed, we often accept them unconsciously without considering either cause or consequence.

Political Myth and the Bill of Rights

The myths surrounding the Bill of Rights are wrapped in the larger fabric of the American Founding and the near-religious reverence bestowed upon the Founding Fathers. Thomas Jefferson, the author of the Declaration of Independence and a catalyst for the Bill of Rights, casts a large shadow over our historical understanding of our individual rights and freedoms. His proclamation that "all men are ... endowed by their Creator with certain unalienable Rights, that among these are Life, Liberty and the pursuit of Happiness" serves as the foundation for our ongoing and persistent belief in the United States as a nation of rights. In Jefferson's formulation, rights are "natural," meaning that they are given not by government but by a creator and they extend equally to all citizens.

Jefferson, of course, fell short of the ideals he expressed as has the American political system he helped to create and shape. The long and sordid histories of civil rights and civil liberties stand at odds with our collective beliefs in the United States as a nation of individual freedoms. Political rights have been anything but "unalienable," and their application has historically been limited to privileged populations and has been highly contingent upon historical context. While it is often noted that the Founding Fathers failed to extend rights beyond white male property owners, they also wasted no time in passing laws limiting criticism of government via the Alien and Sedition Acts.[7]

In contemporary politics, we need look no further than the Patriot Act or more recent scandals involving the National Security Administration's (NSA) access to individual phone records to reveal a willingness to cross the line of individual freedom in pursuit of collective security.[8] Disregard Jefferson's natural rights; the reality has been that the definition of individual rights and their application and extension to specific populations has been the subject of ongoing and contested political debate.[9] Perhaps this is the single most important lesson we can impart: The meaning of individual rights is not now, nor has it ever been, singular, unambiguous, or uncontested. We have the rights we fight to keep.

This is, in part, why myths remain so critical to contemporary political debates. "Rights talk," Harvard Law Professor Mary Ann Glendon contends, dominates and impoverishes our discussion of contemporary political issues, stressing individualism over community and political rights over responsibility.[10] Rights talk is rooted in the mythology that we are a nation of rights. It persists because it corresponds well with our collective identity, it provides a compelling narrative, and it fits comfortably within contemporary political debate. Myths are perpetuated by mythmakers, the political and business leaders who articulate visions of the future and offer interpretations of the past, the news media that reinforces myths in its framing of news and events, and the entertainment media that uses the mythology as a cultural context for story settings. They find a receptive audience in a public that has been long socialized to believe in the broader mythology and that is largely ignorant of the history underlying the creedal beliefs of the American political culture. The result is public opinion that is based more on the mythology than on actual meaning.

Public Ignorance, Myth, and the Bill of Rights

Public opinion scholars have long noted that Americans' political beliefs are poorly formed, unstable, and misinformed.[11] More optimistic

FIGURE I.1. Percentage of Americans Able to Name Specific Rights in the First Amendment

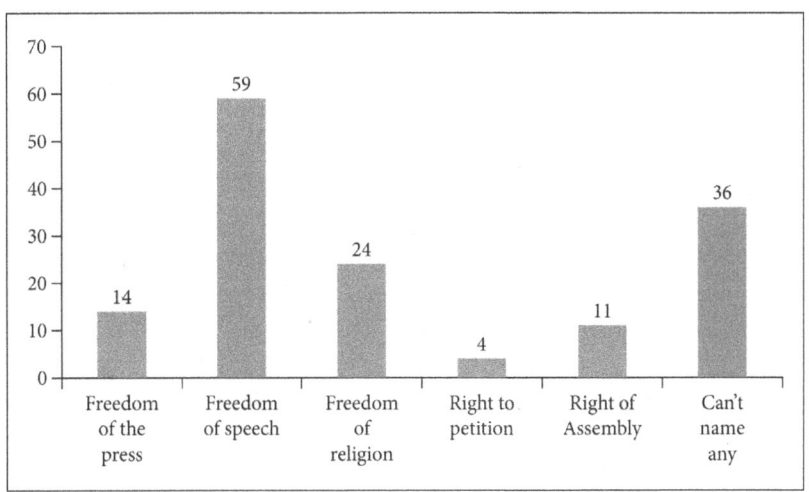

"revisionist" portrayals of the American citizenry emphasize limited information rationality, the ability of citizens to rely on cues and heuristics to make reasonably informed decisions with small amounts of information.[12] Voting on the basis of a candidate's partisan affiliation, for example, serves as a reasonably good substitute to actually learning about the issues. Alternatively, scholars have argued that factual knowledge is a poor indicator of reasoned decision-making, as individuals have poor recall of the facts but easily remember more general impressions. We may forget why we do not like Hillary Clinton, but we do not forget that we dislike her. The impression remains even if the factual underpinnings quickly fade.

When it comes to public understanding of the Bill of Rights, the level of ignorance is astonishing. In 2011, *Newsweek* gave 1,000 citizens a U.S. citizenship test: 38 percent failed and 43 percent did not know the Bill of Rights is the first ten amendments to the U.S. Constitution.[13] Each year, the First Amendment Center conducts the State of the First Amendment Survey to ascertain Americans knowledge and understanding of the protections provided in the First Amendment.[14] The results from 2013, displayed in Figure I.1, display an alarming level of ignorance that, even more alarmingly, has remained relatively constant over time. When it comes to public knowledge of the Bill of Rights, there were no good old days. More than a third of Americans (36 percent) cannot name any of the rights protected by the First Amendment. Moreover, most Americans equate the First Amendment narrowly in terms of freedom of speech (named by 59 percent), and are oblivious to freedom of religion (24 percent), freedom of the press (14 percent), the right to petition (4 percent), and the right of assembly (11 percent).

Somehow out of this morass of ignorance, however, we still believe we are "a nation of rights." When asked to compare the United States to other modern industrialized nations, for example, Americans rate our individual freedoms as our best virtue.[15] Even so, we have no reservation about limiting individual freedom for others, when we feel threatened, or during periods of unrest. As illustrated in Figure I.2, 34 percent of Americans in the 2013 survey said the First Amendment went too far in protecting the rights of American citizens.[16] As can be seen, results to this question vary over time, suggesting public support for the First Amendment is heavily dependent on context and is not tied to some deeper understanding of the U.S. Constitution. In the wake of the 9/11 terrorist attacks, nearly 50 percent of Americans said the First Amendment went too far in protecting individual rights. Faced with an external threat, we are more than willing to limit individual freedom. In an April 2014 column, P. J. O'Rourke went so far as to argue that if the ten individual amendments that comprise the Bill of Rights were put on a national referendum, only three or four would pass.[17] He assessed the chance of passage for the First, Fifth, and Sixth Amendments as "low."

Other surveys provide collaborating evidence into public ambivalence toward the Bill of Rights. Americans, at once, embrace the importance of the Bill of Rights while also recognizing the rights and freedoms it protects are limited. A survey conducted in 2002 by the National Constitution Center,[18] for example, found that nearly three-quarters of Americans

FIGURE I.2. Percentage of Americans Saying the First Amendment of Rights Goes Too Far in Protecting Rights

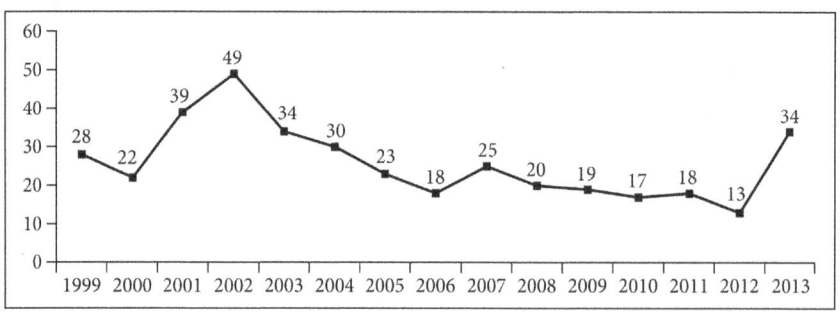

(73 percent) believe the Bill of Rights comes with limits and responsibilities compared to only 24 percent who believe it should be complete and absolute. The same survey found that more than 6 in 10 Americans believe the meaning of rights and freedoms changes with the times while only 1 in 3 Americans believe the meaning never changes.

So what does it mean about our rights if their meaning changes with the political, social, and economic context? For one, we too often misapply the Bill of Rights to contexts where they are not applicable. When Duck Dynasty's Phil Robertson made homophobic and racist comments to *GQ* magazine, A&E executives suspended the popular reality television star. Many conservative politicians—including Louisiana Governor and Rhodes Scholar Bobby Jindal, who presumably should have known better—rushed to Robertson's defense claiming a violation of his First Amendment rights. Phil Robertson certainly had the right to say whatever he wanted, but he was protected only from government censorship and not from his employer. In the end, Robertson won the debate but on economic grounds rather than First Amendment principles. His market value in audience and advertising revenue proved more valuable to A&E than any harm caused by his politically charged comments. Had the Duck Dynasty been less popular, he would have followed in the footsteps of Food Network star Paula Deen, who was dismissed after admitting racially insensitive comments in the past.

Alternatively, we are often slow to extend basic, natural rights to others, despite an abstract commitment to individual freedom and political equality. Our understanding of rights may be rooted in the Declaration of Independence, but our practice of protecting individual rights has been more suspect, more guarded, and more limited. Historically, we have offered, at best, limited protection of individual rights particularly for racial minorities or unpopular groups. African-Americans, for example, received de jure protection only with the passage of the 1964 Civil Rights Act, a hundred years after the civil war and the ratification of the Fourteenth Amendment. Practices of unequal protection (e.g., racial profiling) continue today. Similarly, we continue to debate whether the rights protected by the Bill of Rights should extend to immigrant populations or gay, lesbian, bisexual, and transgendered populations.

Misreading the Bill of Rights: The Top Ten Myths

The myths that we discuss in the remainder of the book reflect various flaws in our historical understanding of the Bill of Rights. Some of these myths are based on a historical misunderstanding created by a collective need to read our own values into a more complex and nuanced political history. The fact that we debated whether a bill of rights was even necessary, for example, is glossed over in most retellings of the American Founding, as if Thomas Jefferson simply reminded James Madison that he forgot to add in protections of individual freedoms. Other myths reflect the gap between belief and action. Our collective unwillingness to apply individual freedom to minority or unpopular groups has been a recurring theme in American political history. Indeed, one might argue that the single most important theme of American political history has involved marginalized groups demanding that the political system live up to its founding ideals.

In the chapters that follow, we discuss ten myths we believe have been most important to our historical understanding and contemporary political debates. The order is not indicative of their importance, but rather of how we believe these myths best fit together historically and politically. At the risk of giving away the ending, these are outlined as follows:

Myth #1: We need a bill of rights to protect our individual freedoms. One of the greatest misunderstandings regarding individual rights involves why the Bill of Rights was added to the U.S. Constitution in the first place. James Madison, the architect of the U.S. Constitution, strongly opposed the Bill of Rights, yet drafted and then advocated for it as a mechanism for assuring ratification of the U.S. Constitution. Madison was not alone. Many of the Founding Fathers saw the Bill of Rights as an unnecessary add-on to a constitution meant to create the political institutions and structures that would define the American polity.

The arguments against the Bill of Rights are instructive and counterintuitive in the context of contemporary governance. Opponents argued that setting a limited number of specified rights would imply only those rights listed in the Bill of Rights would be protected. Despite this history, constitutional fundamentalists, like the Tea Party, routinely argue that no rights should be created beyond those explicitly granted in the U.S. Constitution.

Myth #2: The Bill of Rights applies equally and to everyone. Barron v. Baltimore stands as one of the landmark cases in the early American republic. When the city of Baltimore redirected the water flow and adversely affected an existing wharf, the owner sued for federal government protection under the provisions of the Fifth Amendment. The Supreme Court ruled that the Bill of Rights only protected citizens against federal government action. Even after the Civil War and the ratification of the Fourteenth Amendment, individual rights were guaranteed against state government action only on a case-by-case basis through the process of selective incorporation. In contemporary politics, we often forget that the Bill of Rights does not necessarily (or clearly) protect us from employers or fellow citizens or that their application has been historically uneven.

Myth #3: *Thanks to the First Amendment, no one can tell me what to say (or what not to say).* In American politics, citizens often believe they can say whatever they want. Indeed, no right is more central to democratic governance than the right of free speech. Yet, shortly after ratifying the Bill of Rights, the Founders passed the Alien and Sedition Acts, making criticism of public officials a crime. Similarly, free speech, as defined by the Founding Fathers, would not have necessarily covered nonpolitical or *artistic* expression.

Political protest similarly has a long and storied history in American politics reaching back from the Boston Tea Party to the Civil Rights era and on to the contemporary Tea Party and Occupy Wall Street movements. Despite this history, the constitutional right to protest is poorly understood and little valued. Despite our First Amendment protections, many Americans believe the will of the majority should silence *disruptive* speech. Freedom of expression has been limited not only by government but also by public opinion that supports free speech in the abstract but not in practice.

Myth #4: *A free press is independent from the government and the government officials it reports on.* We are routinely told that a free press is critical to democracy, yet the press has never been free. Indeed, the development of the American news media has been closely tied to government subsidies that allowed the growth of newspapers through reduced postal rates and regulations that protected the broadcast industry from competition by narrowly defining and controlling the public airwaves. In contemporary politics, the press is highly dependent on access to government officials for news and information and corporate advertising for financial support. Popular criticisms of the news media emphasize *liberal biases*, but, more often than not, the news media serve as a mouthpiece for the powerful.

Myth #5: *The United States is a Christian nation.* Religion, unquestionably, played an important role in the American Founding, but the connection between Judeo-Christian traditions and democracy is far looser than most Americans care to believe. Many of the Founding Fathers were best described as deists, believing there was a creator but not one who regularly intervened in human affairs. In an act that would be considered heresy in contemporary politics, Thomas Jefferson literally cut out the parts of the Bible he did not like. The Founding Fathers clearly saw the danger that creating a state religion would pose to republican government and to individual freedom.

Myth #6: *There is a strict wall of separation between church and state.* If characterizations of the United States as a Christian nation are easily discarded, so too are conceptualizations build on the metaphor of a strict wall of separation between church and state. Even if religion has most often been used in ceremonial and symbolic ways, it has never been very far removed from the public sphere.

Myth #7: The Second Amendment was written to protect Americans against criminals. Like much of the U.S. Constitution, the Second Amendment is written in vague, ill-defined language that is the subject of considerable dispute. Does the Second Amendment recognize the need for *a well-regulated militia* or the right of individual citizens to own guns as a mechanism for self-defense? The answer is not particularly satisfying to gun-control advocates or Second Amendment defenders. The Second Amendment was written to assure protections against an overly intrusive federal government and likely extends to individual gun ownership. However, none of our rights are absolute, so there is little reason to believe that the Founding Fathers would recoil at limits on semi-automatic rifles or mandatory background checks for gun ownership. And there is little reason to connect the Second Amendment to protection from criminal behavior. The Second Amendment does not give a right to *stand your ground* and shoot an intruder, but was instead put in place as yet another effort to assure the people were protected against an overly intrusive federal government and that they quickly organize for defense against a foreign invasion.

Myth #8: Too many criminals get off on technicalities. Americans routinely express concerns that our judicial system does too much to protect criminals. The reasons for these protections, however, are rooted not in criminal justice but in politics. The long history of despotism shows ample reason for concern: Authoritarian governments routinely use criminal proceedings to silence political opposition. The importance of these political considerations in the definition of civil liberties is poorly understood and generally unappreciated. This is perhaps most frequently expressed as concern that criminals *get off on a technicality* when the technicality is the Bill of Rights. As a result, Americans show a willingness to scale back individual protections against self-incrimination, search and seizure, and trial by jury if it means putting more criminals behind bars.

Myth #9: If you have not done anything, you should not care if government searches your house or monitors your emails. The right to privacy is not mentioned in the Constitution. The right emerged more than a century later after advertisers used the image of a child without her family's permission. The body of law has grown to include the right to protect one's body, likeness, reputation, and even emotional state. Some protections are firmly rooted in sections of the Fourth Amendment, which limit police search and seizures. As the branch of privacy rights has developed, we shed light on the rights covered by the right to privacy. In doing so, we return to an earlier point: The Founding Fathers never intended for our rights to be limited to those protections specifically spelled out in the U.S. Constitution. We also address our ninth myth: "If you have not done anything, you should not care if government searches your house or monitors your emails." Privacy protections exist not to protect the guilty but to protect the innocent from unnecessary government intrusion. In the chapter, we impugn broad notions of a constitutional right to privacy. We also show the limited protections from governmental intrusions on privacy and reveal the broad areas left unprotected by the Constitution.

Myth #10: *Killing is not cruel or unusual, but torture is.* The language in the Eighth Amendment prohibits "cruel and unusual punishment," but most Americans are willing to let criminals rot in jails. Few Americans sympathize with criminals subject to hard labor, squalid conditions, and overcrowding. But the penitentiary system did not exist at the drafting of the Bill of Rights. Punishments were often swift and public. Jails were reserved for those awaiting trial, not as a form of punishment for committing a crime. In Chapter 10, we examine how our notions of cruel and unusual punishment have changed over the past two centuries. Many of the swift and painful punishments doled out by our Founding Fathers would not be socially acceptable today. Alternatively, many of our contemporary practices would fail colonial definitions of cruel and unusual punishment. In doing so, we address our tenth myth that "killing is not cruel or unusual, but torture is" by critically examining the cruelty of executions. We also challenge conventional thinking about our current plan to *throw away the key* for certain criminals.

We conclude by returning to a central theme. Our collective understanding of the Bill of Rights is clouded in misinformation and ignorance. As a result, the protections are considerably less protective than they may at first appear. Indeed, our freedoms are largely contingent upon historical context and the public's willingness to support the expansion of individual freedoms or, alternatively, to suppress dissent. The good news here is that the larger timeline of American political history has generally revealed an expansion of individual rights and freedoms. We may fairly say that we are freer today than during most of American history. This optimism, however, has to be tempered by the fact that Americans are more than willing to suppress dissent and limit freedom when faced with an external threat. Revelations that the NSA-monitored domestic telephone calls were, for example, largely met with a collective yawn. Similarly, technology allows for greater monitoring of individual behavior, setting up the capacity for more intrusive federal government and a collective loss of individual liberty. If, as we argue, the meaning of individual rights is never set in stone but is instead contested and ambiguous, the future of our political freedom is set, in no small part, by what we allow and what we forbid. Those boundaries will be determined not by definitions of rights that transcend time and place but by the myths that we believe in, the stories we tell about who we are as a people, and how we choose to apply them in contemporary and future contexts.

Notes

1. Often attributed to Mark Twain, the phrase appears to be from J. Frank Dobie, though its origins are not entirely clear.

2. Dan Nimmo and James E. Combs, *Subliminal Politics: Myths & Mythmakers in America* (Englewood Cliffs, NJ: Prentice Hall, 1980).

3. G. K. Chesterton, *What I Saw in America* (New York: Dodd, Mead, and Company, 1923); Seymour Martin Lipset, *American Exceptionalism: A Double-Edged Sword* (New York: WW Norton & Company, 1996).

4. Mary Ann Glendon, *Rights Talk: The Impoverishment of Political Discourse* (New York: The Free Press, 1991).

5. Markus Jäntti, Bernt Bratsberg, Knut Røed, Oddbjørn Raaum, Robin Naylor, Eva Österbacka, Anders Björklund, and Tor Eriksson, *American Exceptionalism in a New Light: A Comparison of Intergenerational Earnings Mobility in the Nordic Countries, the United Kingdom and the United States*, Institute for the Study of Labor, Discussion Paper No. 1938 (January 2006).

6. In their 1980 book *Subliminal Politics*, Nimmo and Combs outline several characteristics of myths. They are credible, socially constructed, dramatic, and taken for granted as reality; see Nimmo and Combs, *Subliminal Politics*.

7. John C. Miller, *Crisis in Freedom: The Alien and Sedition Acts* (Boston: Atlantic-Little, Brown, 1951).

8. Darren Davis and Brian D. Silver, "Civil Liberties vs. Security: Public Opinion in the Context of the Terrorist Attacks on America," *American Journal of Political Science* 48 (2004): 28–46.

9. Stuart Scheingold, *The Politics of Rights: Lawyers, Public Policy, and Political Change* (Ann Arbor: University of Michigan Press, 2004).

10. Glendon, *Rights Talk*.

11. Philip Converse, "The Nature of Belief Systems in Mass Publics," In *Ideology and Discontent*, ed. David Apter (New York: Free Press, 1964, pp. 2012–2261); John Zaller, *The Nature and Origins of Mass Opinion* (Cambridge: Cambridge University Press, 1992).

12. Samuel Popkin, *The Reasoning Voter: Communication and Persuasion in Presidential Campaigns* (Chicago: University of Chicago Press, 1994); Milton

Lodge, Kathleen McGraw, and Patrick Stroh, "An Impression-Driven Model of Candidate Evaluation,"*American Political Science Review* 83 (1989): 399–419.

13. Andrew Romano, "How Ignorant Are Americans?" *Newsweek*, March 11, 2011, available at http://www.newsweek.com/how-ignorant-are-americans-66053 (accessed on February 2, 2014).

14. First Amendment Center, State of the First Amendment Survey Report. Available at http://www.firstamendmentcenter.org/sofa (accessed on December 6, 2013). The survey was conducted in May 2013 and included 1,006 respondents. Specific question wording is as follows: *As you may know, the First Amendment is part of the U.S. Constitution. Can you name any of the specific rights that are guaranteed by the First Amendment?*

15. Lydia Saad, "Americans Consider Individual Freedoms Nation's Top Virtue," *Gallup Politics*, January 7, 2013, available at http://www.gallup.com/poll/159716/americans-consider-individual-freedoms-nation-top-virtue.aspx (accessed on February 2, 2014). The survey was conducted on December 14–17, 2012, and included 1,025 adults interviewed on landline and cellular phones ($N = 400$).

16. State of the First Amendment Survey Report. Specific question wording is as follows: *The First Amendment became part of the U.S. Constitution more than 200 years ago. This is what it says: "Congress shall make no law respecting an establishment of religion, or prohibiting the free exercise thereof, or abridging the freedom of speech, or of the press, or the right of the people peaceably to assemble, and to petition the government for a redress of grievances." Based on your own feelings about the First Amendment, please tell me whether you agree or disagree with the following statement: The First Amendment goes too far in the rights it guarantees. Do you strongly or mildly agree/disagree?*

17. P. J. O'Rourke, "Who Actually Really Wants This Bill of Rights?" *The Daily Beast*, April 12, 2014, available at http://www.thedailybeast.com/articles/2014/04/12/p-j-o-rourke-who-really-actually-wants-this-bill-of-rights.html (accessed on August 6, 2014).

18. National Constitution Center, 2002, Knowing It by Heart: The Constitution & Its Meaning Survey. Survey conducted on November 29–30, 2001, and included 1,002 respondents.

Chapter 1

The Bill of Rights and the Myth of Individual Freedom

We hold these truths to be self-evident, that all men are created equal, that they are endowed by their Creator with certain unalienable Rights, that among these are Life, Liberty and the pursuit of Happiness.

We are often taught that the Bill of Rights reflected the Founding Fathers deep commitment to individual freedom, but these lessons gloss over its obvious omission from the original draft of the constitution. If the Bill of Rights was so important, why was it not included? The deeply unsatisfying answer is that the Bill of Rights was not central to the conversation leading up to the draft; it was an afterthought, reluctantly agreed to as a part of a practical political calculation to assure ratification of the Constitution, mute Anti-Federalist criticisms of the U.S. Constitution, and keep the constitutional framework unaltered. Or perhaps stated differently, it was a crass and cynical political ploy.

This is not to suggest that the Founding Fathers were unconcerned with individual freedom or that they did not believe that individual rights should be protected; only that they did not see the need for written protections enumerated in a defined bill of rights. James Madison, the architect of the Constitution, drafted the Bill of Rights but only with great reluctance, describing it as a "nauseous project."[1] The first ten amendments, in his view, represented only a "parchment barrier" to government infringements and, even worse, implied rights would be limited to those specifically enumerated. Madison believed the institutional checks built into the Constitution and the rights already defined and protected by state constitutions would more effectively prevent government from infringing upon individual liberties than any national bill of rights. Alexander Hamilton, perhaps, makes the argument best in Federalist #84: "[T]he constitution is itself in every rational sense, and to very useful purpose, A BILL OF RIGHTS."[2] There was no need to limit federal government authority (e.g., to restrict freedom of the press), Hamilton argued, where the federal government had no constitutional authority in the first place. By what power could the federal government limit freedom of the press? Limited government, rather than carefully spelled-out rights, was best suited to protecting individual rights and freedoms.

Despite his reluctant authorship, James Madison is fairly described as the "Father of the Bill of Rights"[3] for his role in drafting the amendments and shepherding them through a legislative process with Federalists unconvinced of the need for protected freedoms and Anti-Federalists rightly suspicious of Madison's motives. In letters to Thomas Jefferson, Madison carefully laid out his opposition, much of it rooted in his deep distrust of democracy. If the people demanded restrictions on individual freedom, a written bill of rights would be ineffective against a democratic majority. Explaining his position in a letter to Jefferson, Madison argued: "[R]estrictions however strongly marked on paper will never be regarded when opposed to the decided sense of the public; and after repeated violations in extraordinary cases, they will lose even their ordinary efficacy. Should a Rebellion or insurrection alarm the people as well as the Government, a suspension of Hab. Corp. be dictated by the alarm, no written prohibitions on earth would prevent the measure."[4]

Despite his initial opposition, Madison was not an ideologue but a political pragmatist concerned that failing to address Anti-Federalist criticisms would expose his constitutional framework and the newly constituted federal government to a more radical restructuring. By adding the Bill of Rights, Madison could remove one of the central objections to his new government and broaden support for the federal government. Madison had a more immediate and practical concern as well. Running against James Monroe in a district gerrymandered by his Anti-Federalist political opponent Patrick Henry to assure his defeat, Madison needed to change his position to win election.[5] His decision to take the lead in drafting the Bill of Rights was similarly rooted in political strategy. Madison wanted to control the process to assure minimal damage to an institutional framework he believed was critical to assuring the long-term stability of the new government. Madison's success in this endeavor reflected less on his belief in the necessity of a bill of rights and more on his political acumen.[6] His Anti-Federalist opponents were not fooled and voted against the Bill of Rights even though its absence was their principle objection to the new Constitution.

Understanding this more complex and nuanced political history allows us to imagine what might have been had the Bill of Rights never been added to the U.S. Constitution. For the sake of argument, we can discard the possibility that the new government would have fallen apart under the weight of Anti-Federalist objections. Madison's fears may well have been realized, and the failure to include a bill of rights might have led to a more radical restructuring, but that hypothetical scenario takes us away from the central question: How different would the American political system be if Madison and Hamilton's logic had prevailed and there were no bill of rights? Would we actually enjoy fewer freedoms? Or has the "parchment barrier" limited our freedoms through enumeration? Regardless of how we answer these questions, one conclusion is inescapable: It is a myth to believe that we need a bill of rights to protect individual freedom. That protection is rooted more clearly and definitively in a cultural commitment to individual rights. Where that commitment weakens or erodes, individual liberties are threatened regardless of the constitutional protections.

Can Democracy Exist Without a Bill of Rights?

The short answer is yes, democracies can and do exist without written protections of individual freedoms. They are no less free than the United States. One might quibble over which nations are most free, but the United Kingdom, New Zealand, and Australia—all countries without a constitutional enumerated bill of rights[7]—enjoy political freedoms and individual rights at levels roughly equivalent to the United States. The independent watchdog Freedom House has rated the level of freedom in individual countries annually for over 30 years, including ratings for a number of different subcategories measuring the level of political freedom and protection of civil liberties. The 2014 scores for the United States, the United Kingdom, Australia, and New Zealand are presented in Table 1.1.

As one can quickly discern from Table 1.1, there is little evidence to suggest that a constitutional bill of rights makes the United States freer than these other advanced democracies. Indeed, on several of the

TABLE 1.1. 2014 Freedom House Ratings by Subcategory

	Political Rights			Civil Liberties			
	Electoral Process	Political Pluralism and Participation	Function of Government	Freedom of Expression and Belief	Associational and Organizational Rights	Rule of Law	Personal Autonomy and Individual Rights
New Zealand	12	15	12	16	12	15	15
Australia	12	15	12	16	12	15	15
United Kingdom	12	16	12	15	12	15	15
United States of America	11	16	10	15	11	14	15

Source: Freedom House, "Freedom in the World 2014" available at http://www.freedomhouse.org/report/freedom-world-2014/ (accessed February 18, 2014).

scores—including freedom of expression and belief, associational and organizational rights, and rule of law—the United States scores below one or more of these countries. We need not quibble over one- or two-point differences. Each of these countries is rated as *free* and the differences are relatively small. The larger point is that a bill of rights is not necessary or sufficient for protecting individual freedom. Something else is clearly at play: the cultural commitment and the political resources necessary to protect individual freedom.

Implicit in the argument for a written bill of rights is a decidedly undemocratic premise. Trust for enforcement of rights should reside in the hands of unelected judges farthest removed from "democratic" political pressures.[8] Or perhaps stated differently, we need judges to protect us from our own democratic impulses to deprive minority groups of their rights and freedoms. In fairness, the history of democratic decision-making does not instill one with great confidence in the ability of democracies to protect individual rights. Not only are intolerant "illiberal" governments often and increasingly elected,[9] but ballot measures in states that allow referendum and initiative campaigns often work to the disadvantage of minority interests.[10] The "tyranny of the majority" is not simply a misplaced Madisonian fear; it is a reality that infects even the most liberal democratic governments on a regular basis.

If democratic institutions provide no guarantee of constitutionally protected rights, creating a constitutionally binding bill of rights jealously guarded by unelected judges may seem like a reasonable alternative. The history of American jurisprudence where the courts have often outpaced democratically elected representatives in supporting civil liberties and civil rights is instructive on this point. We would be at least two steps behind in protecting individual freedom had decisions been left entirely to the U.S. Congress.

Yet the same history should also serve as a cautionary tale. For nearly a century and a half, federal judges did very little to protect individual freedom, particularly for transgressions committed by state governments or private entities. Judicial protection of individual liberties may surpass the protection of legislatures alone, but it has been, at best, uneven and, for substantial periods of American history, nonexistent. Judges are, by no means, infallible as guardians of individual liberty, and while they may be further removed from political pressures, they remain products of a broader political, economic, and social context.

In the worst case scenario, judges may resist broader cultural changes. Prior to "the stitch in time that saved nine," the U.S. Supreme Court actively resisted legislative efforts to restrict business activities and protect the rights of workers to organize and engage in collective bargaining. Even today, judges who adhere to the principles of judicial restraint and original intent believe that the courts should not invent rights that are not clearly spelled out in the Constitution. The irony here should be immediately apparent as their philosophy embodies the Founders fears that an enumerated bill of rights would limit individual freedom.

Judicial ineffectiveness may also reflect the nature of courts as political institutions. While the Supreme Court has great discretion over its agenda, it cannot simply make up cases to express an opinion. It depends on cases winding their way through the lower and appellate court structures and the agreement of four Supreme Court justices to actually hear the case. The protective capabilities of the courts depend greatly on the cases at hand, which, in turn, depend on capable, willing, and resourceful litigants. Individuals, in other words, must not only be willing to fight for their legal rights but must also have the economic and political resources to wage the battle all the way to the Supreme Court.

Examining the adoption of the Canadian Charter of Rights and Freedoms in 1982 and its consequences for subsequent court rulings, political scientist Charles Epp concluded that the effectiveness of this Canadian bill of rights depended not on the written protections incorporated into the charter but on the support structure for legal mobilization.[11] That is, a bill of rights is most effective where individuals have the resources to challenge existing statutes and legal decisions. Since individual plaintiffs often lack these resources, political groups organized and committed to a legal strategy and financially capable of finding and supporting test cases are critical to this process. Perhaps stated differently, the landmark decision in *Brown v. Board* is unthinkable without the legal and financial support of the National Association for the Advancement of Colored People (NAACP).[12] More broadly, the "rights revolution," Epps argues, depended less on activist judges or constitutional text and more on engaged interest groups capable of mounting a sustained legal strategy.[13]

Federal Judge Learned Hand, widely considered the most influential federal judge to have never sat on the Supreme Court, expressed this limited view of constitutional rights eloquently in his 1944 speech, "The Spirit of Liberty," delivered in New York's Central Park. "I often wonder whether we do not rest our hopes too much on constitutions, upon laws and upon courts. These are false hopes; believe me, these are false hopes. Liberty lies in the hearts of men and women; when it dies there no constitution, no law, no court can save it; no constitution, no law, no court can even do much to help it. While it lies there it needs no constitution, no law, no court to save it."[14]

The presence of a bill of rights may, however, affect the type of rights protected. In Australia, where no bill of rights exists, a rights revolution occurred, but the focus was on the expansion of political rights as opposed to legal rights. Regardless, the balance of evidence seems to support Madison and Hamilton and the decision to leave the Bill of Rights out of the Constitution. Cultural commitment, rather than constitutional protections, is the driver of individual freedom. This is why—in the American context—the definition and application of rights has changed over time. The text of the Bill of Rights is no different than when it was originally drafted or when it was made applicable to state government actions via the Fourteenth Amendment in 1868, yet its meaning has changed dramatically. To say that our speech is constitutionally protected in 2014 means something far different than in 1868 not because the First Amendment has changed but because we read the First Amendment differently in a post-industrial digital age than in the rural agrarian society of the American founders or in the industrial age of late 1800s.

The Value of Constitutional Protected Rights

Before we conclude that a bill of rights has no value and move on, we should take a step backward and ask the question in a different way: What is the worth of the Bill of Rights to individual freedom? Or, perhaps more pointedly, what would we lose if the Bill of Rights were removed from the U.S. Constitution?

Notice the slight change in the framing of the question. In the previous section, we asked whether rights *could* be protected in the absence of clearly articulated constitutional protections. The answer was an unequivocal yes as constitutional protections are neither necessary nor sufficient guarantees of individual freedom. The United Kingdom enjoys a wide range of rights even though those rights are protected primarily by statute and common law and not by a constitution. Legal support systems, cultural commitments to individual freedom, public opinion, and the broader political, economic, and social context all influence the protection of individual liberties. A constitution alone is–as Madison feared–little more than a "parchment barrier."

We should be careful, however, not to take this logic too far and conclude that the Bill of Rights does not matter at all. Even if fallible, imperfect, and contextually contingent, constitutionally protected rights matter specifically because they lift individual rights and freedoms above statutory law. The explicit expression of rights in a constitution is not only a reflection of a nation's political values, but they give those values a preferred legal status.

This point has not been lost on political and legal observers in the United Kingdom who routinely call for constitutionally protected bill of rights that extend beyond the reach of the British Parliament. Great Britain may well enjoy a wide range of freedoms, but many Brits are concerned those rights are too precariously protected when they could potentially be revoked by Parliament at any time. Writing in 1983, political scientist Glenn Abernathy argued that relying on Parliament may be inadequate to protecting individual freedoms, particularly during an age when the administrative reach of government has been growing during periods of crisis. As he concludes, "reliance upon Parliamentary action alone without some form of a Bill of Rights still leaves the way open for at least as frequent legislation which is restrictive of human rights as for legislation to protect those rights."[15]

More recently, in 2012, the British government officially visited the issue by creating the Commission on a Bill of Rights. The commission called for a new UK Bill of Rights that would encode current protections provided under the Human Rights Act of 1998 and the European Convention on Human Rights.[16] The recommendation was not without its critics and the process illustrated the difficulty of discussing rights in contemporary politics. To merely encode protections seemed a superficial remedy when rights are already protected by Parliament. On the other hand, extending the bill of rights opened the door to an array of questions. What rights should be protected? And which rights should be left out?

On the other side of the Atlantic, the case for the Bill of Rights has perhaps been made most convincingly by Supreme Court Justice William J. Brennan. Brennan begins his defense by acknowledging the deficiencies. The Bill of Rights is "painted with a flat brush rather than etched with a jeweler's pin,"[17] he observes, meaning the definition of individual rights and the willingness of courts to protect these rights are necessarily vague and contingent on the times. Neither the flexibility in the written language nor the variance in meaning, however, detracts from the "real" value of the Bill of Rights. For Brennan, its inclusion in the U.S. Constitution makes it more than a mere "parchment barrier" because the Constitution makes it enforceable. This is particularly important during times of crisis when individual freedoms become expendable in pursuit of greater security. During these periods, a constitutionally protected bill of rights becomes an important weapon protecting individual freedom against the tyranny of the majority. American history teaches us that a written document is not fail safe; it requires the political will for enforcement but, Brennan argues, it is better than the alternative of moral arguments without written protections. As Justice Brennan concludes, "I know of no surer weapon in that fight against our own fear and intolerance than an entrenched, enforceable bill of rights."[18]

Conclusions

The mythology that defines the American polity often begins (and ends) with the question of those individual freedoms constitutionally protected by the Bill of Rights. We are, it is argued, a nation of rights, where the rule of law is elevated above the democratic impulse, where individual freedom trumps the collective will. Yet if we imagine a world in which the Bill of Rights was never drafted, it is hard to imagine that we would be any less free. Our interpretation of individual rights is heavily contingent on the political, economic, and social context, so much so that it is fair to say that the rights we enjoy today scarcely resemble the freedoms as envisioned by the Founding Fathers. A legal framework that elevates individual freedoms above and beyond the province of statutory law unquestionably assists in the fight to define and expand individual rights, but it is neither necessary nor sufficient as a guarantor of freedom. Far more important is a citizenry committed to individual freedoms as a pillar of democratic governance. Should that pillar falter, the legal framework outlined by the Bill of Rights will do little to protect against a majority intent on taking rights away from an unpopular minority. Which is to say, the Bill of Rights matters not because of any inherent meaning or power invested in the written text but because we choose to value it as an expression of our political identity. If we value its protections less, it becomes considerably less powerful.

Notes

1. Jack N. Rakove, "James Madison and the Bill of Rights," In *This Constitution: From Ratification to the Bill of Rights,* ed. American Political Science Association and American Historical Association (Washington, DC: Congressional Quarterly, 1988).
2. Alexander Hamilton, Federalist #84, *The Federalist Papers.*

3. Paul Finkelman, "James Madison and the Bill of Rights: A Reluctant Paternity," *The Supreme Court Review* (1990): 301–347.

4. As quoted in Finkelman, "James Madison and the Bill of Rights," 332. The original source is a letter from Madison to Jefferson, October 17, 1788.

5. Andrew Burstein and Nancy Isenberg, *Madison and Jefferson* (New York: Random House, 2013).

6. Robert Goldwin, *From Parchment to Power: How James Madison Used the Bill of Rights to Save the Constitution* (Washington, DC: AEI Press, 1997); Finkelman, "James Madison and the Bill of Rights," 301–347.

7. In the United Kingdom and New Zealand, a bill of rights exists, but the rights are statutorily granted rather than constitutionally protected. In Australia, no bill of rights exists; see Jeffrey Goldsworthy, Tom Campbell, and Adrienne Stone, *Protecting Rights Without a Bill of Rights: Institutional Performance and Reform in Australia* (Hampshire, Great Britain: Ashgate Publishing, 2006).

8. James Allen, "Bill of Rights and Judicial Power–A Liberal's Quandary," *Oxford Journal of Legal Studies* 16 (1996): 337–352.

9. Fareed Zakaria, "The Rise of Illiberal Democracy," *Foreign Affairs*, November/December 1997, available at http://www.foreignaffairs.com/articles/53577/fareed-zakaria/the-rise-of-illiberal-democracy (accessed on February 18, 2014).

10. Daniel C. Lewis, *Direct Democracy and Minority Rights: A Critical Assessment of the Tyranny of the Majority in the American States* (New York: Routledge, 2013); Donald Haider-Markel, Alana Querze, and Kara Lindaman, "Lose, Win, or Draw? A Reexamination of Direct Democracy and Minority Rights," *Political Research Quarterly* 60 (2007): 304–314.

11. Charles Epp, "Do the Bill of Rights Matter? The Canadian Charter of Rights and Freedoms," *American Political Science Review* 90 (1996): 765–779.

12. *Brown v. Board of Education*, 347 U.S. 483 (1954).

13. Charles Epp, *The Rights Revolution: Lawyers, Activists, and Supreme Courts in Comparative Perspective* (Chicago: University of Chicago Press, 1998).

14. From "The Spirit of Liberty" Speech given by Learned Hand in 1944. The full text can be found in William Safire, *Lend Me Your Ears: Great Speeches in History* (New York: W.W. Norton & Company, 2004).

15. Glenn Abernathy, "Should the United Kingdom Adopt a Bill of Rights?" *American Journal of Comparative Law* 31 (1983): 431–479, especially 479.

16. Commission on a Bill of Rights, "A UK Bill of Rights: The Choice Before Us," December 18, 2012, available at https://www.justice.gov.uk/news/press-releases/cbr/the-commission-on-a-bill-of-rights-report-a-uk-bill-of-rights-the-choice-before-us (accessed on August 6, 2014).

17. William J. Brennan, "Why Have a Bill of Rights?" *Oxford Journal of Legal Studies* 9 (1989): 425–440.

18. Ibid., 440.

Chapter 2

Equally and for Everyone? Protecting Citizens Against the Federal Government

We hold these truths to be self-evident, that all men are created equal, that they are endowed by their Creator with certain unalienable Rights, that among these are Life, Liberty and the pursuit of Happiness.

The unanimous Declaration of the thirteen united States of America, July 4, 1776

The meaning of the words carefully spelled out in the Declaration of Independence may seem obvious in their intent, but they co-existed with the inequality of slavery, property requirements for voting, and the patriarchal and sexist treatment of women. The distinction was an easy one for the Founders who saw no contradiction between the "equal" natural rights that existed in a state of nature and the political and social inequalities that defined civil society.[1] Well versed in the philosophies of Thomas Hobbes and John Locke, they recognized that a functioning government required giving up some measure of personal freedom and fully accepted that some in society had to give up more than others. Inequalities in opportunities, rights, and outcomes were deeply ingrained into the fabric of the American Founding and widely accepted as political, economic, and social realities.

The implications of the Declaration of Independence's call for equality were not lost on the declaration's readers: Massachusetts freed its slaves, while southern states edited the language from "all men" to "all freemen" to leave no question that certain inequalities would persist despite the revolution and any clarion call for natural rights for all men (or all persons).[2] In contrast to the Declaration of Independence, the U.S. Constitution did not include the word *equality* until the ratification of the Fourteenth Amendment in 1868. Assuring equal treatment before the law was neither the intent nor the purpose of a constitution designed to create a governing framework and not to protect individual rights.

Images of Thomas Jefferson as the reluctant slave owner and philosopher tortured by the contradictions between the abstract ideals expressed in the Declaration of Independence and his personal reality as slave owner are themselves part of a larger mythology that paints the founding ideals as aspirational and Jefferson as a visionary constrained by his times. The remarkable piece of this history is how quiet Jefferson remained on the issue of slavery and how little he did to address it even in comparison to many of his contemporaries. Jefferson was more comfortable with the contradiction and more willing to accept the inherent and presumed inequality that provided the foundation for slavery than we want to believe or than we teach in our American history courses.[3]

Jefferson, of course, was not alone; nor was he unique on this point.[4] The U.S. Constitution was not designed to create or assure equality but instead built inequality into its institutional framework. The separation of powers, checks and balances, and federalism were designed to perpetuate existing inequalities—not eliminate them—by making it difficult for the have-nots to use their political power to redistribute economic wealth. Democracy was not the solution; it was the threat, solved by an institutional framework that thwarted the majoritarian impulse. The addition of the Bill of Rights to James Madison's institutional framework did little to change this reality. Indeed, who is protected by the Bill of Rights and against what (and whom) are perhaps the central questions of American constitutional history. Gordon S. Wood, a noted historian of the American Founding, questioned: "[I]n republican America where there was no longer any Crown or any prerogatives, did bills of rights make sense? What was the need of protecting the people's rights from themselves?"[5] Or stated differently, exactly who was the Bill of Rights supposed to protect and what was it supposed to protect them from?

In the previous chapter, we discussed whether a bill of rights was necessary to protect individual freedom. Here, we take a slightly different turn and explore whom the Bill of Rights has protected. We discover that the interpretation and application of the Bill of Rights has been remarkably uneven and highly contingent on historical context. In doing so we uncover our second myth—"[T]he Bill of Rights applies equally and to everyone."

The Limited Protection of the Bill of Rights

For nearly a century the Bill of Rights did little to protect citizens against federal government action, state governments, or private economic interests. The document so widely celebrated as the defining statement of American freedom was mostly ineffective and forgotten. Law professor and legal scholar Akhil Reed Amar notes the "remarkably small" role played by the Bill of Rights during the American Founding, observing that "no federal judge invalidated the Sedition Act of 1798,"[6] an early frontal assault on freedom of expression designed to silence critics of John Adams' Federalist Administration. The mistake in reviewing the historical record is to believe that the Bill of Rights did little to protect individuals against state governments or private economic interests but maintained protections against the federal government during this early period. The reality is the Bill of Rights did little to protect individual rights prior to the Civil War and the adoption of the Fourteenth Amendment against any government (federal or state). Moreover, it was only recently that Americans began to think about and debate issues first and foremost in the language of individual rights.

Perhaps no case better illustrates the limited application of the Bill of Rights against state governments during this early period than the landmark decision in *Barron v. Baltimore*. When the city of Baltimore redirected water flow and adversely affected an existing wharf forcing it to close, the owner sued for federal government protection under the provisions of the Fifth Amendment as an unlawful taking of property. The Supreme Court ruled that the Bill of Rights protected citizens only against federal government action and not against a state government unlawfully taking property. Even on questions of federal government infringements, it was unclear what protection citizens needed from their elected representatives. Did they really need protections against the people elected to represent them? If they did, what did this say about democracy?

Akhil Reed Amar contends that the original intent of the Bill of Rights was not to protect individual rights but to empower majorities so that they could exercise control over their elected representatives,[7] that is, to assure they were responsive to constituent concerns. Contemporary interpretations focusing on individual rights, he argues, owe far more to the

Fourteenth Amendment than to the Founding Fathers or to original intent. "Like people with spectacles who forget that they are wearing them," Amar writes, "most lawyers read the Bill of Rights through the lens of the Fourteenth Amendment without realizing how powerfully that lens has refracted what they see."[8] The same might be said of the contemporary Tea Party movement and civil libertarians who stress the emphasis placed on individual rights and freedoms in America's Founding documents. Couched in the language of original intent, their view is a historical revision rooted in a contemporary reinterpretation of individual rights.[9]

Even after Civil War and the ratification of the Fourteenth Amendment, individual rights were protected from state government infringement only on a case-by-case basis through the slow and gradual process of selective incorporation. Legal scholar Jamal Greene calls the Fourteenth Amendment "a failure in its time," noting its successes only came much later and on the backs of subsequent generations.[10] This failure occurred despite the relatively clear language in the Fourteenth Amendment forbidding the states from denying citizens "equal protection of the laws" without due process of the law.

Despite its failures in the short term, the ratification of the Fourteenth Amendment stands as a critical turning point in our social and political understanding of the Bill Rights, as increasingly Americans began to think in terms of protected rights and individual freedoms. Political science professor Barry Alan Shain attributes this shift to Abraham Lincoln's successful "sleight of hand" in the Lincoln–Douglas debates in which Lincoln vastly extended the meaning of Jefferson's "all men are created equal" beyond its historical intent and toward to its literal meaning. Lincoln's political opponent, Stephen Douglas, offered the historically accurate but less inspiring interpretation of Jefferson's famous phrase by noting that the Founders meant those words to apply only to "white men" and not to "all men."[11] Nevertheless, it is Lincoln's expansive interpretation and not Founders' intent that prevailed, though it is perhaps worth noting that it took a Civil War and another hundred years for Lincoln's interpretation to win the day.

Winning the rhetorical battle may have meant the end of slavery, but it did little to assure equal treatment before the law. Not only were state-supported inequalities created and legally justified via *Plessey v. Ferguson* and other court rulings, but the question of whether the state could protect individuals from private economic interests remained unanswered. Lochner era court rulings (1905–1937) protected individual rights as contract rights, thus ceding considerable authority to private economic interests to impose unsafe workplace conditions on an economically vulnerable labor market. Individuals effectively gave up their rights for a company paycheck. During this period, the Supreme Court overturned laws on the minimum wage, child labor, and the regulation of insurance and banking industries. It is a healthy reminder that courts are often less stalwart defenders of individual rights than legislatures as much depends on the configuration of the nine justices on the Supreme Court at any given time as well as the broader contours of social, economic, and political power. Perhaps ironically, these rulings were cast as efforts at protecting individual rights to enter into contracts free of government interference. The practical effect was that the Constitution provided little or no protection against an employer. The Lochner era ended with the 1937 decision in *West Coast Hotel Co. v. Parrish* and the "stitch in time that saved nine," in which the court upheld minimum-wage legislation to avoid Franklin Roosevelt's court-packing scheme.

While the courts have never fully embraced the expansion of the Bill of Rights as protections against employers, the cultural shift during the New Deal era was nevertheless profound. Like Lincoln before him, Franklin Roosevelt expanded *rights talk* by proposing a second bill of rights rooted in economic protections and economic security. Economic rights have, of course, never risen to the level of constitutional amendment, but the way Americans thought about rights was profoundly influenced during this period, as was the expectation that such rights would be protected by the federal government and through the courts. The conservative backlash to protect individual rights against government infringement was also rooted in an expanding *rights talk*. When Duck Dynasty's Phil Robertson made anti-gay comments and was temporarily suspended by his network A&E, it was conservative *small government* politicians, like former vice presidential nominee Sarah Palin and Louisiana Governor Bobby Jindal, who decried the suspension by his employer as a violation of his First Amendment freedoms. Similarly, religious conservatives have strongly advocated protecting individual religious freedoms against requirements to provide information and/or access to birth control in the workplace. Were such rights left to original intent, it is unlikely that one's religious beliefs are an adequate defense against requirements created by receiving a paycheck.

Arguments in favor of expanding or contracting rights do not map neatly on to a liberal–conservative continuum, as one's ideological position often depends on what rights and whose rights are being discussed. Conservatives had little tolerance when National Basketball Association star Mahmoud Abdul-Rauf refused to stand for the national anthem as a protest against *tyranny and oppression*. Groups across the ideological spectrum frame issues in the language of rights as a way of influencing larger policy discussions and public opinion across a wide range of issues. Questions of whether health-care plans should be required to provide birth control, for example, take on a different meaning when they are cast as a question of the right of the individual employee to refuse to provide birth control on religious grounds as opposed to an individual right to privacy to obtain medical treatments that some health professional might find morally repugnant or religiously unacceptable.

Protecting individuals against discrimination by private economic interests has greatly expanded the federal government's authority. To effectively enforce the Civil Rights Act of 1964, President Lyndon Johnson relied on a sweeping interpretation of the U.S. Constitution's commerce clause. Broadly interrupting *commerce* allowed the federal government to regulate business activity and effectively end *whites-only* business practices. As a more general rule, applying the Bill of Rights equally across populations required (and requires) a larger and more active federal government and highlights one of the most important value dimensions underlying American politics: the tradeoff between individual freedom and equality. Unabridged, political freedom would allow for discrimination in all its shapes, forms, and facets. Equal protection of the law, in contrast, requires a government strong enough and large enough that it can effectively protect individuals not just against federal or state government intrusions but also against the actions of their fellow citizens whether in the form of individual action, organized groups, or private businesses. The paradox here is hopefully apparent: We cannot protect individual freedom without giving up some measure of individual freedom. This is the cost of living in a civil society. What rights are protected (and which are not), and which individuals have to give up some measure of their freedom to protect the rights of others is an inherently, inescapable, and ongoing conversation.

The conversation over rights has grown in size and importance. Princeton historian Daniel Rogers observes that "rights talk" is now an ingrained feature of our legal system, reflected in the number of lawyers per capita and the number of legal claims made on the basis of individual rights.[12] The language of rights is powerful, he observes, because of "its open-endedness, its invitation to think at cross-purposes to history, custom, and massively entrenched convention and to measure against original principles of justice." Under this framework, the meaning of rights could expand beyond the narrow definitions of enumerated rights and beyond the narrow province of white male property owners. Though not there yet, it allowed the possibility of transforming Jefferson's rhetoric into a democratic reality. The underbelly of this transformation was that a narrow focus on rights too often defined issues in terms of individualistic needs and protections rather than in the language of community.

Those questions aside, the larger transformation has been clear and unequivocal. We are a nation where speaking in the language of rights is not only expected but also defines issues and sets parameters around potential solutions. If the reality is that rights have been unevenly applied across time and populations, and highly contingent upon context, the sustaining myth is that we all share in a set of natural rights that are inviolate and cannot be infringed. It is a myth that is given breath by our Bill of Rights, encoded into the U.S. Constitution as one of our founding documents.

Protecting Women

The story of how women came to be protected by the Bill of Rights furthers the general point that rights are dependent on the broader social, political, and economic context while adding important nuance and detail. The Bill of Rights and the U.S. Constitution are, in fact, "gender neutral" as none of the protections spelled out in the Bill of Rights specifically exclude (or include) women.[13] Yet women were also conspicuous by their absence.

Voting rights were intentionally left to state governments where women were routinely denied voting rights. In the aftermath of the Civil War and the ratification of the Fifteenth Amendment providing that the right to vote would not be denied on the basis of "race, color, or previous condition of servitude," women's groups were angered by their exclusion from the Fifteenth Amendment. Suffragists Susan B. Anthony, whose image would eventually be featured on a one-dollar coin, and Elizabeth Cady Stanton argued that educated women would be better voters than former slaves. Women's groups made more progress in individual states, gradually earning the right to vote throughout the western United States[14] but did not receive full constitutional protection, via the Nineteenth Amendment (1920), until 50 years later.

Voting rights were the most visible but hardly the sole source of inequality. Women were generally not allowed on juries nor given other rights (or responsibilities) as American citizens. Under the doctrine of coverture, married women had few legal rights to buy property, enter into contracts, or earn wages separate from, or without the approval of, their husbands. Coverture was gradually whittled away by Married Women's Property Acts, laws passed at the state level beginning in 1839 that granted women the right to enter into contracts, own property, and earn a salary. Notably, this was done more out of economic necessity and the desire to protect family property than any abstract commitment to equal rights.[15] What is important to note is that absent state legislative action, the gender-neutral language of the U.S. Constitution and the Bill of Rights not only failed to provide women with equal protection of the law but was also interpreted to permit explicit discrimination. In the case of women's rights, the courts often moved behind more democratic political institutions.

Until 1976, laws treating men and women differently needed to show only a sufficient rationale for the discrimination (via the rational-basis test). This is notably a far less demanding standard than the *strict scrutiny* applied to legal discrimination on the basis of race. Most laws easily passed this fairly low constitutional bar. Subsequent court rulings have raised the bar for laws affecting women to an *intermediate* level of scrutiny, increasing the burden of proof and placing it more clearly on governments for laws and legislation that treated men and women differently. Even so, legislation that discriminates on the basis of sex is not assumed on its face to be unconstitutional as is the case with race.

Legal discrimination against women has often been wrapped in the cloak of *protection* rather than inferiority. Women, for example, received greater protection from labor laws than men and were kept from combat duty and draft requirements because of sex-based differences. Without denying the importance of these biological differences, many of the rationales offered were the result of culture and socialization, expectation and belief, and not biology.

The widespread acceptance of sex-based inequality is perhaps best illustrated by resistance to the Equal Rights Amendment (ERA), first proposed in 1923 and never ratified. Consider first the relatively straightforward language:

- *Section 1. Equality of rights under the law shall not be denied or abridged by the United States or by any State on account of sex.*
- *Section 2. The Congress shall have the power to enforce, by appropriate legislation, the provisions of this article.*

- *Section 3. This amendment shall take effect two years after the date of ratification.*

In a country where rights are ingrained into the fabric of our national identity and *rights talk* defines much of our contemporary debate, a statement proclaiming that rights should not be "denied or abridged" on the basis of sex might seem uncontroversial. Indeed, when the ERA was revived in 1971 in the wake of the liberalization of the 1960s, its passage seemed both quick and assured. Yet, despite a long and enduring history of sex-based discrimination, opposition to the ERA took a familiar and predictable form. First, it was argued it was not needed because women were already protected by the gender-neutral language of the U.S. Constitution and Bill of Rights. Second, it was argued that the ERA would harm women's issues by removing legal protections that already existed in the law, including workplace protections, sexual assault laws, alimony, and draft requirements for military service and combat duty. Opponents further argued that the amendment be the first step down a slippery slope to gay rights because the word *sex* could be extended to protect gay and lesbian individuals. Framed in terms of the potential harm to women, the ERA generated significant grassroots opposition, led by Phyllis Schlafly and Stop ERA, among conservative religious women that ultimately proved its undoing.[16]

Though significant gains have been made, full equality for women has proven to be elusive. Currently, it is estimated that a woman earns 77 cents for every dollar earned by a man, and while this number is often contested, there is little doubt that significant barriers remain to *equal protection of the laws* for men and women. At least one legal scholar argues that the Bill of Rights has hindered rather than facilitated women's progress in this area. "Although many historical inequities would have persisted without the Bill of Rights," writes law professor Mary Becker, "the Bill magnifies these inequities." Indeed, it is only the contemporary era that women's constitutional protections have approached the protections provided to men,[17] yet another fact that reinforces our basic conclusion in this chapter: The application of the Bill of Rights has always been uneven and dependent on the broader social, economic, and political context.

Extending Protections to Lesbian, Gay, Bisexual, and Transgender

Recent and controversial battles over lesbian, gay, bisexual, and transgender (LGBT) rights further illustrate the point. First, it is only in recent decades that the question of *equal protection* for LGBT populations could be seriously raised as a civil rights issue. For much of American history, discrimination against gay and lesbian populations was both culturally acceptable and legally enforced. Second, public opinion has changed dramatically on whether homosexuality is a trait individuals are born with or a *choice*, whether discrimination against gays and lesbians in employment and housing should be allowed (or prohibited), and whether civil unions and same-sex marriage are acceptable. Across a range of issues affecting LGBT populations, public opinion has liberalized and grown increasingly tolerant, particularly among younger Americans. As a general rule, legal decisions and antidiscrimination policies have followed—rather than led—these changes in public opinion. Public opinion has likewise followed active campaigns to change public perception and increase support for gay and lesbian equality. What equality exists for gays and lesbians was not simply granted; it first had to be demanded, and then it had to be won.

Consider that as recently as 1986, in the case of *Bowers v. Hardwick*, the Supreme Court ruled that the right to privacy did not extend to protect the "right of homosexuals to engage in acts of sodomy." A decade later, in *Romer v. Evans*, the Supreme Court extended the Fourteenth Amendment to overturn a Colorado state constitutional amendment disallowing antidiscrimination policies protecting gay and lesbian residents. And, in 2003, the Supreme Court overturned the *Bowers v. Hardwick* decision in *Lawrence v. Texas*, effectively ending state provisions designed to criminalize same-sex relations. Notably, in Louisiana, not only are anti-sodomy laws on the books but the law was being enforced by a sting operation in East Baton Rouge as recently as 2013.[18] In 2014, the Louisiana House of Representatives voted 27–67 at the urging of the Family Forum to keep the state's anti-sodomy provisions on the books despite the fact that they are unenforceable. Louisiana is hardly alone as Alabama, Florida, Idaho, Kansas, Michigan, Mississippi, North Carolina, Oklahoma, South Carolina, Texas, and Utah still have unenforceable but symbolically significant anti-sodomy laws in effect.

The criminalization of sexual preference may stand as the starkest expression of inequality, but other forms of inequality exist as well, including physical violence and intimidation and discrimination in employment, housing, marriage, and adoption. The arguments around these issues take a familiar form as supporters argue that a historically discriminated-against group deserves the same rights and protections enjoyed by everyone else, while opponents argue that such *special rights* are unnecessary and that LGBT groups already enjoy the same protections as other citizens. Whatever one's take on these arguments, public opinion is clearly moving in the direction of greater equality. First, the public has long supported laws forbidding discrimination against gays and lesbians as long as such laws are framed specifically as antidiscrimination measures. This includes discrimination in the workplace, in schools, and in housing.[19] Second, public support for same-sex marriage has increased consistently over time to the point where it now enjoys majority support in national opinion polls. In 1996, more than two in three Americans (68 percent) believed same-sex marriages *should not* be recognized as legally valid. By 2013, a majority of Americans (54 percent) said same-sex marriages *should* be legally recognized.[20]

Overall, greater equality for LGBT populations is the result of changes in the broader political, social, and economic contexts, and is not the result of rights enumerated in the Bill of Rights or constitutional protections proscribed over 200 years ago.

Immigration and Foreign Nationals

One of the more curious of the Tea Party stances given their near-religious reverence for the U.S. Constitution is their disregard for the Fourteenth Amendment's definition of a citizen. Specifically, the Fourteenth Amendment states: "All persons born or naturalized in the United States, and subject to the jurisdiction thereof, are citizens of the United States and of the State wherein they reside." This seemingly simple clause in relatively clear language confers citizenship to children born in the United States regardless of their parents' bloodlines. Perhaps stated more simply, children born to foreign parents on U.S. soil are automatically citizens regardless of the nationality or citizenship of their parents. This clause and its subsequent interpretation has drawn the ire of various commentators and politicos who refer to these children in derogatory terms as *anchor babies* and argue that they should not receive citizenship nor, by extension, constitutional due process protections. The Bill of Rights, they contend, should not apply to someone just because he or she happened to be birthed on U.S. soil. Regardless of one's view of this particular issue, the central question and controversy is similar to those discussed throughout this chapter. Just who should be protected by the Bill of Rights? If the answer is to protect only U.S. citizens, how does one define citizenship? Should the definition be based on place of birth (jus soli) or on bloodlines (jus sanguinis)?

As the critics of the citizenship clause correctly observe, the intent of the Fourteenth Amendment was not to confer citizenship on children based on place of birth but it was instead designed to remedy the Dred Scott decision and assure states did not deny citizenship to former slaves.[21] Even so, in its first application in 1884, the Supreme Court ruled that being born on U.S. soil did not guarantee citizenship to Native Americans born on reservations. By 1898, however, the Supreme Court had reversed course in *United States v. Wong Kim Ark* and ruled that a child born to Chinese immigrants inside the United States was a citizen under the provisions of the Fourteenth Amendment. This has been the prevailing interpretation of the citizenship clause ever since. In 1982 in the case of *Plyer v. Doe*, the Supreme Court extended these protections, deciding that state-provided benefits, specifically public education, could not be denied to children of illegal immigrants.

The rights and protections guaranteed to U.S. immigrants and foreign nationals currently living in the United States received renewed attention in the aftermath of the 9/11 terrorist attacks. Should noncitizens receive the same due process protections as citizens? Should they be provided equal treatment before the law? Before answering, it is worth noting that the Bill of Rights does not specify that its protections should apply only to U.S. citizens. Consider the First Amendment's strongly worded prohibitions—"Congress shall make no law"—against establishing a religion or prohibiting the free exercise of religion. At no point does the text limit the First Amendment's application to citizens.[22] Georgetown law professor David Cole quotes James Madison in support of a broad application of the Bill of Rights to include noncitizens, arguing that because noncitizens owe "a temporary obedience, they are entitled, in return, to their protection and advantage." Regardless, foreign nationals generally do not enjoy the same level of protection as citizens, as laws discriminating against them need pass only a rational-basis test. Thus, the courts have allowed deportation, confinement, and military tribunals instead of criminal courts, particularly during periods when national security concerns are heightened. The 9/11 attacks yielded policies (government surveillance and Patriot Act) that constricted everyone's freedoms but limited the freedoms of immigrants and foreign nationals even more.

Concerned about growing populations of illegal immigrants, Arizona raised the stakes further by requiring police officers to check immigration status provided they had a *reasonable suspicion* to do so. While civil libertarians quickly pointed out the dangers of racial profiling and the threat to individual freedom, the Supreme Court upheld this portion of the law, and reinforced our broader conclusions: The Bill of Rights has never applied equally and to everyone.

Notes

1. Barry A. Shain, "Rights Natural and Civil in the Declaration of Independence," In *The Nature of Rights at the American Founding and Beyond*, ed. Barry Alan Shain (Charlottesville: University of Virginia, Press, 2007).

2. Henry Wiencek, "The Darkside of Thomas Jefferson," *Smithsonian Magazine*, October 2012.

3. Paul Finkelman, "Thomas Jefferson and Antislavery: The Myth Goes On," *The Virginia Magazine of History and Biography* 102 (1994): 2, 193–228.

4. Barry Allan Shain tells the story of Lord Dunmore, who offered to free the slaves in Virginia in 1775 (p. 133). The act was widely condemned as a British violation of property rights. See Shain, "Rights Natural and Civil in the Declaration of Independence."

5. Gordon S. Wood, "The History of Rights in Early America," In *The Nature of Rights at the American Founding and Beyond*, ed. Barry Alan Shain (Charlottesville: University of Virginia Press, 2007).

6. Akhil Reed Amar, "Creation, Reconstruction, and Interpretation of the Bill of Rights," In *The Nature of Rights at the American Founding and Beyond*, ed. Barry Alan Shain (Charlottesville: University of Virginia Press, 2007).

7. Akhil Reed Amar, *The Bill of Rights: Creation and Reconstruction* (New Haven: Yale University Press, 1998).

8. Ibid., 7.

9. Richard Primus, *The American Language of Rights* (Cambridge: Cambridge University Press, 1999).

10. Jamal Greene, "Fourteenth American Originalism," *Maryland Law Review* 71, 4 (2012): 978–1014.

11. Shain, "Rights Natural and Civil in the Declaration of Independence." Shain separately argues that it is a mistake to attribute intent solely to Jefferson as the author of the Declaration of Independence, which was a public document edited and revised by others. He further contends that it is a mistake to read the declaration as a novel expression of rights, but instead should be read as a revolutionary document designed to explain to the world why the colonists (via grievances) were revolting.

12. Daniel Rogers, "Rights Consciousness in American History," In *The Nature of Rights at the American Founding and Beyond*, ed. Barry Alan Shain (Charlottesville: University of Virginia Press, 2007).

13. The word *male* does not appear until the Fourteenth Amendment, Section 2, which guarantees the right to vote.

14. Western states were not necessarily more liberal, but used the right to vote to attract women to states with large male populations.

15. Joan Hoff-Wilson, "The Unfinished Revolution: Changing Legal Status of Women," *Signs* 13 (1987): 7–36.

16. Donald Critchlow and Cynthia Stachecki, "The Equal Rights Amendment Reconsidered: Politics, Policy and Social Mobilization in a Democracy," *Journal of Policy History* 20, 1 (2008): 157–176.

17. Mary E. Becker, "The Politics of Women's Wrongs and the Bill of 'Rights': A Bicentennial Perspective," *The University of Chicago Law Review* 59 (Winter, 1992): 453–517; Joan Hoff-Wilson, "Women in American Constitutional History at the Bicentennial," *The History Teacher* 22 (1989): 1, 145–176.

18. Jim Mustian, "Sheriff's Office Sets Up Park Stakeouts to Ensnare Gay Men," *The Baton Rouge Advocate*, July 28, 2013, available at http://theadvocate.com/news/police/6580728-123/gays-in-baton-rouge-arrested (accessed on February 17, 2014).

19. Paul Brewer, *Value War: Public Opinion and the Politics of Gay Rights* (Lanham, MD: Rowman & Littlefield, 2008).

20. http://www.gallup.com/poll/1651/Gay-Lesbian-Rights.aspx (accessed on April 16, 2014). Specific question wording is as follows: *Do you think marriages between same-sex couples should or should not be recognized by the law as valid, with the same rights as traditional marriages?*

21. Margaret Tebo, "Who's a Citizen?" *ABA Journal* 93 (2007): 1.

22. David Cole, "Are Foreign Nationals Entitled to the Same Constitutional Rights as Citizens?" *Thomas Jefferson Law Review* 25 (2003): 367–388, especially 371.

Chapter 3

The Myth of Unlimited Free Speech: Limiting Freedom of Expression the American Way

In 1977, the Nazi Party of America petitioned to march in the predominantly Jewish community of Skokie, Illinois. The request would have been offensive in any community, but many of the local residents in Skokie were World War II concentration camp survivors. Without question, the intent of the Nazi Party was to exercise their First Amendment freedoms to offend Jewish residents in the streets of their local community.

This story, regularly retold as a landmark First Amendment victory, well illustrates the fundamental trade-offs inherent in the Bill of Rights and its explicit protection of free speech. When does your right to express offensive and reprehensible political views interfere with my right to be left alone? In a free society, do I have a right to not be offended by intentionally provocative, offensive, or racist speech? The lesson most often drawn from this history is that in the United States we allow hateful and repugnant speech as a protected First Amendment freedom. In return, our own right to say whatever we want, whenever we want is also carefully protected. A quick history of the First Amendment reveals this is more myth than reality; speech can be (and has been) limited across a range of contexts. The First Amendment is not now—nor has it ever been—absolute.

In this chapter, we dissect the myth that in the United States, we can say whatever we want, whenever we want. While abstract support for free speech is quite strong and we believe in our own rights to political expression, our willingness to extend those rights to others is severely limited. Or perhaps stated differently, our belief in the First Amendment is heavily conditioned upon how strongly we agree (or disagree) with whoever is speaking. Courts and legislatures have also been more than willing to punish speech that is obscene, libelous, provocative, and/or racists. As with our other political freedoms, free speech is very much dependent on who is speaking and the broader social, economic, and political context. When we, as a nation, feel at risk or threatened, our rights shrink and contract.

Political Tolerance and American Democracy

The language of the First Amendment is quite clear, declaring that "Congress shall make no law respecting an establishment of religion, or prohibiting the free exercise thereof; or abridging the freedom of speech or of the press; or the right to peaceably assemble, and to petition the Government for a redress of grievances." Given this language, it is perhaps not surprising that the Supreme Court decided in favor of the Nazi Party and against the people of Skokie, Illinois, in 1977. The right of the Nazi Party to march was held to be paramount to the right of the people in Skokie to be free of offensive, hateful, and intentionally provocative speech. Notably, despite winning the legal battle, the Nazis never marched in Skokie but instead marched elsewhere in Chicago, a healthy reminder that the First Amendment may have protected Nazis from government interference but not from the people of Skokie. The First Amendment only goes so far.

The concept of political tolerance—allowing speech or protest activity that we disagree with—is at the core of classic democratic theory, and is deeply embedded into the mythology of American political culture. It is neatly captured in the quote most often misattributed to Voltaire: "I disapprove of what you say, but I will defend to the death your right to say it."[1] The operative word in the phrase is *I disapprove* as it is easy to argue in favor of free speech for ideas we agree with but much harder when the speech is factually wrong, morally repugnant, offensive, or profane. The willingness to allow for dissenting, even offensive, opinions is perhaps the defining characteristic of a democratic political culture: Without dissenting voices, there is only the illusion of freedom and choice.

Political dissent, and by extension political tolerance, is most often defended in the American political culture in the language of the marketplace of ideas with its deeps roots in the philosophy of John Stuart Mill and the writings of John Milton, and which later took root in the Supreme Court. The logic is fairly straightforward: Bad ideas cannot sustain themselves where there is a free exchange of information and opinion and where individuals are free to reach their own opinions. Censorship either keeps the truth from being spoken, an outcome that threatens the foundation of democratic society, or keeps misinformation from being disputed and corrected. Left unstated and unchallenged, misinformation runs just beneath the surface of political discourse, and grows like a cancer infecting and destroying democratic governance.

More broadly, Mill and others have argued that freedom of expression aids in the intellectual development and education of citizens, making for a better and stronger democratic political system. Given the freedom to express their own ideas while also being exposed to the widest possible range of political views allows individuals to grow and develop as citizens. Thomas Jefferson expressed this sentiment eloquently in his first inaugural address: "If there be any among us who would wish to dissolve this Union or to change its republican form, let them stand undisturbed as monuments of the safety with which error of opinion may be tolerated where reason is left free to combat it."[2] Errors in perception, Jefferson believed, would not withstand a fair trial based on fact and reason.

In light of contemporary political psychology, Jefferson's faith in the capacity of the democratic citizen is largely misplaced. Not only are citizens often uninformed, but they are also often willfully misinformed, choosing to believe misinformation even in light of factual corrections.[3] Moreover, correcting misperceptions does not necessarily weaken or change beliefs, but instead reinforces them, pushing adherents to believe more strongly. The marketplace of ideas, it would seem, is based on the faulty assumption that fact is more relevant to the direction and/or intensity of political belief than it really is.

Perhaps even more troubling and relevant to the current discussion is the slippage in support for free speech when expressed as an abstract principle (free speech is good) versus its specific application (free speech should be extended to groups I don't like). As long as the sentiment remains in the abstract, free speech is widely supported by an American public that embraces the principle of freedom of expression. According to a 2009 survey, for example, 99 percent of U.S. citizens believe it is very important (78 percent) or somewhat important (21 percent) "for people to be free to express unpopular political views, without fear of being harassed."[4] Few items of American public life, particularly during this time of partisan polarization, achieve this type of consensus-level support from the American public.

Indeed, throughout the long history of public opinion research, public support for freedom of speech has been not only overwhelming but also widely perceived as a defining characteristic of the American political system. Being an American means believing in freedom of speech. For example, when asked what makes the United States unique relative to other nations, citizens routinely cite freedom of expression. In a 2013 survey, 61 percent of Americans identified freedom of speech as a right they would put on the list of protected freedoms if asked about their freedoms by a visitor from another country. No other freedom comes close. Freedom of religion finished second with 36 percent followed by the right to bear arms at 22 percent.[5] Americans overwhelmingly connect *freedom* and *liberty* to freedom of speech.

As we move beyond the abstract to specific application, support for free speech dissipates quickly. Samuel Stouffer's groundbreaking work, *Communism, Conformity, and Civil Liberties*, found mass intolerance as U.S. citizens routinely said they would not extend First Amendment freedoms to socialists, communists, or atheists. This included majorities who opposed allowing communists to speak publicly or teach in colleges or universities, and who supported removing books written by communists from public libraries.[6]

The good news in Stouffer's study was that education and political influence were associated with greater political tolerance and greater support for the "rules of the game." Mass intolerance was subsequently less of a problem for the overall political system than might otherwise be expected because more educated and tolerant political elites "guarded" the system against the intolerant and ignorant masses.[7] Rather than embracing the free exchange of ideas, Americans instead expressed concern that bad ideas can lead to bad consequences and must be censored, a view largely shared by the U.S. Supreme Court throughout much of American history.

Context and specifically the perception of an external threat also played a role in determining individual-level tolerance. The more an individual perceived the overall political system was at risk from an external threat, the less tolerant he or she was of targeted groups. During the red scare, for example, the willingness to extend freedoms to communists necessarily dissipated. Similarly, in the immediate aftermath of 9/11, citizens grew increasingly intolerant of Muslims and other groups who incorrectly appeared to be Muslim and/or of Arabic descent.[8] Sikhs, for example, who are from India but regularly wear turbans, were routinely targeted in the United States in the aftermath of 9/11. Americans not only displayed intolerance but also misapplied that intolerance to the wrong target groups.[9] The importance of threat has been confirmed in comparative studies, which find that individuals, including political elites, are less tolerant in nations that border a perceived (or real) enemy. Israel, for example, is considerably less tolerant than the United States because Israel faces more immediate and proximate military threats.[10]

Outside of a specific context of a heightened threat, Americans may display greater forbearance and political tolerance, but even here they fall far short of the bar set by the classic democratic political theory. Work subsequent to Stouffer's 1955 landmark study found growing tolerance as the United States emerged from the 1950s, McCarthyism, and the red scare into the more liberal and socially tolerant 1960s.[11] With the direct threat of communism minimized and without elites stoking the fires of intolerance, public tolerance of socialists, atheists, and communists increased over this time period.

This work would subsequently be challenged as capturing intolerance only toward left-leaning groups, thus missing intolerance toward groups on the right and overstating overall tolerance levels. Indeed, when individuals were free to choose their own least-liked groups, political intolerance was gauged to be at surprisingly high levels, thus casting doubt on evidence that Americans were growing more tolerant over time.[12] While overall levels of intolerance might be alarming, intolerance has limited effects on democratic governance because the targets of intolerance are widely dispersed rather than narrowly focused. Or perhaps stated differently, because we hate lots of different people, our intolerance is less troubling in terms of its democratic consequences. Hate widely dispersed is hate that has been thinned to more manageable levels.

Broadly speaking, Americans may believe the First Amendment allows them to say anything they want, but they are often unwilling to extend that freedom to others they disagree with. This is not a trivial concern as meaningful public support for individual freedom often sets the parameters around individual freedom.

The Supreme Court and Free Speech

One of the tenets of the U.S. Bill of Rights (discussed in Chapter Two) is that trust is placed in unelected judges to be more stalwart defenders of constitutional rights than legislators or the general public. Where legislators may bow to the pressure of public opinion, judges with lifetime appointments would, in theory, be relatively immune to such pressures. Such a view is well represented in the answer Justice Antonin Scalia gave to a question about flag burning following a speech at the University of Freiburg in Switzerland:

> *I don't like that result, and I if that was up to me, IF I WERE KING—I would take scruffy, bearded, sandal wearing IDIOTS who were going around burning the flag, and I would put them in jail. But, since I'm an originalist, I have to look at the First Amendment and say you know, what did the First Amendment mean, and I cannot avoid the conclusion, it was a guarantee of freedom of expression. YOU HAVE A RIGHT to criticize, to condemn the flag, the Supreme Court, the government. I mean, that what the First Amendment is about.*[13]

Yet, if justices often subscribe to a content neutral view when discussing the First Amendment, the evidence suggests that they lose their objectivity in deciding individual cases. First, Supreme Court justices are much more likely to support free speech when they agree with the speaker.[14] That is, conservative justices are more likely to support free speech in cases where the speaker is also conservative. Second, the Supreme Court does respond to public opinion though there is some question as to whether the effect is direct (public opinion influences court decisions)[15] or indirect (public opinion influences the composition of the court, which influences decisions).[16] Regardless, Supreme Court decisions change with the tenor of the times to reflect the broader social, political, and economic context.

National Security Versus Free Speech

Perhaps nowhere is the importance of context more apparent than in decisions where the court is asked to balance free speech against national security. In different times and contexts, the court has moved from not protecting speech (primarily by communists or socialists) to providing broad and substantive free speech protections based on the marketplace of ideas. Over time, there is a trend toward more liberal interpretations of the First Amendment, but this expansion has been more cyclical than linear, expanding during some periods and contracting during others.

As we noted previously, the Founding Fathers wasted little time in making it a crime to criticize the government via the Alien and Sedition Acts. The Adams administration pursued prosecutions and secured convictions against a number of offenders, mostly editors and publishers of local newspapers. While Thomas Jefferson pardoned everyone convicted under the Sedition Act, this early period illustrates the limits of free speech even in the wake of ratifying the First Amendment. More broadly, the guarantees provided in the First Amendment are only as good as our collective fidelity to the basic tenets of freedom of expression and our commitment to the importance of political dissent to a democratic society. Where that commitment is lacking, the First Amendment is necessarily limited and weakened.

Between 1798 and 1917, the Supreme Court treated the First Amendment with "pervasive hostility," rarely ruling favor for free speech.[17] In the definitive work on this period, legal scholar David Raban notes that the courts never articulated a coherent approach to free speech cases and tended to defer to legislative and administrative decisions that punished (but did not censor) speech. Even truth was seen as an inadequate defense when speech was perceived as harming the public welfare. In *Gompers v. Bucks Stove & Range Co.* (1911), for example, the Supreme Court distinguished between "normal speech" protected by the First Amendment and "verbal acts"—in this case advocating for a union boycott—which were not protected.[18] Similarly, in *Mutual Film Corp v. Industrial Commission of Ohio* (1915), the Supreme Court ruled that the exhibition of films was a profit-making business and could subsequently be censored.[19] Speech could be limited during this period not if it incited illegal activity but if it created the potential for "bad tendencies," where bad tendencies were broadly defined under the logic that it was impossible to foresee the consequences of a speech.

The more libertarian view toward free speech, which jealously guards political speech, extends those protections to symbolic acts (such as flag burning) and to other mediums and to *artistic* expression, occurred slowly and over time. The articulation of a judicial doctrine underlying what speech is protected (and what speech is not) only really began to take shape in the wake of World War I and the arrests of individuals advocating the overthrow of government or articulating an ideological critique of capitalism.

In 1917, Congress enacted the Espionage Act, making it a crime to interfere with the prosecution of World War I. One year later, the Sedition Act followed, making it a crime to criticize the government, the flag, the draft, or the war. Prosecutions under the Sedition Act were upheld in the landmark decision of *Schenck v. United States* in which Justice Oliver Wendell Holmes outlined the "clear and present danger test," allowing speech to be limited if it was likely to be followed by illegal actions.[20] So, for example, distributing leaflets encouraging young men to dodge the draft during World War I was speech that created the very real possibility that individuals would, in fact, dodge the draft, and could subsequently be limited. By contemporary standards, the clear and present danger test may sound restrictive, but at the time it represented a more libertarian and expensive interpretation of the First Amendment.

The most prominent prosecution and conviction was in 1918 of Eugene V. Debs, a Socialist Party candidate for president, a union organizer, and an antiwar activist. Consistent with the *Schenck* decision, the Supreme Court held that by praising those who had been convicted for obstructing the draft, Debs was interfering with the war effort, thus presenting a clear and present danger. Perhaps ironically, Debs began the speech that led to his arrest by noting the limited protection of the First Amendment: "I realize that, in speaking to you this afternoon, there are certain limitations placed upon the right of free speech. I must be exceedingly careful, prudent, as to what I say, and even more careful and prudent as to how I say it. I may not be able to say all I think; but I am not going to say anything that I do not think."[21] Debs's precautions were apparently inadequate as he was subsequently jailed, prosecuted, and convicted. Debs acknowledged and accepted this possibility in his speech: "I would rather a thousand times be a free soul in jail than to be a sycophant and coward in the streets."

Curiously, later in that same year, Justice Oliver Wendell Holmes offered in *Abrams v. United States* what may be the single most important dissent in the history of American jurisprudence by articulating that "the best test of truth is the power of the thought to get itself accepted in the competition of the market."[22] While Holmes never specifically used the term *marketplace of ideas*, the dissent articulated that free expression of opinion was the best antidote to speech that only advocated ideas and did not yield to illegal behavior or outcomes. The specific case involved the distribution of leaflets criticizing U.S. foreign policy during World War I. Holmes drew the distinction between his opinions in *Schenck* and *Debs* by noting the leaflets were "silly" and written by unknown persons with no real consequence. While the dissent would form the basis of more liberalizing decisions in the future, the Supreme Court rejected Holmes's opinion in *Abrams v. United States* by a 7–2 vote and upheld the convictions.

The paradox inherent in the clear and present danger test should be apparent. Speech could be limited only if it might prove to be effective in mobilizing action. Debs, who offered powerful oratory guided by a belief that the existing economic and political systems were immoral, could be prosecuted and convicted, while speech that was ineffectual or *silly* required no restraint. The marketplace of ideas would be open only to less-threatening and persuasive forms of expression.

Fighting Words

If speech can be limited to protect national security, it can be also limited when its intent is to incite an illegal or violent response, that is, when the words spoken can be fairly labeled as *fighting words*. The law in this particular area is murky as the phrase *fighting words* is vague and ill-defined. Lower court rulings have subsequently been inconsistent in their interpretations. After establishing the fighting words exception in *Chaplinsky v. New Hampshire* (1942), the Supreme Court has generally found the exception unexceptional, opting instead to protect free speech rights against incitement to violence.

In 1942, Walter Chaplinsky, a Jehovah's Witness, was convicted for calling a local New Hampshire official "a God damned racketeer" and "a damned fascist."[23] His conviction was upheld on the basis that his speech was not an expression of an idea and subsequently lacked social value. Despite the Chaplinsky ruling, the courts have mostly allowed speech that is intentionally offensive, vulgar, or profane. Flag burning, for example, does not count as fighting words even if the act might incite a violent response, nor does wearing a jacked that says "Fuck the Draft" or shouting profanities at police officers.

In *Cohen v. California* (1971), Justice Harlan articulated the majority opinion in the "Fuck the Draft" case, noting that while profanities may be distasteful, "one man's vulgarity is another's lyric."[24] The inclusion of a profanity did not necessarily void the speech of any redeeming social value. In *City of Houston v. Hill* (1987), Justice Brennan made the point more explicit, observing that "[t]he freedom of individuals verbally to oppose or challenge police action without thereby risking arrest is one of the principal characteristics by which we distinguish a free nation from a police state."[25] Indeed, the most common use of the "fighting words" exception has been to give police officers authority to arrest uncooperative or unruly individuals on the basis of their speech rather than their actions. The courts have looked askance at such practices, holding that police officers should be trained to handle such tirades and subsequently should also be held to higher standard than private citizens. If the First Amendment is to have any value, it must extend to criticisms of police action.

The courts have also protected more outrageous and offensive forms of speech, including the uncivil protests of the Westboro Baptist Church at military funerals with signs reading "God Hates Fags" and "Thank God for Dead Soldiers." The Supreme Court overwhelmingly (8–1) sided with Westboro, holding that even repugnant and offensive speech in the context of a military funeral must be protected.[26] In the majority opinion, Chief Justice John Roberts observed that we cannot react to the "pain" of intentionally hurtful speech by punishing the speaker. The lone dissenter in the case, Justice Samuel Alito, drew a line between free speech and the right to verbally assault individuals. The digital age adds unique wrinkle to this question: By what standard should we judge threats posted on Facebook or via other social media? Is it enough to show that a reasonable person would find the language threatening or does it require proving subjective intent?[27] In the case at hand, can an estranged husband post "I'm not gonna rest until your body is a mess, soaked in blood and dying from all the little cuts," on Facebook, under the pretense that he was not threatening his estranged wife just letting off a little steam?[28]

Whether or not exceptions to the fighting words doctrine are allowed by the courts often boils down to a fairly straightforward question: Is the exception content neutral or does it punish particular points of view? In the Westboro decision, the church had, in fact, followed the law for allowable protests, including time and place restrictions. As such, their "crime" was the offensive content of the speech and not the manner or the place in which they spoke. Content neutral restrictions, requiring permits for protests or not allowing speech in particular areas or at specific times, can be upheld provided they are universally applied.

This brings us to two important implications for free speech and fighting words. First, speech may be limited where it fails to advance the expression of ideas and where the speech lacks social value. Simply shouting random profanities may not be protected. Shouting profanities at a police officer, in contrast, must be protected because there is inherent political content in challenging police authority. We should add a corollary that although you have a right to be uncivil or rude to a police office, it is best to avoid doing so. Your rights can be violated and you can still spend a night in jail. Second, speech may be limited as long as any restrictions are content neutral. The Westboro Baptist Church can be legally required to stay a thousand feet away from a military funeral as long as other groups are subject to the same restrictions and as long as the restrictions are not unreasonable. An interesting application of this principle has been in states with *adopt a highway* programs in which volunteer groups help to clean roads and highways. When racist groups, like the Ku Klux Klan in Missouri, the National Alliance in Kentucky, and the Klan again in Georgia, apply for such programs, they must be evaluated on the basis of the same content neutral criteria as other organizations.

Speech Codes on Campus

It is only a slight extension to consider free speech restrictions on college campuses as a tool for minimizing the adverse consequences of race or gender biases on student retention and degree attainment. While such limits are often dismissed as mere *political correctness*, there are compelling arguments for restricting such speech. Left unchallenged, these biases can have negative effects on the educational experience of racial minorities, women, and LGBT communities and can adversely affect the broader intellectual climate. Perhaps stated differently, free speech and open intellectual inquiry are not served well by racial, sexist, or homophobic invectives.

The adoption of speech codes and other related policies illustrates the trade-off inherent in creating an environment that minimizes offensive and oppressive language versus an environment that allows the fullest range of political expression. Do we trust that an open conversation can effectively address prejudice and misperception, or should we set boundaries around what is acceptable speech? Where violations occur, should we treat them as teachable moments or punishable offenses? In many ways, this is the same trade-off faced by the Supreme Court in deciding whether to allow the Nazis to march in Skokie: Is your right to be left alone more (or less) important than my right to say whatever I want, whenever I want?

On U.S. college campuses, the tendency has been to err on the side of not offending minority groups. This is despite court rulings that cast doubt on the constitutionality of overly vague university speech codes and harassment and incitement policies that punish speech as well as action. For example, these codes often prohibit any *verbal or physical* behavior, and specifically prohibit certain types of speech. According to a 2014 study, 58 percent of public universities and colleges had policies (or speech codes) that "clearly restrict protected speech."[29] Most of these policies were aimed at speech that might be fairly limited (e.g., incitement, obscenity, and harassment) but were often misapplied and broadly construed by overly zealous university administrators.[30] As a result, there is no shortage of anecdotes of students or faculty punished for innocuous speech or behavior. For example, universities have suspended a faculty member for a "threatening" joke in class about an exam that was a "killing spree," defined harassment to include offensive op-eds in student newspapers, and limited students from handing out copies of the U.S. Constitution or gathering signatures for petitions outside of tightly defined and restricted free speech zones. The very existence of free speech zones raises the obvious question of why a public university is not, by definition, a free speech zone, particularly when the speech in question is often inherently political (handing out political flyers) and not commercial (handing out information on drink specials or credit card applications).[31]

In fairness, one might argue this is a false trade-off. You can express most ideas without being offensive, racist, sexist, or homophobic. Moreover, one of the primary functions of a university should be to teach students to engage in civil debate and deliberative reflection. Yet the fear of running afoul of speech codes may well lead reasonable and well-intended students and faculty to engage in self-censorship by avoiding difficult conversations and by not expressing thoughts that might not be *politically correct*. The best strategy may be simply not to talk about it at all. In a 2010 study, only 36 percent of college students and 19 percent of faculty *strongly agreed* that it was "safe to hold unpopular positions on campus."[32] Taken out of context, the statistic is a little misleading as the vast majority of students (81 percent) agreed that it was safe to hold unpopular views on campus. Even so, roughly 1 in 5 students did not agree *and* college seniors—as compared to college freshmen—were less likely to strongly agree that college campuses were safe for unpopular views. After four years on campus, students were less likely to strongly agree that campuses are safe place to express unpopular ideas.

In the marketplace of ideas, unexpressed thoughts cannot be countered or discussed, nor can one gain insight into someone else's unique life experiences and perspectives. At least some college professors have dealt with the problem by avoiding discussion on sensitive topics. Others have adopted *trigger warnings* to caution students that specific sections of the course may be offensive so that students can opt out of discussions and lectures. Either way, the open and free debate that defines an idealized version of the college experience is often limited by concerns that discussions of sensitive topics may give way to charges of racism or sexism.

Limiting free speech is not solely the work of left-wing groups or political correctness run amok. Conservative groups, like Accuracy in Academy, use students to report on professors who are—in their view—indoctrinating students into left-wing ideologies. Accuracy in Academy has developed a list of 100 arguments against tenure, a list of faculty considered to be indoctrinating students into liberal beliefs. Included on the list are a Noble Prize winner whose work on economic inequality has been definitive and the director of the Innocence Project, a legal research team designed to assist those individuals wrongfully convicted of crimes. Conservative commentator David Horowitz similarly compiled a list of the 101 most dangerous academics in America in his book *The Professors*.[33] The goal of such works is not to engage in the marketplace of ideas but to create a chilling effect on the free expression of ideas and to send the unmistakable message to college professors that they are being monitored.[34]

The politicization of the university has meant that university students and faculty often sit between liberal groups seeking to enforce speech codes that minimize racial and gender biases and conservatives intent on exposing liberal college professors for teaching critical or ideological perspectives. The result is that college campuses, which might be idealized as bastions of free speech, often limit expression as a means to creating a more welcoming and enriching learning environment. Were they to be challenged in court, it is likely that many university policies would be found unconstitutional. This has not, however, stopped colleges from adopting and enforcing speech codes and harassment and incitement policies. This reality reinforces the point that having First Amendment protections does not mean they will be respected by state or local authorities who may knowingly violate free speech protections in pursuit of other policy-related goals. Free speech can be protected only where it is challenged.

Obscenity

Pornographic images, text, and video are pervasive online. Estimates are that there are 25 million porn sites accounting for 12 percent of all websites. While accurate estimates of the overall economic value of online porn are difficult to ascertain, some estimates are as high $2.8 billion.[35] Despite its pervasiveness, obscenity is not protected speech and can be limited by federal and state governments. Before moving forward, we should note that not all pornography is obscene. Nude photographs, for example, may have great artistic value or they may be deeply offensive and lacking in artistic value. Both are pornographic, but only the latter is obscene. The challenge, of course, is in developing a working definition of what might be fairly considered offensive and void of artistic merit. The Supreme Court has generally floundered, reverting back to an only slightly more clearly articulated version of Justice Potter's observation that "I know it when I see it." The current definition, articulated in *Miller v. California* (1973), is a three-prong test riddled with ambiguity:[36]

- Whether the average person, applying contemporary community standards, would find that the work, taken as a whole, appeals to the prurient interest.
- Whether the work depicts or describes, in a patently offensive way, sexual conduct specifically defined by the applicable state law.
- Whether the work, taken as a whole, lacks serious literary, artistic, political or scientific value.

The questions with such a definition abound. What is an average person? What are contemporary community standards? How do we define *community*? And who determines whether a work lacks serious literary, artistic, political, or scientific value? Isn't such *value* inherently subjective?

By the court's current interpretation, *community* is defined as a local community, thus allowing for variance in the definition of what constitutes obscenity as one travels from New Orleans, Louisiana, to Bismarck, North Dakota, and from Portland, Maine, to Los Angeles, California. Yet the court has also recognized that local community standards have to be applied within a broader national context. The movie *Carnal Knowledge* (1971), for example, could not be defined as obscene simply because it included nude scenes and sexual content.

In the postmodern age where an expanding definition of art has opened the doors to more offensive, provocative, and symbolic acts or expression, determining *artistic* value proves even more vexing than defining community standards. The arrest of the rap group 2 Live Crew in Hollywood, Florida, for obscenity, for example, sparked a still unsettled debate over the meaning of artistic expression. The album "As Nasty as They Wanna Be" was unquestionably sexually explicit, misogynistic, and profane, but did it possess *serious artistic value*? In 1990, U.S. District Judge Jose Gonzales ruled the album was obscene, the first album ever to receive such a designation, calling it "an appeal to dirty thoughts and the loins, not to the intellect and the mind."[37] Henry Louis Gates Jr., at the time a Duke University literature professor, had argued the songs served as powerful parodies of racial stereotypes. Music critic John Leland traced the history of rap music and argued the music and the lyrics made a unique contribution to American music. In 1992, an appellate court struck down the obscenity ruling opening the door to a wider range of profane—but not necessarily obscene—artistic expression.

While it might be a mistake to imbue 2 Live Crew with undue social, political, or legal significance, the doors have subsequently swung open to *artistic* expression that would have been considered obscene in an earlier time. Arguing that pornography has adverse and harmful consequences, social conservatives and feminists reason that the courts should do more to limit pornography as political expression. Radical feminist Andrea Dworkin, for example, contended that pornography served to legitimize and incite harm to women.[38] Conservative Irving Kristol similarly argued that, just as great works of art can serve to enlighten and expand our understanding of our world, pornography (and obscenity) can dehumanize us and narrow our understanding of that same world.[39] For Kristol, the issue is quite clear: "[I]f you care for the quality of life in our American democracy, then you have to be for censorship," though he also adds that there is cost to artistic expression that quickly sinks to the lowest common denominator. Allow all expression, and our political and artistic expression gets dumber, crasser, and more profane.

The reasoning here brings us back to the marketplace of ideas and the role of the First Amendment in protecting *political* expression but not necessarily protecting commercial expression or nonpolitical speech. If speech does not further the exchange of ideas and information, if it does not enhance democratic governance by attempting to inform or persuade citizens, then, arguably, there is little reason that it should be protected by the First Amendment. The Supreme Court, however, has mostly rejected this argument, opting instead to extend First Amendment protections to obscene nonpolitical artistic expression. As a result, speech challenging government in the immediate aftermath of a terrorist attack is more likely to be limited than a singer, an artist, or an actor engaged in profane speech or acts.

Libel

The First Amendment has never protected the intentional spreading of misinformation to defame a person or, for that matter, to sell a product. In the context of English common law, even truth was no defense for a charge of seditious or blasphemous libel. In 1734, however, Philadelphia attorney-Andrew Hamilton defended printer Peter Zenger against charges of seditious libel made against New York's governor by arguing the published statements were true. Zenger's acquittal established truth as a defense against libel and helped to expand the definition of protected speech, particularly speech critical of governing authorities.

In 1964, these protections were extended even further in *New York Times Co. v. Sullivan*.[40] The case involved local Alabama officials trying to use libel laws to get back at outsiders critical of how local law enforcement treated civil rights protestors. The advertisement, which served as the basis for the libel claim, did indeed include factually incorrect information, but it was not at all clear that the advertisement harmed the reputation of Sullivan, a local public safety commissioner. The Supreme Court ruled that because the case involved a public official, the statements must be shown not only to be untrue but also to have been made with *actual malice*, meaning knowledge that the statements were untrue, or a reckless disregard for their truth. More broadly, the court's ruling can be seen as an effort to minimize the effect of libel laws on the willingness of citizens to criticize public officials. Where the target is an *average citizen*, that is, not a public figure, the bar for demonstrating libel is considerable lower.

Subsequent decisions have followed a similar logic. In *Hustler v. Falwell* (1988), for example, the court ruled that a parody, which was obviously false, could not possibly defame its target.[41] In this case, the parody showed the Moral Majority's Jerry Falwell in incestuous relationship with his mother in an outhouse.

Campaign Spending as Speech

One area were political speech has remained relatively unrestricted is in the right to spend unlimited sums of money during political campaigns. In *Buckley v. Valeo* (1976), the Supreme Court never quite equated campaign spending with free speech but instead drew on the analogy that campaign spending is to speech as gasoline is to a car.[42] Without campaign spending, political campaigns could not go very far. Even this right, however, was not without limits. While the Supreme Court has allowed unlimited *independent* spending on political spending, it has allowed limits on contributions to candidates and parties as a mechanism for addressing the *appearance of corruption* in political campaigns. Notably, the appearance of corruption—and not the reality—was enough to justify contribution limits.

Citizens United v. FEC (2010) is often pointed to as the case that opened the floodgates to virtually unlimited campaign spending, but the reality is that at least one mechanism (independent spending) had been in place since 1976.[43] The Super PACs that emerged in the wake of *Citizens United* simply provided the organizational might and political will to allow for a more rapid infusion of politically interested cash. The result has been that wealthy citizens (Koch brothers, George Soros, and others) are spending ever-increasing amounts to influence U.S. elections, thus amplifying their *speech* above the din of other voices. The political system is subsequently more responsive to the preferences of wealthier Americans.

No other industrial democracy defines *speech* in this way. First, most provide some form of free radio or television time for candidates and parties to communicate directly to voters. Second, most provide some form of public funding, limiting the candidates' reliance on private donations. There no connection made between *speech* as a protected right and campaign spending, nor is there any evidence that limiting spending limits the scope of political debate. Indeed, in American politics, campaign spending is filtered through political candidates who focus spending on campaign messages that can be communicated effectively in a 30-second television or radio ad, on a direct mail piece, or in a robocall to targeted households. Public financing in European democracies has encouraged the growth of a wider range of political parties, including labor parties on the left and Christian Democrats on the right. Overall, there is scant evidence that campaign money expands the range or depth of political debate.

By roughly equating political speech with campaign spending, the Supreme Court's decisions unintentionally narrowed the scope of civic dialogue, encouraged the use of polarizing *wedge* issues, and shrunk the time available for campaign communications to 30-second ads. This is not a limit on speech per se, but it is unquestionably a limit in terms of its consequences for the broader conversations that define politics.

Conclusions

In 1971, unsuccessful Supreme Court nominee Robert Bork observed: "The law has settled upon no tenable, internally consistent theory of the scope of the constitutional guarantee of free speech."[44] In contemporary America, we tend to think of the First Amendment as broadly protecting freedom of expression. Indeed, there is much truth here as the First Amendment today is interpreted much more broadly than during any time in American history. Yet, even broadly interpreted, the First Amendment has its limits. It does not necessarily protect speech against the needs to maintain national security nor does it protect fighting works, obscenity, or libel.

More generally, the interpretation of the First Amendment by the Supreme Court may have unintentionally hurt the quality of democratic public life. Endorsing campaign spending as speech has yielded a politics of 30-second ads, exaggerated claims, and polarizing messaging. Expanding protections of artistic expression has encouraged a popular culture that rewards shock value with media attention and sales. As a result, the marketplace of ideas remains relatively stagnant even as the amount and volume of speech have increased exponentially.

Notes

1. The source of the quote was Evelyn Beatrice Hall, who wrote the famous sentence as representative of Voltaire's political beliefs.

2. Thomas Jefferson, "First Inaugural Address in the Washington, DC," Wednesday, March 4, 1801, available at http://www.bartleby.com/124/pres16.html (accessed on April 27, 2014).

3. Brendan Nyhan, Jason Reifler, and Peter Ubel, "The Hazards of Correcting Myths about Health Care Reform," *Medical Care* 51 (2013): 127–132; Brendan Nyhan and Jason Reifler, "When Corrections Fail: The Persistence of Political Misperceptions,"*Political Behavior* 32 (2010): 303–330.

4. World Public Opinion: A Study of 24 Nations, conducted by WorldPublicOpinion.Org, available at http://www.ipu.org/idd-e/report09.pdf (accessed on April 28, 2014).

5. Full question wording is as follows: If someone from another country were to ask you to make a list of the specific rights and freedoms you have as a resident of the United States, what would be the first thing you would put on the list? (Open ended, coded with precoded list). "Balancing Act: The Public's Take on Civil Liberties and Security," conducted by the Associated Press-NORC Center for Public Affairs Research, August 12–29, 2013, and based on interviews with 1,008 adults.

6. Samuel Stouffer, *Communism, Conformity, and Civil Liberties: A Cross-Section of the Nation Speaks Its Mind* (Garden City, NY: Doubleday, 1955).

7. James Prothro and Charles Grigg, "Fundamental Principles of Democracy: Bases of Agreement and Disagreement," *Journal of Politics* 22 (1960): 276–294; Herbert McClosky, "Consensus and Ideology in American Politics," *American Political Science Review* 58 (1964): 361–382; see John Sullivan and Henriet Hendriks, "Public Support for Civil Liberties Pre- and Post-9/11," *American Review of Law and Social Science* 5 (2009): 375–391 for a review of this literature.

8. Darren Davis and Brian Silver, "Civil Liberties vs. Security: Public Opinion in the Context of the Terrorist Attacks on America," *American Journal of Political Science* 48, 1 (2004): 28–46; Darren Davis, *Negative Liberty: Public Opinion and the Terrorist Attacks on America* (New York: Russell Sage Foundation, 2006).

9. It is perhaps worth noting that the number of attacks was relatively small.

10. Michael Shamir, "Political Tolerance among Mass and Elites in Israel: A Reevaluation of the Elitist Theory of Democracy,"*Journal of Politics* 53 (1991): 1018–1043.

11. Allen Williams, Clyde Nunn, and Louis Peter, "Origins of Tolerance: Findings from a Replication of Stouffer's Communism, Conformity, and Civil Liberties," *Social Forces* 55 (1978): 394–408; Clyde Nunn, Harry Crockett, and Allen Williams, *Tolerance for nonconformity* (San Francisco: Jossey-Bass Publishers, 1978); James A. Davis, "Communism, Conformity, Cohorts, and Categories: American Tolerance in 1954 and 1972–3," *American Journal of Sociology* 81 (1975): 491–513.

12. John L. Sullivan, James Piereson, and George Marcus, *Political Tolerance and American Democracy* (Chicago: University of Chicago Press, 1982).

13. Quoted in Adam Liptak, "For Justices, Free Speech Often Means 'Speech I Agree With,' " *New York Times*, May 5, 2014, available at http://www.nytimes.com/2014/05/06/us/politics/in-justices-votes-free-speech-often-means-speech-i-agree-with.html?_r=0 (accessed on May 6, 2014). Original source is from a speech at the University of Freiburg in Switzerland on March 28, 2006, available at www.aparchive.com (accessed November 7, 2014).

14. Lee Epstein, Christopher Parker, and Jeffrey Segal, "Do Justices Defend Speech They Hate? In-Group Bias, Opportunism, and the First Amendment," paper presented at the 2013 annual meeting of the American Political Science Association, Chicago, IL.

15. Kevin McGuire and James Stimson, "The Least Dangerous Branch Revisited," *Journal of Politics* 66 (2008): 1018–1035; Barry Friedman, *The Will of the People: How Public Opinion Has Influenced the Supreme Court and Shaped the Meaning of the Constitution* (New York: Farrar, Straus and Giroux, 2009).

16. Helmut Norpoth and Jeffrey Segal, "Comment: Popular Influence on Supreme Court Decisions," *American Political Science Review* 88 (1994): 711–716.

17. David Raban, "The First Amendment in Its Forgotten Years," *Yale Law Journal* 90 (1981): 514–595; David Raban, *Free Speech in Its Forgotten Years* (Cambridge: Cambridge University Press, 1997).

18. *Gompers v. Buck's Stove and Range Co.*, 221 U.S. 418 (1911).

19. *Mutual Film Corporation v. Industrial Commission of Ohio*, 236 U.S. 230 (1915).

20. *Schenck v. United States*, 249 U.S. 47 (1919).

21. "The Canton, Ohio Speech, Anti-War Speech," available at https://www.marxists.org/archive/debs/works/1918/canton.htm (accessed on May 7, 2014).

22. Justice Oliver Wendall Holmes dissenting in *Abrams v. United States* (No. 316), 250 U.S. 616, November 10, 1919, available at http://www.law.cornell.edu/supremecourt/text/250/616 (accessed on April 27, 2014).

23. *Chaplinsky v. New Hampshire*, 315 U.S. 568, 62 S. Ct. 766, 86 L. Ed. 1031 (1942), U.S. 851.

24. *Cohen v. California*, 403 U.S. 15 (1971).

25. *City of Houston v. Hill*, 482 U.S. 451 (1987).

26. *Snyder v. Phelps*, 562 U.S. ___ (2011).

27. Elonis v. United States, 13-983 U.S. ___ (2015)

28. David Savage, "Supreme Court appears unlikely to protect Facebook Threats," *Los Angeles Times*, December 1, 2014, available at http://www.latimes.com/nation/la-na-supreme-court-facebook-threats-free-speech-20141201-story.html (accessed on December 7, 2014).

29. Spotlight on Speech Codes 2014: The State of Free Speech on Our Nation's Campuses, Foundation for Individual Rights in Education, available at http://www.thefire.org/spotlight/reports/ (accessed on May 25, 2014).

30. There is a cottage industry of books detailing individual cases of university overreach. Greg Lukianoff, *Unlearning Liberty: Campus Censorship and the End of American Debate* (New York: Encounter Books, 2014); Alan Charles Kors and Harry Silverglate, *The Shadow University: The Betrayal of Liberty on America's Campuses* (New York: The Free Press, 1998); Dinesh D'Souza, *Illiberal Education: The Politics of Race and Sex on Campus* (New York: The Free Press, 1991).

31. Faculty have often done themselves no favors when it comes to free speech by using *academic freedom* to engage in blatantly partisan activity on campus and/or using university funds. The ethic guiding faculty writing should be that it is based on research and not polemics, and that it should be oriented toward the rigorous standards that define academic disciplines. Yet many faculty abuse the privilege.

32. Eric L. Dey and Associates, *Engaging Diverse Viewpoints: What Is the Campus Climate for Perspective Taking?* (Washington, DC: Association of American Colleges and Universities, 2010).

33. David Horowitz, *The Professors: The 101 Most Dangerous Academics in America* (Washington, DC: Regnery Publishing, 2006).

34. Notably, if college professors are trying to liberalize students, they are not very good at it. While there is a *liberalizing effect* of a college education, it appears to have less to do with classroom lectures than with intellectual development and an understanding the world is not black and white, and to interactions with peers with different backgrounds, worldviews, and experiences.

35. David Futrelle, "Sex on the Internet: Sizing Up the Online Smut Economy," *Time*, April 4, 2012, available at http://business.time.com/2012/04/04/sex-on-the-internet-sizing-up-the-online-smut-economy/ (accessed on May 29, 2014). According to the article, the growth of online pornography appears to be limited

by online piracy and free online porn. Online webcams are currently the growth industry.

36. *Miller v. California*, 413 U.S. 15 (1973).

37. Billy Johnson, Jr. "7 Ways the World Went Crazy with 'As Nasty As They Wanna Be,'" *Rolling Stone*, February 7, 2014, available at http://www.rolling stone.com/music/news/7-ways-the-world-went-crazy-with-as-nasty-as-they-wanna-be-20140207 (accessed on June 5, 2014).

38. Andrea Dworkin, *Pornography: Men Possessing Women* (New York: E.P. Dutton, 1989), paperback edition.

39. Irving Kristol, "Pornography, Obscenity, and the Case for Censorship," *New York Times Magazine*, March 28, 1971, available at http://www.rense.com/general87/obscenity.htm (accessed on June 6, 2014).

40. *New York Times Co. v. Sullivan*, 376 U.S. 254 (1964).

41. *Hustler Magazine, Inc. v. Falwell*, 485 U.S. 46 (1988).

42. *Buckley v. Valeo*, 424 U.S. 1 (1976).

43. *Citizens United v. Federal Election Commission*, 558 U.S. ___ (2010).

44. Robert H. Bork, "Neutral Principles and Some First Amendment Problems," *Indiana Law Journal* 47 (1971): 1–36, especially 20.

Chapter 4

The Myth of a Free and Independent Press

No experiment can be more interesting than that we are now trying, and which we trust will end in establishing the fact, that man may be governed by reason and truth. Our first object should therefore be, to leave open to him all the avenues to truth. The most effectual hitherto found, is the freedom of the press.

—Thomas Jefferson, Letter to John Tyler (1804)

Only a free and unrestrained press can effectively expose deception in government.

—Hugo Black, Concurring Opinion in New York Times Co. v. United States

The freedom of the press is one of the greatest bulwarks of liberty, and can never be restrained but by despotic governments.

—George Mason, The Virginia Declaration of Rights

A popular Government without popular information, or the means of acquiring it, is but a Prologue to a Farce or a Tragedy, or perhaps both. Knowledge will forever govern ignorance: And a people who mean to be their own Governors, must arm themselves with the power which knowledge gives.

—James Madison, Letter to W.T. Barry (1822)

For the newspaper is in all literalness the bible of democracy, the book out of which a people determines its conduct. It is the only serious book most people read. It is the only book they read every day.

—Walter Lippmann, Liberty and the News (1920)

Freedom of the press is the staff of life for any vital democracy.

—Wendell Wilkie, Letter to W.N. Hardy (1940)

A democracy ceases to be a democracy if its citizens do not participate in its governance. To participate intelligently, they must know what their government has done, is doing and plans to do in their name. Whenever any hindrance, no matter what its name, is placed in the way of this information, a democracy is weakened, and its future endangered. This is the meaning of freedom of press. It is not just important to democracy, it is democracy.

—Walter Cronkite, *Leading Journalists Tell What a Free Press Means to America* (1984)

One need not look hard or long for a list of quotes exalting the role of a free press in a democratic society. Democracy requires informed citizens. To be informed, citizens need reliable, credible, and independent sources of information. An independent news media uncensored and free of government control not only serves this function but arguably serves as the linchpin of democratic governance. If information is the lifeblood of democratic governance, a free and independent press is the primary—though certainly not monopoly—supplier of political news and information.[1]

The importance of the news media to democratic governance is further evidenced by the behavior of authoritarian regimes. Authoritarian governments tightly control news coverage to assure citizens receive only the information the regime wants heard framed in the most favorable possible light. Unfavorable news and critical opinions are censored or punished and sources of information are closely monitored and controlled. While controlling information is more difficult in a digital age, authoritarian countries like China censor Internet access and Web page content to limit criticism. China is hardly alone. In their 2013 report "Freedom on the Internet," Freedom House found that 34 of 60 countries (and not just authoritarian regimes) had moved to restrict Internet access and content. This includes blocking and filtering content, surveillance of Internet activity, and passing new and restrictive laws and subsequent arrests.

In authoritarian systems, the news media cannot adequately perform its surveillance function (alerting citizens to what they need to know) or its watchdog function (exposing official corruption and wrongdoing). Government is subsequently allowed to operate in the absence of important institutional controls and citizens are often left uninformed, misinformed, or both.

The alternative to a state-controlled media, a free and independent press, is unquestionably more desirable both at a practical and a theoretical level. Yet this simple comparison of a *free press* and *state-controlled* media defines a *free press* only as a negative, giving neither shape nor form to a fuller and richer understanding of what independent media are supposed to do. What exactly constitutes a free press? Does a free press require an absence of government regulation? Does this mean the press must operate entirely independent of government subsidies, favorable policies, and/or favorable treatment? Broad and ill-defined, a *free press* can take on very different forms and shapes depending on the social, economic, and political contexts.

In the United States, a *free press* has generally meant a press functioning as a corporate entity within the confines of economic markets but outside of direct government control. The press may not be directly censored by government, but its primary function is not to inform or engage citizens (despite the rhetoric of journalists and journalism professors); it is to attract an audience and sell advertising. Private economic forces and not government censors shape decisions about news content and influence the structure and format of news programming. While media scholars often emphasize the "social responsibility theory" of the press over libertarian models,[2] the goal of private media is to not to further democratic governance but to make a profit. Or perhaps stated differently, journalism schools may teach social responsibility as a theory to aspiring journalists, but media corporations operate largely as economic actors. In fact, in Western democracies, governments have done more to prop up the news media through economic subsidies than to censor them.

Duke University economics professor James Hamilton's excellent book *All the News That Is Fit to Sell*[3] provides the most comprehensive assessment of why these motives—furthering democratic governance and selling the news—often work at cross-purposes. *Sellable* content is not always the richest or most informative content. When asked, consumers will tell pollsters or focus group moderators they prefer hard news and substance but their socially desirable responses are a poor cover for their actual behavior. Given the choice between a story on health-care policy and kittens, they almost inevitably select the kittens.[4] Studies of news attentiveness find that more substantive thematic news stories attract less attention and less emotional engagement than episodic news,[5] that horse race news coverage attracts more attention than issue coverage during election campaigns,[6] and that uncivil crosstalk may have negative long-term consequences like declining political trust but it attracts viewers' eyes and ears in the short term.[7] In a digital age, incivility becomes a tool for breaking through the noise and attracting attention.[8]

More to the point, competitive markets can drive down the overall quality of news as producers search for the largest audience share and largest profit.[9] Civic knowledge and engagement, when (and if) they occur, are fortunate by-products of selling the news but are not factored into Nielsen Ratings and have little bearing on metrics of a successful news (or entertainment) program. Too often, selling the news means lowering the quality of the news product or sensationalizing content to reach a target audience. During the broadcast era, this meant targeting the news to the median consumer and an objective and neutral presentation of information. During the digital age, this has meant targeting niche and often partisan news audiences, thus adding to an already fragmented and polarized political context. The news audience for any given program may be smaller in contemporary politics, but it is also more easily defined for advertisers seeking to narrowly target advertising messages.[10]

Hamilton also observes, however, that it would be a mistake to believe that the U.S. media system has functioned on the basis of the same economic principles as those affecting the production of manufacturing goods. For one, the news industry has long benefited from direct economic subsides—most often in the form of reduced postal rates—that assured industry profitability and growth; government regulation that effectively limited competition, particularly during the era of broadcast news when the *public* airwaves were tightly controlled; and press briefs, video feeds, and other institutional supports from political actors and government agencies that help reduce the costs of news production.[11]

Far too much of *the news* is given to news media outlets, which publish or broadcast it with little or no editing. In 2005, for example, controversy erupted when it was revealed that Bush administration's video news releases (VNR) were played on local television news programs with little or no editing and often without attributing the Bush administration as the original source of the news story. By providing pre-packaged *free* news, the Bush administration fed into the profit-maximizing strategies driving news organizations and effectively communicated the news in favorable terms for the administration. While this serves as a particularly egregious and controversial example, anyone who has ever written a press release understands the trick is to make your news easier to cover by giving journalists a neatly wrapped story, quotable sources, catchy headlines, and abbreviated content. The *best* press releases (or VNR) from a public relations standpoint make it into the news with little or no editing. With the advances in social and digital media allowing for the easier creation and dissemination of content, contemporary politicians can bypass traditional news media altogether by posting blogs, tweeting out reports, and posting Facebook statuses to communicate directly with followers.

Thanks to the First Amendment, the U.S. news media may be largely *free* of direct government censorship, but they remain heavily dependent on government resources for the production of the news. Daily press briefings, for example, feed the White House press corps with access to official sources and news stories. More broadly, this illustrates an important observation: News stories are not created by journalists in isolation but are created, pushed, and framed by public officials, political candidates, and interest groups. A free press may challenge public officials, but it is just as often used by those same officials as a tool for governing, persuading the opposition and announcing official policy positions.[12]

This brings us to our fourth myth: A free press is independent from the government and the government officials it reports on. Not only have news organizations benefited from generous government subsidies throughout American political history, but they are also reliant on official government sources for news. The news that we see, hear, or read on a daily basis often originates not in the newsroom but in the offices of elected officials, interest groups, and other political actors using the news media to push an ideological or policy-oriented agenda. This "negotiation of newsworthiness"[13] is so prevalent that every citizen should ask the following questions when reading or watching a news story that is not event-centered breaking news:[14] Exactly who is behind this story? And what are they trying to get out of it? Seen in this light, the news media are less a bystander and more of an active participant in the governing process than is commonly believed or recognized.

The Logic of a Free Press

Journalism schools often turn to Thomas Jefferson to defend an independent and free press. Jefferson not only famously said, "were it left to me to decide whether we should have a government without newspapers, or newspapers without a government, I should not hesitate a moment to prefer the latter,"[15] but he also frequently lauded the importance of a free press in his personal letters. Jefferson is not alone. Throughout American history, the news media have been seen as instrumental to democratic governance.

Lost in such laudatory discussions is the fact that a free press is but a means to an end (and not the end itself). The goal is not a free press but the informed citizenry that a free press should, in theory, help to produce. An independent press is an essential mechanism because it provides the communication channels necessary—but not sufficient—for citizens to become informed, engaged, and capable of challenging ruling party elites.

To understand this distinction, it is helpful to recall that the news media at the time of the American Founding were not neutral and objective purveyors of information but partisan players, funded and supported by the political parties. They existed not to inform a mass audience but as partisan instruments whose purpose was to persuade and mobilize an elite audience. It is only more recently that a *free press* has taken on connotations that imply nonpartisan objectivity. This highlights an important point and a recurring theme throughout this text: The definition of a free press, like all of the protections and freedoms provided by the Bill of Rights, is highly contingent on the social, economic, and political contexts. The free press that exists today is not the free press experienced or imagined by Thomas Jefferson or James Madison.

What then did the Founders envision in free press? Most likely, they viewed the press as a vehicle for partisan dissent and a mechanism for challenging government officials. It is important not to take this logic too far as the Federalist Party quickly made use of the Alien and Sedition Acts to jail printers and publishers for criticizing President John Adams. Arguably, at least some of the Founders believed a free press only meant the absence of prior restraint, thus allowing for punishment after publication. You were *free* to criticize the president, but that criticism might earn you jail time. Of course, not all of the Founders—particularly Thomas Jefferson—agreed with this assessment, and most viewed a free press as able to criticize public officials and avoid any resulting reprisals. Both Jefferson and his principal rival, Alexander Hamilton, recognized and used the press as weapons in their very personal and partisan disputes over the direction of the country.

Given the nature of the partisan press that existed at the time, it is unlikely that the Founders envisioned a press independent of political influence or as detached and objective purveyors of the *truth*. Indeed, one might well argue that the American Founders would have been less surprised by the partisan slant of *Fox News* than the more *objective New York Times*. On the other hand, they would have been far more comfortable with the more elitist *New York Times* than the more populist and lowbrow *Fox News*. As evidence to this point, consider that the *letters to the editor* that comprised the Federalist Papers were intended for a very limited but highly literate population.

Transitioning the Press: The Common Denominator in Changing Media Systems

With the shift to steam-powered printers in the 1830s, printing newspapers became cheaper and more efficient. The result was the penny press, an expanded news audience and competition for readers, and increasingly sensationalized news content. Unlike the partisan press of the founding era, the penny press was funded by sales and advertising and was subsequently less overtly political but also less substantive than newspapers funded by the political parties. The availability of cheap newspapers aided democratic goals by expanding literacy, but the cost was a lower quality, less political, more human interest news product that appealed to a mass audience. While the role of yellow journalism in starting the Spanish-American War is often overstated in historical accounts, William Randolph Hearst's declaration to artist Frederic Remington that "[y]ou furnish the pictures and I'll furnish the war" was symptomatic of the sensationalized but impactful news content that spoke well beyond the events of the day. Sensationalized news stories, Hearst and Joseph Pulitzer, his rival publisher at the New York World, quickly learned, sold more copies.

The competitiveness of this period lead to perversities in content, and sensationalized and over-hyped news, and called into question the credibility of news organizations. The subsequent crisis in credibility opened the door to the possibility of the *New York Times*, a newspaper dedicated to objective and credible reporting. The need to secure advertising revenues to pay for content further fueled the impetus for *objective* news as most advertisers preferred neutral (as opposed to politicized) content to reach the largest possible audience.

This economic model fit well even as the new technologies of radio and television challenged printed newspapers as the primary source of public information. The era might be best characterized as having limited choice in news content and limited competition for readers or viewers. In most communities, a single newspaper dominated the local market, and while the local and national television news programs competed for viewers, the competition was limited to three networks and was directed at a median viewer, politically moderate and generally not deeply passionate about politics.

This model was challenged first by the widespread adoption of cable and the creation of cable news networks. Cable expanded the amount of choice in television viewing, thus increasing competition for broadcast news channels, while the development of the first 24-hour news network (*CNN*) created pressure to fill 24 hours of content. One solution was the "Crossfire"-style program pitting competing ideological and partisan viewpoints in less than civil conversations. Such formats not only attracted viewers but were cheaper and easier to produce than investigative news stories. As audiences and advertising revenues shrank for any one particular source, the appeal of such formats was further magnified. Alternatively, news channels also increased the relatively cheap production of sensational and celebrity-based news. You might not see great depth in content but you could certainly keep up with the latest news about Britney Spears or Lindsay Lohan. *Fox News* added an additional challenge by carving out an ideological niche for disaffected conservative news viewers, an approach later adopted by MSNBC to capture the liberal viewing audience. More choice in news channels did not yield to higher quality news but to news heavily tilted toward specific partisan views.

The development and widespread adoption of the Internet expanded choice further with predictable and mostly unfortunate consequences. Partisans found more news that confirmed their existing worldviews, while the less partisan and less engaged watched other channels. To some degree, this is likely overstated as partisans do more news grazing than is commonly realized, but even their grazing is done with an eye to confirmation rather than enlightenment.

The principle connecting definitions of a *free press* across these unique time periods and media systems is the absence of direct government control and/or public ownership. Notably, this does not preclude press ownership by political parties or the use of the press for explicitly political purposes. During the early American republic, the Jeffersonian Democratic-Republican presses were used to attack the ruling Federalist government (though not without consequence). During the muckraking period defined by sensationalism and yellow journalism, a free and independent press was able to investigate government corruption and incompetence, shedding light on abuses and creating a groundswell for political reform. While muckraking served a social purpose, that is, exposing government corruption and promoting reform, it also provided tangible economic rewards through newspaper sales. The economic model drove the production of information, not its social or political value.

When the *New York Times* established the norm of objectivity as a guiding principle for the news media, the free press became defined as a purveyor of truth, where truth was defined as factually accurate and political neutral accounts of the news of the day. This too was an economic strategy designed to capture an audience fed up with sensational and incredible news stories. In the contemporary media system, the *free press* functions without a clear anchor, thus serving multiple functions. The norm of objectivity has withered but not yet died, investigative journalism has become more difficult to fund and subsequently more rare, and there are signs of a return to a more partisan press. Despite all these changes, the common denominator in the definition of a free press remains: the absence of direct government control, though notably not the absence of government or political influence. In democratic governance, a free press can only be so free. If it is not constrained directly by political forces, it is influenced by them. If a free press is not subject to government control, economic forces directly influence the quantity and quality of news.

The Press and Democratic Accountability

This reality raises troubling concerns for democratic theory and the assumption that a free and independent press can effectively inform citizens and enhance democratic governance. A government-supported or -controlled news media cannot effectively serve as a voice for partisan dissent, nor can it effectively perform the surveillance functions necessary to inform citizens of breaking events or the watchdog functions necessary to provide a check on government corruption and abuse of power. Even absent overt efforts to control or censor content, a government-supported press provides an incentive to curry favor with the powerful via positive news coverage. Presidents and other elected officials, for example, can grant special access to favored reporters or news channels, increasing the odds of positive coverage. If the media provide the coverage many politicians crave and find necessary to govern, government officials control access to information, decision-makers, and news stories.

The late Tim Cook described the news media as a political institution critical to governing strategies of political elites. A news statement from President Obama on Russia, for example, is not just making news and informing audience; it is also part of the governing process.[16] President Obama, in this scenario, needs the news media to effectively govern.

Yet political actors are not powerless in cultivating news coverage. They can decline interviews, limit public appearances, and make it more (or less) difficult for journalists to find relevant information and cover critical news stories. In November 2013, more than 30 news organizations, including the Associated Press, the *New York Times*, and *Fox News*, sent the White House a letter protesting limited access to President Obama. *New York Times* photographer Doug Mills compared the White House to the Telegraph Agency of the Soviet Union (TASS), while other journalists noted the Obama administration provided even less direct access to daily events than the Bush administration.[17] Whether the charge is true or not, controlling access is a critical tool for press relations.

Moreover, even when access is granted, it is often limited. Reporters' interviews with public officials, for example, are now increasingly attended by "minders," public relations specialists who serve to interject, clarify comments, and/or end the interview if the questioning becomes uncomfortable or unpleasant.[18] Most reporters play along to get the official on record. Ron Fournier of the *National Journal* places the trend in the context of a media system that advantages politicians over journalists:

> Minder madness joins the surge of "background briefings" and the decline of access to decision-makers as evidence that the White House—and other big institutions—are manipulating the press. It's that, but it's also something worse: It's evidence that journalists are ceding control when they should be seizing it, accepting canned news rather than breaking it.[19]

He argues reporters should not play the game and should instead set the ground rules for the interview and be willing to walk away. To do so, however, means risking the limited access that has been granted and potentially losing an important story. Regardless, it is a mistake to believe that journalists can operate entirely independently of the political actors they report on. While journalists have their own set of leverage in crafting news stories, so too do public officials.

Harvard political scientist Thomas Patterson, whose masterful book *Out of Order* described the contrary and unrealistic expectation set upon the media by a dysfunctional political system,[20] has recently offered yet another reason why politicians can effectively manipulate press coverage. Most journalists lack the substantive knowledge to challenge more knowledgeable public officials.[21] The result is that journalists are often overreliant on sources and carefully adhere to norms and routines that can be easily manipulated by policy-makers and their PR teams. Consider, for example, news coverage of science controversies (e.g., stem cell research, climate change, or evolution) where there is a public controversy but little doubt among scientists. The journalistic norm is to balance coverage giving the misimpression that there is a rough equivalence on the two sides of the controversy. The anomalies, those scientists whose views significantly depart from the scientific community, are often able to make statements that go unchallenged by journalists who lack the necessary substantive knowledge. The same issue confronts journalists covering policy decisions, budget making, and other aspects of the political process.

The broader conclusion is simple and straightforward: A weakened free press empowers politicians and government officials at the expense of the news media and, arguably, democratic accountability.[22]

How Policy Decisions Create the Press

A *free press* is not only subject to influence and manipulation by political elites, it is also dependent on government policy. It is a mistake, for example, to assume that media industry growth is the result of technological innovation or business acumen rather than policy-related decisions. The development of radio unquestionably transformed American politics, but the specific media system that developed as a result of technological innovation reflected calculated political decisions. Historian Paul Starr's outstanding history of the origins and creation of the American media system stands as the most authoritative work in this area, carefully documenting how government policy gave rise to modern communication systems.[23] By subsidizing postal rates, for example, government encouraged the growth of daily newspapers and indirectly contributed to the creation of a more literate and informed citizenry.

As technology advanced—first the development of the telegraph and then telephone and radio—political decisions about control over media systems emphasized private ownership as opposed to public control. These decisions uniquely defined the American media system and made it distinct from European systems, which placed greater emphasis on public ownership. In Starr's analysis, markets were a mixed blessing in the development of the U.S. media system. Markets expanded access to new technologies, especially relative to Europe, and opened up new channels of communication, yet they also threatened democratic accountability by placing control of these systems in the hands of large corporate interests.

Western Union's monopoly over the telegraph, for example, raised important issues about democratic accountability. Should one company have so much control over the nation's information infrastructure?

By comparison, in European democracies, greater emphasis was placed on public ownership. Hence, the British Broadcasting Corporation (BBC) was funded with public dollars via an annual television license fee charged to British households with television sets. The result was, arguably, more substantive content, though notably not content that is necessarily more popular. A poll conducted by the *Telegraph* in November 2013 found that 70 percent of British citizens wanted the license fee abolished or cut.[24]

During much of the broadcast era, the regulation of the public airwaves meant the voices Americans heard on television and radio were oriented toward a median consumer, politically moderate and middle of the road in terms of culture and taste. The growth of first cable television and then the Internet presented a fundamental challenge by expanding the number of channels available and easing barriers to entry for creating and disseminating original content, though for a variety of reasons the challenge was more apparent than real. First, the development of cable television fits into the broader pattern of government regulation that helped establish local monopolies and limit competition. As cable was developing, it was simply not feasible to have multiple companies creating cable networks. The parallel would be to have multiple water companies providing competing sewage and plumbing systems to a single home. To encourage the development of cable networks, local governments partnered with cable providers giving them local monopolies in exchange for the initial investment necessary to build infrastructure. Second, while the growth of the Internet (Al Gore jokes aside)[25] was initially spurred by government investment and research, it quickly ceded control to private corporations as soon as its money-making potential was clear.[26] This has been a recurring pattern in the development of American media systems, initial government investment to spur growth gradually ceding to private ownership advantaged by government policy and support during the industry's developmental phase.

Cable and the Internet provided a natural synergy as cable providers were able to leverage existing advantages in cable networks directly into control over high-speed Internet access. The existence of local monopolies has limited competition and innovation to the disservice of consumers.[27] As a result, U.S. consumers pay more for slower service than in other Western democracies. Just as Western Union controlled the flow of information via the telegraph, cable giants Comcast and Time-Warner control much of the information flow via high-speed Internet access. A proposed merger of these two cable giants would further consolidate ownership though it would do little harm to local competition as each enjoys regional monopolies.

When it comes to content, the implications are less clear. Marketing guru Seth Godin argues that widespread adoption of digital media effectively ended the era of the mass market, replacing it with niche markets that celebrate uniqueness and creativity.[28] Consider, for example, the array of television programming (*Breaking Bad, Dexter, Mad Men*, etc.) that would have been unlikely during a broadcast era. Online, Godin argues, authentic voices that can speak to specific and defined audiences (or tribes) can gain resonance and influence. Meaningful impact comes not from speaking to median consumers but by connecting to people who care to make a difference.

Not all accounts are so celebratory. Documentary filmmaker Astra Taylor observes that while the Internet tore down many industry hierarchies and opened up media systems, it also left content creators scrambling to be "internet famous" without adequate resources and support systems to build a successful career or body of work.[29] If Andy Warhol gave everyone 15 minutes of fame, Internet fame is even more fleeting, less meritorious, and more random.

Within the contexts of academic research, scholarship is divided on the consequences of digital democracy. For many authors, digital technologies are a tool for enhancing democratic governance, opening the gates to new voices, and engaging the public.[30] Other scholars offer more pessimistic assessments arguing that the democratic effects of the Internet have been greatly overstated. While the Internet has transformed politics, it has not fundamentally altered the balance of power between democratic citizens and democratic elites.[31] If the power of the Internet is in organization, it is yet another tool for the politically engaged to expand their influence.

Narrowing in on the role of a free press in a democratic society, scholars have found that niche news creates insular ideological communities, lessens public understanding of differing points of view, and increases partisan polarization.[32] As historian Paul Starr observes,

> The digital revolution has unquestionably been good for freedom of expression—for the free expression, that is, of opinion. It has also been good for freedom of information—for making previously inaccessible information more

widely available. But it has not been so good for freedom of the press, if one understands that freedom as referring not merely to the formal legal rights but to the real independence of the press as an institution.

Television, as a medium, offered candidates the opportunity to speak directly to voters, bypassing political party elites and traditional news media gatekeepers. Prior to the widespread diffusion and adoption of cable television and then digital media, however, the broadcast spectrum was too limited for candidates and parties to take full advantage of unmediated communication. Digital and social media, in contrast, allow candidates and parties with significant Facebook and Twitter followers to bypass the traditional news media altogether. Why speak to the press when you can speak directly to your followers?

A number of recent campaigns have subsequently been organized around tightly controlled campaign events, limited and unscripted access to the news media, and aggressive social media campaigns to engage and mobilize followers. Traditional media outlets complain that such tactics violate the spirit of an independent press, yet it is worth recalling the concept of the "negotiation of newsworthiness" in which candidates control access and journalists write news stories. Political campaigns cannot guarantee a favorable coverage, but candidates are under no obligation to guarantee reporters access to candidates or campaign events. Seen in this light, alternative channels for connecting directly with voters strengthens candidates and public officials—at least those with relatively large followings—relative to journalists. Relatively unknown candidates, especially political amateurs, remain dependent on traditional media to reach voters. Thus, the advantage is to candidates, such as incumbents, who already enjoy institutional advantages.

If the digital age provides the illusion of greater diversity in content and wider range of voices, it is worth stepping back to consider the economic underpinnings of the American media system. The illusion is the plethora of channels for news and information; the reality is that ownership remains concentrated and under corporate conglomerate control. The *Big Six* media corporations (Comcast, Disney, Fox News Corp., Time-Warner, Viacom, and CBS) still control much of the media content in the United States. ABC, for example, is owned by Disney, which also owns ESPN, Pixar, and Miramax. In the online world, Google has emerged as one of the largest and most powerful media companies in the world, as have Amazon and Yahoo. In radio, Clear Channel is an unquestioned behemoth with over

800 radio stations throughout the country. The growing diversity in channels for news and entertainment then reflects the technology capacity rather than diversity in ownership and political perspective. Even in an age with declining profits and lower barriers to entry, media concentration of ownership is the norm rather than the exception.

The Political and Economic Challenge

The challenge digital media present for democratic accountability pales in comparison to the profound and enduring economic crisis it has spurned. Traditional business models have proven inadequate to a digital age in which information moves quickly and freely from user to user. Notably, even though the traditional news audience is shrinking, this is less a crisis in demand than in understanding how to translate the creation of original news and information into a profitable business model. The consumption of news and information far exceeds consumption during the broadcast era, when the availability of news was necessarily limited and routinized around the nightly newscast or morning newspaper. News can now move instantaneously and news consumers can seek (and find) updated information instantaneously. The most politically engaged are plugged in at all times, and while the politically disengaged can avoid most political news, it continues to find them via incidental exposure on Facebook and Twitter.[33] The economic challenge is finding a way for news organizations to profit from the production of news and information and its consumption so that—at least in theory—they can produce higher quality news and analysis.

The political challenge is seeking mechanisms to assure that a free press fulfills the information needs of democratic governance and that citizens are learning about issues and not simply confirming pre-existing attitudes and beliefs. Or worse, that they are not turning away from politics altogether in favor of sports and entertainment.[34] Choice, Princeton political science professor Markus Prior has observed, expands participatory biases and further polarizes an already polarized electorate.

The long-term outlook for traditional media outlets is not particularly promising. First, increasingly citizens are getting their news online rather than via traditional news outlets. In 2001, only 13 percent of Americans reported getting their news online.[35] By 2013, half of Americans reported getting news online. This has corresponded with a long term trend toward declining newspaper readership. In 2001, 45 percent of Americans reported getting their news from a daily newspaper compared to 28 percent in 2013. The trends are even starker when looking at younger Americans. If you are under 25 years old, odds are you are getting your news free online rather than from traditional media sources.

Curiously, much of online news is *pass-through* readership or commentary based on original reporting from a leading newspaper (e.g., *New York Times, Washington Post, Wall Street Journal*), suggesting that the role for traditional media is less diminished than it is transformed by the new realities of digital media. Thought of in this way, this is not a crisis in the demand for news and information but rather in developing a business model in the context of public expectations that online news is free and instantly available. Experiments by newspapers in setting up paywalls have generally helped but have not successfully replaced revenues lost to a declining readership. And while online advertising revenues have grown dramatically, they have not replaced the income lost from declining subscriptions, traditional print advertising, and classified ads.

While journalism professors often lament the decline of these traditional news sources,[36] the background story is of an industry that was remarkably profitable in an era when the supply of information was restricted and which was slow to adapt to new realities. Local newspapers, for example, controlled access to valuable local advertising markets and generated tremendous revenue from traditional print advertising and classified ads. Increasingly, advertisers have direct access to these consumers and carefully target ads to key demographic and psychological profiles. Perhaps even more damaging to newspaper profitably, *Craig's List* and other online resources have cut deeply into classified advertising revenues.

In response, local newspapers cut staff, raised prices, and increased their reliance on wire service news stories that were readily available online. Less-original content at a higher price may have made sense to the executive editors, chief financial officers (CFOs), and corporate boards of large newspaper chains maintaining profit margins and intent on satisfying their corporate boards, but consumers—not surprisingly—balked at the trade-off. Even so, there is a fair point to be made about how the rapid growth of digital media has challenged our understanding of the role of a *free and independent* press in a democratic society. That understanding was predicated on the assumption that the news media could serve the needs for an informed democratic citizenry while operating in a market economy.

The *social responsibility* of the news industry has always been overstated by journalists and media scholars, particularly relative to market considerations. Yet the myth worked as long as the number of suppliers was fairly limited. What happens when competition increases and choice in information sources grows exponentially? The competitive pressures drive down quality, citizens opt into polarized news sources or out of news altogether, and the ability of a *free press* to further the goals of democratic governance is increasingly questioned.

For historian Paul Starr, the result is that American news media have grown to resemble European news media with smaller audiences and increasingly politicized content. The history lesson, Starr argues, is that government should do what it has done in the past, subsidize the news industry not by *propping up* old media but by encouraging experimentation in content and delivery via mobile, digital, and other new technologies. If past is prologue, such investments can pay tremendous dividends in terms of the development of an information infrastructure and an informed citizenry. Just as mail subsidies encouraged the growth of the newspaper industry and subsequently a more informed citizenry, incentives can encourage the development of mobile news devices, apps, or content that might at once aid the news industry while also furthering a free and independent press capable of informing the public.

From Watchdog to Guard Dog: A Case Study in Controlling the Press

In the movie *Kill the Messenger*, Jeremy Renner plays Gary Webb, a Pulitzer Prize–winning journalist from the *San Jose Mercury News* who uncovers a link between the Contras in Nicaragua and the domestic narcotics trade in the United States.[37] While the story provided no direct evidence that the CIA was responsible for, or directly involved in, the domestic drug trade, the story did show that the CIA turned a blind eye to and even actively protected allies involved in the illegal drug trade and participating as the Contra opposition in Nicaragua. The story, which broke on Sunday, August 18, 1996, and was published as a three-part series, was initially backed by *San Jose Mercury News* editorial team, including executive editor Jerry Ceppos. When the *Washington Post* initially challenged the series, Ceppos supported the story commenting that "[w]e strongly support the conclusions the series drew and will until someone proves them wrong. What is even more remarkable is that four experienced Post reporters, re-reporting our series, could not find a single factual error. The Post's conclusions are very different—and I believe, flawed—but the major facts aren't. I'm not sure how many of us could sustain such a microscopic examination of our work, and I believe Gary Webb deserves recognition for surviving unscathed."[38]

Ceppos greatly overstated his willingness to stand by the story. By May 1997 and under pressure from the nation's leading newspapers, Ceppos caved, turned on the story, and effectively threw his reporter under the bus. He did not wait for the proof that the story was wrong; the ensuing controversy and the pressure from elite media outlets were apparently sufficient to change his mind. In a column published on May 11, Ceppos wrote that the story "fell short of my standards" and acknowledged the newspaper lacked proof the CIA knew of the Contras drug connections. In fairness, Ceppos never intended the column to serve as a retraction of the entire story, but it was treated as such by the *New York Times* and other mainstream media outlets, and it began the process of killing the story and marginalizing Gary Webb, the journalist who wrote the series. Webb was not allowed to write a response or to publish the additional evidence he had gathered in support of his findings. Even worse, Ceppos began actively limiting Webb's assignments and placed him in the suburban Cupertino bureau away from the story and his family, moves that eventually lead to Webb's resignation from the *Mercury News* and effectively ended his career as a journalist.

On a story of this magnitude, why did the *Washington Post*, the *New York Times*, and the *Los Angeles Times* side with the powerful? According to Associate Press reporter Robert Parry, who was writing similar stories, many of these news organizations were bowing to pressure from Reagan supporters intent on protecting his legacy as president.[39] The conservative *Washington Times* began the criticism of the Dark Alliances series, which was eventually picked up by the *Washington Post* and other mainstream news outlets. The push-back from these leading newspapers was partly the result of pressure from the powerful and partly a reaction to criticism from Gary Webb and others for not getting on and staying on a story that disproportionately affected the African-American community.[40] Under pressure for not covering the story adequately, they attacked the credibility of the reporter, his story, and his newspaper.

What is perhaps most remarkable is later evidence largely vindicated Gary Webb's reporting. Even the CIA confirmed "the C.I.A.'s connection to Central American drug dealers" in 1998.[41] The Justice Department would similarly and subsequently release the Bromwich Report, which also found that the CIA was aware of—but not responsible for—Contra involvement in the narcotics trade. These later stories, however, received little play as the Washington media was by that time enraptured with Monica Lewinsky's blue-stained dress and Kenneth Starr's report as special prosecutor. While the story might have been overhyped by the *Mercury News* and its conclusions might have overreached toward the sensational, much of its content later proved to be factually accurate.

Subsequent professional and academic analyses of the story have mostly yielded the same conclusion: The faults with the story resided not with Gary Webb's reporting but with the lack of "competent editing."[42] Associated Press reporter Robert Parry concluded that much of the problem came from the editors who, hoping for a Pulitzer Prize, overhyped the CIA's role in the domestic drug trade. Tim Graham, writing in the *Columbia Journalism Review*, similarly placed the blame on Webb's editors, noting that "[t]he editors are supposed to be the gatekeepers," but they failed to perform their role in this particular case.

Alas, being mostly right did not protect Gary Webb from retribution, hence the title of the movie. Nor did incompetence keep his editors from securing promotion and advancing within the newspaper industry. While Webb was being forced out, executive editor Jerry Ceppos was given an *ethics* awards for his May 11 column and promoted, eventually becoming a vice-president at the Knight-Ridder newspaper chain. In what is perhaps an ironic twist, he later entered academics first at the University of Nevada-Reno and later at Louisiana State University, where he teaches *media ethics* and trains future journalists. Having been marginalized from investigative journalism, Gary Webb committed suicide in 2004. "What's especially troubling about this new 'Dark Alliance' tale," wrote reporter George Hodel, "is that the investigative spotlight was turned off not by the government, but by the national news media."[43]

While most news stories lack the drama and the significance of the Dark Alliances series, the story pulls back the curtain on one of the most enduring and important myths created by the Bill of Rights: that the First Amendment by its mere existence secures a free and independent press. The reality is, of course, much more complicated. Economic determinants of the news mean that content is necessarily constrained by audience considerations and advertising pressures. Political considerations mean that the news media need access to official government sources for content, quotes, background, and other sources of information. The norms and routines adopted by journalists mean that they are often overly dependent on official government sources. As a result, the news media often echo rather than challenge official statements. Where they do present a more sustained challenge it is most often because opposition party leaders are pushing an issue or a viewpoint and not because the news media are acting independently of the broader context.

In contemporary politics, the willingness to challenge official sources has perhaps grown, but it is also increasingly politicized and partisan. *Fox News*, for example, under the control of Republican strategist Robert Ailes, was tightly aligned with the Bush administration but is a consistent critique of the Obama administration. MSNBC offered the liberal alternative with anchors Rachel Maddow and Christopher Hayes often defending liberal views and causes while CNN maintained a traditional formula of event-centered, celebratory-oriented and sensational news story.

Notes

1. Other sources of information include candidates, parties, and interest groups. These sources present biased information and are subsequently discounted in theories of the press. It is worth noting, however, that biased information is not always uninformative and may be important in mobilizing action.

2. Fred Siebert, Theodore Petersen, and Wilbur Schramm, *Four Theories of the Press* (Urbana-Champaign, IL: University of Illinois Press, 1963).

3. James Hamilton, *All the News That Is Fit to Sell: How the Market Transforms Information into News* (Princeton, NJ: Princeton University Press, 2004).

4. This is, of course, a gross overgeneralization to make the point. The politically engaged often select news content over kittens.

5. Kimberly Gross, "Framing Persuasive Appeals: Episodic and Thematic Framing, Emotional Response, and Policy Opinion," *Political Psychology* 29 (2009): 169–192.

6. Shanto Iyengar, Helmut Norpoth, and Kyu S. Hahn, "Consumer Demand for Elections News: The Horserace Sells," *Journal of Politics* 66 (2004): 157–175.

7. Diana Mutz, "Effects of 'In Your Face' Television Discourse on Perceptions of Legitimate Opposition," *American Political Science Review* 101 (2007): 621–635.

8. Susan Herbst, *Rude Democracy: Civility and Incivility in American Politics* (Philadelphia: Temple University Press, 2010).

9. Johanna Dunaway, "Markets, Ownership, and the Quality of Campaign News Coverage," *Journal of Politics* 70 (2008): 1193–1202.

10. Nearly two-thirds of local television news stations (65.7 percent) reported a profit in 2012. "Local TV News Stations Profitability," *Pew Journalism Project*,

available at http://www.journalism.org/media-indicators/local-tv-news-stations-profitability/ (accessed on August 1, 2014). And despite the criticism for partisan bias, *Fox News* is highly profitable, earning $869 million in 2011. Jesse Holcomb, Amy Mitchell, and Tom Rosenstiel, "Cable: By the Numbers," *The State of the News Media 2012, Pew Center's Project for Excellence in Journalism* available at http://stateofthemedia.org/2012/cable-cnn-ends-its-ratings-slide-fox-falls-again/cable-by-the-numbers/ (accessed on August 1, 2014). Newspapers similarly remain profitable though the margins are declining and the outlook remains relatively bleak.

11. The news industry, in this respect, is not all that different from other industries they report on in which powerful established companies enjoy better access to policy-makers and favorable regulatory environments.

12. In his seminal work *Governing with the News*, political scientist Tim Cook referred to this interplay between politicos and journalists as the "negotiation of newsworthiness."

13. Tim Cook, *Governing with the News* (Chicago: University of Chicago Press, 1998).

14. It is worth noting that much *breaking news* is the result of staged events and that the term itself is overused by news stations to attract views. Breaking news events are also quickly politicized as elected officials, candidates, and political parties spin events to help set the narrative and gain a political advantage over the opposition.

15. Jefferson also added a corollary that citizens must receive the newspapers and be capable of reading them.

16. Cook, *Governing with the News*.

17. Catherine Taibi, "Journalists Protest Restrictions on Photographing Obama, Compare White House to Soviet Union," *Huffington Post*, November 21, 2013, available at http://www.huffingtonpost.com/2013/11/21/white-house-photographers-protest-restrictions_n_4317284.html (accessed on July 24, 2014).

18. Paul Fahri, "And Minder Makes Three: For White House Interviews, It's Never Just One-on-One," *Washington Post*, July 23, 2014, available at http://www.washingtonpost.com/lifestyle/style/and-minder-makes-three-for-white-house-interviews-its-never-just-one-on-one/2014/07/23/678b5e34-1084-11e4-98ee-daea85133bc9_story.html (accessed on July 24, 2014).

19. Ron Fournier, "How White House Reporters Can Reclaim Their Beat," *National Journal*, July 24, 2014, available at http://www.nationaljournal.com/white-house/how-white-house-reporters-can-cowboy-up-and-reclaim-their-beat-20140724 (accessed on July 24, 2014).

20. Thomas Patterson, *Out of order* (New York: A. Knopf, 1993).

21. Thomas Patterson, *Informing the News: The Need for Knowledge-Based Journalism* (New York: Random House, 2013).

22. One can easily argue the press is less important to democratic accountability than competitive political parties. The theory of indexing, for example, argues

that press criticism is dependent on divisions among political elites; see Lance Bennett, "Toward a Theory of Press-State Relations," *Journal of Communication* 40 (1990): 103–125.

23. Paul Starr, *The Creation of the Media: Political Origins of Modern Communications* (New York: Basic Books, 2004).

24. Tim Ross, "BBC License Fee Should Be Cut or Scrapped, Poll Finds," *The Telegraph*, November 2, 2013, available at http://www.telegraph.co.uk/culture/tvandradio/bbc/10423117/BBC-licence-fee-should-be-cut-or-scrapped-poll-finds.html (accessed on July 15, 2014). The 70 percent number is a little misleading as 49 percent said it should be abolished while 21 percent said it should be cut.

25. Former vice president Al Gore was famously criticized for claiming that he invented the Internet. Not only was Gore's statement taken out of context and exaggerated for political purposes, he actually did play a role in the initiative to develop an information super highway, including sponsoring legislation.

26. Robert McChesney, *Digital Disconnect: How Capitalism Is Turning the Internet Against Democracy* (New York: The New Press, 2013).

27. Ibid.

28. Seth Godin, *We Are All Weird Now: The Myth of Mass and the End of Compliance* (The Domino Project, 2011).

29. Astra Taylor, *The People's Platform: Taking Back Power and Culture in a Digital Age* (London: Fourth Estate, 2014).

30. Clay Shirky, *Here Comes Everybody: The Power of Organizing Without Organizations* (New York: The Penguin Press, 2008).

31. Matthew Hindman, *The Myth of Digital Democracy* (Princeton, NJ: Princeton University Press, 2009).

32. Natalie Stroud, *Niche News: The Politics of News Choice* (Oxford: Oxford University Press, 2011); Markus Prior, *Post-Broadcast Democracy: How Media Choice Increases Inequality in Political Involvement and Polarizes Elections* (Princeton, NJ: Princeton University Press, 2007).

33. Yongwhan Kim, Hsuan-Ting Chen, and Homero Zuniga, "Stumbling upon News on the Internet: Effects of Incidental News Exposure and Relative Entertainment Use on Political Engagement," *Computers in Human Behavior* 29 (2013): 2607–2614.

34. Prior, *Post-Broadcast Democracy*.

35. Pew Center for the People & the Press, "Amid Criticism, Support for Media's 'Watchdog' Stands Out," August 8, 2013, available at http://www.people-press.org/2013/08/08/amid-criticism-support-for-medias-watchdog-role-stands-out/ (accessed on July 17, 2004).

36. One former newspaper editor we worked with used to bang on his desk and shout "we must save print."

37. The movie is based on a book of the same name by Nick Schou. Nick Schou, *Kill the Messenger: How the CIA's Crack-Cocaine Controversy Destroyed Journalist Gary Webb* (New York: Nation Books, 2006).

38. Gary Webb, "Taking a Dive on Contra Crack: How the Mercury News Caved in to the Media Establishment," *Fairness and Accuracy in Reporting*, March 1, 2005, available at http://fair.org/extra-online-articles/taking-a-dive-on-contra-crack/ (accessed on October 13, 2014).

39. Robert Parry, "Gary Webb's Death: American Tragedy," *Consortium News*, December 9, 2006, available at http://www.consortiumnews.com/2006/120906.html (accessed on June 19, 2014).

40. Susan Paterno, "The Sad Saga of Gary Webb," *American Journalism Review*, June/July 2005, available at http://ajrarchive.org/article.asp?id=3874 (accessed on June 19, 2014).

41. Ibid.

42. Ibid.

43. George Hodel, "Hung Out to Dry: 'Dark Alliance' Series Dies," *The Consortium*, 1997, available at http://www.consortiumnews.com/archive/crack9.html (accessed on July 17, 2014).

Chapter 5

The Myth of a Christian Nation

Transcending the letter and the spirit of the law is the myth that the United States is a Christian nation. Unlike other topics and chapters in this book, this one is not firmly rooted in an amendment; rather, it addresses an overarching construct—*a metamyth*—of who we are (or selectively purport to be) as a people and a county.

Accepting the *Oxford Dictionary*'s definition of a myth as "a traditional story, especially one concerning the early history of a people or explaining some natural or social phenomenon, and typically involving supernatural beings or events," or revealing "a widely held but false belief or idea,"[1] the Christian nation concept provides a textbook example of both points. Over the course of history and with increasing richness, the story is told of divinely inspired settlers, Founders, and framers who set forth to establish a land of religious liberty. The "history of a people" is intimately connected to "supernatural beings," but in a singular sense—there was and is, according to the myth, only one true God. Of course, myths do not present themselves literally or deliberately as false, and the purpose of this chapter is not to debate the anthropomorphic tendencies of mortals to create belief systems. The goal is to expose the evolution and impact of the Christian nation myth on American life and law.

Early History

Myths endure because we romanticize the past. Especially with regard to religion, our desire to make sense of and solve problems seemingly beyond our control is to invoke a higher order—not to create a new one, but to keep the old one as a sort of fixed constellation from which we have drifted, but to which we can always navigate back. Throughout our history we have perpetuated the myth of a righteous and godly people who braved the sea in search of religious liberty. Upon reaching *the new world*, they did what no other country in their history did: They established laws that protected their religious beliefs. When the bond with their distant ruler became unbearable, they revolted. Our historical heroes, vital to any myth, declared our independence, defeated the Goliath, and created a nation rooted in, and in furtherance of, American exceptionalism. Central to these remarkable accomplishments is an Almighty God.

Defenders of the faith-based history of our nation find some evidence for the argument made in the preceding paragraph: Many settlers did flee religious persecution. In the colonies, they did establish religion. The Declaration of Independence includes four theological references. Our Constitution was dated "in the year of our Lord one thousand seven hundred and Eighty seven."[2] Does this loose assemblage of historical anecdotes uphold the myth or challenge it?

On the faith of our forefathers

A commonly held myth is that our Founding Fathers and the framers of the Constitution were divinely inspired. Such inspiration presumes, of course, fidelity to the source. On this count, the facts do not necessarily, or at least categorically, support the myth. To be sure, the Founders and framers were enlightened individuals. Compared to the average citizen, and as a result of the laws from which they benefitted and to which they would contribute,[3] they were highly educated. As such, many (but not all) were critical and sometimes even suspicious of the motives of organized religion and the unscientific nature of belief systems. In the truest sense of the word, they were *enlightened.*

Application of this term is perilous because it is so politically, semantically, and discursively loaded. It can easily, but inappropriately, strike the reader as tantamount to saying "having seen the light of reason, they rejected religion." It is not that simple. The foundation of thought was simply broader and more critically examined. Drawing inspiration from, and contributing to, what would become known as the Enlightenment, prominent statesmen like Thomas Paine, Thomas Jefferson, James Madison, and Benjamin Franklin relied more on Isaac Newton, Francis Bacon, and John Locke than on the gospel. They were deists. All were born into Puritan environments and grew up as practitioners of the faith, but through the breadth and depth of their education and experiences, increasingly championed reason and empiricism over blind faith and devotion. Deists like Jefferson could, therefore, acknowledge a watchmaker God but reject the superstitious and authoritative aspects of organized religion. They could, and did, to varying degrees rebel against what they perceived to be the corrupting influences of clerics, clergy, and evangelicals. While some, most prominently Paine, have become legends for their scholarship and activism in defense of deism, most others, like Jefferson, wove their thinking into the craft of government. In his classic essay *The Age of Reason*, a pamphlet for which he was arrested and imprisoned in Paris in 1793–1794, Paine advocated freethinking, reason, and a watchmaker/creator God in place of superstition, revelation, and a corrupt Christian establishment.[4] This, from the same author as *Common Sense*, a document so vital to our nation's quest for independence that John Adams famously wrote, "Without the pen of the author of *Common Sense*, the sword of Washington would have been raised in vein."[5]

In our nation's collective memory, Paine is pushed to the side so that actors like Jefferson could take center stage. While history has shown that Jefferson's politics were indeed radical,[6] he was not and is not historically relegated to the station of radical or activist; indeed, he is revered. He is the author of the *Declaration of Independence* and not a pamphlet supporting it. He provided us with a wall of separation dividing church and state (which, as the next chapter shall demonstrate, has brought with it an enduring myth and consequences of its own). He is on record as proclaiming "I am a Christian." But, in context, and through his own writings—many from personal correspondences authored in the wake of rekindled friendships during and after his political career—we find evidence of his deistic beliefs and religious tolerance.

Whether describing himself as a Christian in his letter to Benjamin Rush in 1803 ("I am a Christian in the only sense in which he wished any one to be; sincerely attached to his doctrines, in preference to all others; ascribing to himself every human excellence"), or as "a real Christian" in his letter to Charles Thompson in 1816, we see Jefferson tempering the meaning of his faith to a simple core belief. Yes he acknowledges a god, but not uncritically, as he writes most compellingly in his letter to Peter Carr during the year of the Constitution's drafting: "Fix reason firmly in her seat, and call to her tribunal every fact, every opinion. Question with boldness even the existence of a god; because, if there be one, he must more approve the homage of reason, than that of blindfolded fear."[7] And it remains instructive to note that the legendary president is (less) famous for his own revision of the Bible, removing from it the Old Testament and much of the New Testament, save its moral teaching. In sum, Jefferson would have argued that, absent the corruption and supernaturalism, there is a sound moral code.

As for the faith of the founding generation writ large, the broad strokes of denominational history create a pair of myths belying two important facts: first, that the people must have wanted organized religion, and second, that they must therefore have been deeply religious. To these observations, historian David Sehat notes that "[h]istorical demographers and sociologists have shown that in 1776 only 17 percent of the national population belonged to a church. It appears that an official religion governed an indifferent population for much of the colonial period."[8] This raises the issue of religious establishment.

On establishment

It is true, as the next chapter indicates, that at the time of our nation's independence, as many as 11 of the original 13 colonies maintained established religions, all under the umbrella concept of Christianity, but as Martin Marty notes,

> [m]ost settlers had brought with them the habits and those associated with establishment, or at least they were highly aware of the human cost of contesting such establishments, whether, for example, in "Christian Massachusetts" or "Christian Virginia." Those in power who continue to support formal church establishment and its corollaries in the colonies had fourteen centuries of precedent and habits behind them. Religious establishment was the only world they knew, and it was marked by a polity that they patrolled and from which they benefitted.[9]

This is not a mea culpa for establishment; it is an acknowledgment of the fact that ideas, beliefs, and practices, like luggage, travel with us. It was part of the world they knew that they brought with them. And like the garments that fill our luggage, over the course of time—and often sooner than we expect—we remove and replace our practices when we find or need room to grow. Clearly, the colonies that established official religions did so as small-scale sovereigns and in a perceived effort to represent and protect its citizens. But the country rapidly grew and diversified. Less than

50 years after the colonies became states, established religions and other legal restrictions (such as those requiring assessments and oaths and restricting citizenship and participation) were largely gone. From the beginning of our nation's history, there has been more diversity than is typically acknowledged. The myth of the Christian nation has resulted in a very bland and homogenous picture book of who the settlers were and what they looked like. We see a mini England, even though Germany, Scotland, and Scandinavia were among our first settlers. We see Christianity instead of the diversity of denominations that came to define the early American religious landscape. And we forget the premium settlers and statesmen alike placed upon national unity.

As alluded to earlier in text, by 1833, the primary and prohibitive vestiges of state-established religions were largely dismantled, not through the decisions of the courts or interference by the federal government, but through the volition of the states themselves. As the next chapter indicates, states (especially the newly forming ones) looked to the past (their own history) and to the present (their current demographics) and around them for inspiration and models for change. Predictably, as established religion fell from state constitutional mantles in place of new, tolerance-based preferences for protecting the rights of citizens to act in accordance with their own conscience, religious groups mobilized to "restore religion to its rightful place." In light of the emerging "Christian heterodoxy"[10] and the disestablishment of state churches, and in opposition to the presumed immorality of freethinking deists, Ezra Stiles Ely—in a move that failed utterly but signaled a new tactic for addressing church–state issues—proposed "a new sort of union, or, if you please, a Christian party in politics," proclaiming "[w]e are a Christian nation: we have a right to demand that all our rulers in their conduct shall conform to Christian morality; and if they do not, it is the duty and privilege of Christian freemen to make a new and a better election."[11]

The failure of Ely's movement is attributable to pressure from both sides—the freethinkers, obviously, but also other religious organizations that viewed his position as divisive, immoderate, and opportunistic. There was a moderating tendency at work, revealing an undercurrent of unity among the religious and compatible with Derek H. Davis's thesis defining religious pluralism as the essential element of the nation's quest for unity and order.[12] This quest for unity compels us to return to the national level and to finally identify the foundation of our true exceptionalism.

On the language of the Constitution

The establishment clause discussion, earlier in text, is restricted to the states for a number of reasons, not the least of which is that if the myth of a Christian United States is true and deeply rooted in our past, then it would certainly have been stated explicitly in our national charter. The fact of the matter is that our history is replete with examples of deference: As the new nation-in-the-making—a federal government, no less—was taking shape and ultimately dependent on the support of the states, would it have made any sense to begin the road to ratification with provisions that would have dismantled existing state constitutions, laws, and rights? The answer is no. Given the robust debates between the Federalists and the Anti-Federalists, as well as the long stretch of relative autonomy and sovereignty enjoyed by the states, asking them to vote on a document requiring them to recognize the supremacy of the new Constitution and federal government was quite enough. But it was not simply or really a fear of failure that motivated the framers; it was a genuine and highly intentional interest in mapping out a sound federal model, leaving intact what the states had already created while drafting a document for what would become a nation. It is hard not to overstate that point: The Constitution did not alter or validate an existing government; it envisioned, designed, and established an entirely new one.

Starting from scratch, the Founders had every opportunity to infuse religion in general and Christianity in particular into the document, but they did not. Just as the framers of the state constitutions looked back and around them for inspiration, so too did the Founding Fathers. They could have easily adopted language and rules from the states, but with this new slate they had an opportunity to do otherwise. They nobly resisted whatever temptations existed to create a constitution unencumbered by religious dogma, rules, or restrictions. Even in the one place where the door was wide open and Christian hegemony could have been codified—oaths of office—the framers refused to walk through. This door was closed securely in the third section of Article VI:

> The Senators and Representatives before mentioned, and the members of the several state legislatures, and all executive and judicial officers, both of the United States and of the several states, shall be bound by oath or affirmation, to support this Constitution; but no religious test shall ever be required as a qualification to any office or public trust under the United States.

The Constitution was ratified without a single word on Christianity or religion.

Immediately after ratification in 1789, work began on the Bill of Rights. Whether viewed as a continuation or refinement of the mechanisms by which government operates or as a separate statement on the rights of the people,[13] the Bill of Rights shows no evidence of religious preference. Indeed, the freedom of religion portion of the First Amendment at once prohibits the Congress from creating a national church and from compelling citizens to act in accordance with beliefs that are not their own. Specifically, "Congress shall make no law respecting an establishment of religion, or prohibiting the free exercise thereof." While debating the amendment, the first Senate did propose that Christianity be established as our official religion but the House rejected the proposal, reinforcing the general principle in opposition to establishment and the specific principle of a Christian nation.

If the Christian nation myth were true, our national charter would certainly have included language to that effect. Quite the opposite is true. In the two locations where the framers could have seized the opportunity to solidify Christianity's place in law, politics, and history, they not only passed but also made certain that the door would be closed to any attempts to do otherwise. This does not equate to hostility toward religion. The framers' actions do not constitute a secular-humanist victory or a Christian defeat; they are merely expressions of neutrality in defense of the citizens' rights to believe and practice according to the dictates of their own consciences. Accordingly, the restraint of the framers may well provide the best evidence we have of American exceptionalism.

Beyond Constitutionalism

That's what the Constitution says, but what does it mean?

The word *privacy* appears nowhere in the Constitution, yet we know from *Griswold v. Connecticut*[14] that privacy rights exist. From that liberty we have extrapolated abortion rights in and from *Roe v. Wade*[15] and even expanded the rights of the criminally accused based on the court's ruling in *Katz v. United States*,[16] so it is not unreasonable to wonder whether a similar course has been or can be charted through judicial decisions involving God and politics.

Clearly, as with several controversial issues for which there is no clear textual foundation or signal, questions do not come before the court in yes or no form; they give the court something to go on in an attempt to steer it in a particular direction. Sometimes, as in the case of *Church of the Holy Trinity v. United States*,[17] the court bites.

In this case, Justice David Brewer, a devout Trinitarian Protestant, proclaimed on behalf of the U.S. Supreme Court that "this is a Christian nation, shall it be believed that a Congress of the United States intended to make it a misdemeanor for a church of this country to contract for the services of a Christian minister residing in another nation?"[18] Clearly, he thought the answer should be no and rejected a strict interpretation of the law forbidding labor contracts with foreign persons in deference to the church and its ministers accordingly.

Thirty-nine years later, in the case of *United States v. Macintosh*, a pacifist divinity professor at Yale University was denied his application for naturalization for citizenship. Based on his beliefs, the Canadian applicant indicated his willingness to "support and defend the Constitution and laws of the United States against all enemies, foreign and domestic, and bear true faith and allegiance to the same,"[19] but not through the use of physical force or violence. The court was unsympathetic to his claim and held that "[i]t is not within the province of the courts to make bargains with those who seek naturalization. They must accept the grant and take the oath in accordance with the terms fixed by the law, or forego the privilege of citizenship."[20] His application for citizenship was rejected.

In what could have been decided strictly on the basis of the Act's clear terms and (pro-government) intended effects, Justice George Sutherland's obiter dicta gratuitously echoed Brewer: "We are a Christian people ... according to one another the equal right of religious freedom, and acknowledging with reverence the duty of obedience to the will of God."[21] In his dissenting opinion, Chief Justice Hughes, without referencing Christianity, argued in a manner not inconsistent with a core principle associated with the framers that his right to citizenship ought to have been upheld as it grounded in his freedom of conscience. Although Hughes did not speak for the majority, his opinion would have conferred a right based in part on the freedom of conscience that lies at the heart of many religious beliefs, including those of the Founding Fathers. Conversely, Sutherland's Christian nation proclamation, though utterly impotent as a matter of constitutional law, was associated with a deprivation of a right based on the same foundation.

These two cases represent the beginning and the end of *Christian nation* rhetoric in the court, each without resolving a single question at law in furtherance of or opposition to a religious right or establishing a privileged place for Christianity in the United States. So far, in terms of constitutionalism and constitutional law, the Christian myth falls.

One nation under God?

The Christianity-infused nationalistic ruling in *Macintosh* brings to mind a series of cases that straddle the fence between speech and religion, namely, those involving the flag salute and the pledge of allegiance. In 1940, a Lillian and William Gobitis were expelled from their Pennsylvania school for refusing to salute the flag and recite the Pledge of Allegiance. Suit was brought on behalf of the Gobitises, claiming that as Jehovah's Witnesses, they had a free exercise right to opt out of a compulsory activity that required them to pledge allegiance to an object instead of their God and to refuse the *Roman salute* of the flag, which—according to the custom of the time—required the hand held high, arm extended fully in front of the body. As Jehovah's Witnesses, they were aware of the history of persecution that resulted in members of their faith being arrested and sent to concentration camps for refusing to salute Hitler with the same gesture. Writing for a court unsympathetic to their claim, Justice Frankfurter argued that under the valid secular policy test, the state had a legitimate right to foster patriotism through compulsory participation in the Pledge and salute. Clearly, religious liberty was secondary to the national interest.[22]

Three years later, the court heard *West Virginia Board of Education v. Barnette*, a case remarkably similar to *Gobitis*. The circuit court in *Barnette* upheld the right of Jehovah's Witness students to recuse themselves from participation, arguing that "[t]he salute to the United States' flag is an expression of the homage of the soul. To force it upon one who has conscientious scruples against giving it is petty tyranny unworthy of the spirit of the Republic, and forbidden, we think, by the United States Constitution."[23] The U.S. Supreme Court agreed, striking down the West Virginia law.

Although these cases do not represent mainstream Christianity, they merit inclusion because they help us locate a line where speech and religion rights merged—once favorably, once unfavorably in the opinion of the court (despite essentially similar circumstances)—and where religion will ultimately become defined in specifically Christian terms. It is important to know *Gobitis* and *Barnette*, not just for their precedential value, but for an interesting before and after view of litigation and decision-making surrounding legal change. By extension, and as we will see in the following text, this seemingly minor legal change reconfigures the Christian nation myth as an interactive variable of God and country.

In 1954, as Cold War tensions mounted between the United States and the Soviet Union, Congress added two little words to the Pledge of Allegiance: "under God." Now American schoolchildren could raise their hands to their hearts and pledge allegiance to a flag representing "one nation, under god." And during the Red Scare, that was simply something that Soviet schoolchildren could not do. "We" were a godly nation; "[t]hey" were a godless nation. American government had figured out the galvanizing effect of God and country and in so doing had essentially proclaimed, through the words of millions of schoolchildren daily, that we are a Christian nation.

A generation after its inclusion in the Pledge of Allegiance, the Supreme Court agreed to hear the case of *Elk Grove Unified School District v. Newdow*.[24] Michael Newdow's daughter was a student in the Elk Grove Unified School District, where the Pledge of Allegiance was recited daily. He brought suit alleging that the expectation of participation and having to listen to the voluntary recitation of the "under God" statement in the Pledge even if she opted out violated his daughter's First Amendment rights. As the case argued that the school—as an extension of the state—had no authority to require teachers to lead the Pledge, it was presented as an establishment clause case.

The district court dismissed the case for lack of standing, arguing that as the noncustodial parent of the child, he could not represent her interests in court. On appeal, the ninth circuit court rejected that argument and decided in Newdow's favor, ruling that the 1954 Pledge of Allegiance requirement in the school district did violate the establishment clause. In March of 2004, the U.S. Supreme Court heard the case. On June 14 the public anticipation and speculation ended when the court issued its decision. To the disappointment of many, the court sidestepped (by never addressing) the constitutional question and, like the district court, held that as the noncustodial parent, Newdow lacked legal standing. Three justices—Chief Justice William Rehnquist, Sandra Day O'Connor, and Clarence Thomas—wrote concurring opinions indicating that the policy requiring teachers to lead the Pledge is constitutional.

Most recently, the Massachusetts Supreme Court decided on May 9, 2014, that the Pledge of Allegiance, including the words "under God," does not violate the rights of students and that the statute requiring teachers to lead the Pledge does not violate the establishment clause.[25] Using language familiar to both the *Barnette* and *Newdow* opinions, the Massachusetts court held that the Pledge of Allegiance is a patriotic exercise, not a religious exercise, and although plaintiffs reported feeling excluded, marginalized, and stigmatized, these claims were insufficient to merit a decision otherwise. By using bullying and being ostracized as points of contrast (the students were stigmatized but not ostracized, for example), the court tacitly suggested that there is a fine line that divides the type of impact on students that may ultimately have determined (or will determine) the outcome.

In New Jersey, a case is presently pending that challenges the state's Pledge of Allegiance statute. Unlike the Massachusetts or the Elk Grove law, the New Jersey policy does not require students who have *conscientious scruples* about the exercise to recite the Pledge or salute the flag, but they must remain standing to show respect for the flag. A few red flags are therefore apparent. First, requiring students to stand to show respect for the flag is compulsory; it compels the students to abide by the dictates of the school and not their own conscience. Second, requiring students to show respect for the flag raises questions familiar to the flag desecration case of *Texas v. Johnson*.[26] The court was fairly clear about how we assign meaning to and comprehend our symbols, and although Supreme Court Justice Antonio Scalia has suggested that he would change his vote in the case if he could (he originally voted to protect flag burning as protected speech), he nevertheless instructed us to counter desecration with consecration, reminding us of our options. In the present case there are no options.

With the tacit consent of the courts and the mostly willful behavior of schoolchildren coast-to-coast, the myth of a Christian nation is perpetuated daily as they dutifully or passively chant the mantra of being one nation under God. This has been the case for 60 years, but has it moved us any closer to being a Christian nation? After a long slumber, the wait-and-see question is whether the recent surge in *one nation under God* cases indicates that the principle is more common or more *vulnerable* than ever.

Religion, not Christianity

As we have seen from our discussion of the founding generation, due to theological hegemony in the colonies, religion very much meant Christianity. But with the growth and diversity of the nation, its people and their belief systems, it became necessary for the Court to define religion. It stumbled through the process in *Reynolds v. United States* (1879), regarding the Mormon Church, revealing a tendency to regulate what is new and what was unknown to the framers. For the Mormons, it was a true uphill battle, for all of the questions commonly asked to determine a religion's bona fide status yield answers that are not particularly conducive to the protection of their rights. On history, it had a short one. In terms of congregational membership, it had a small one. In terms of a doctrine of faith—something around which there were sincere beliefs and devotion—it was hard to tell, for the history of the church is rivaled by the mystery of the church. For seemingly anachronistic attributes, the court could simply say no, as it has on the subject of polygamy. And let us not forget that the Mormon religion moved westward in search of a tolerant territory and, along the way, was met with lethal force in Missouri. It was indeed difficult for the court to view the Mormon Church as a bona fide religion, but it was very easy for it to decide that polygamy is unconstitutional. But over the course of time, and as with Jehovah's Witnesses, tolerance did, slowly, evolve.

In some cases, the novelty of a church clearly intrigued the court and it issued protections accordingly. Consider for example *Wisconsin v. Yoder*. In its effort to preserve and protect as much of beliefs and practices of the faith as possible, the court carved out exceptions to existing compulsory educational laws for Amish students. In *Employment Division v. Smith*, the court managed to avoid the question of whether the Native American practice of ingesting peyote was as constitutionally sound as consuming a transubstantiated part of the lord and savior in another religion by focusing instead on the drug policies that applied after the fact. In the *Church of the Lukumi Babalu Aye v. City of Hialeah* case, the court grappled with something it knew almost absolutely nothing about—Afro-Caribbean-based Santerian beliefs and practices that included ritualistic animal sacrifice—but about which it learned and proclaimed it a bona fide religion.

In still other ways, there remain vestiges of historical bias: Sunday blue laws, the recognition of holy days. But these have largely become cultural artifacts, often disassociated from whatever religious tradition they once represented. And while Christian churches have occupied the greatest number of court dates, its presence is a function of numbers—in terms of both members and years in service in the United States. Christianity's representation in American jurisprudence is no more a body of evidence in defense of it as it is in opposition to it. The freedom of religion itself, its social pluralism and its jurisprudence, have stemmed whatever tendency or cause may have given or can give rise to a Christian nation.

It's political

"Religious organizations seek by political means what the Constitution prohibits."[27] The Constitution is protected by a number of sturdy walls and remains relatively impervious to change, unless the change comes from constitutional interpretation. Further, accomplishing what is prohibited has two meanings: getting away with something illegal or trying to influence change through other means. On this latter dimension, organized interests categorically surged in and since the early 1970s. Accompanying the waves of social, legal, and political change that marked the transition from the 1960s to the 1970s, morality and technology—a seemingly unlikely and unintended combination—took root in fertile soil. Situated in the dialectic of morality and disseminated with increased efficiency through new media and technology, religion and its corresponding organizations were able organize, mobilize, and expand their reach like never before, and with little to no organized opposition. Indeed, as Barbara Hinkson Craig and David O'Brien have observed in their classic book, *Abortion and American Politics*, it was in the lull period after *Roe v. Wade*, when the advocates for abortion rights rested briefly, that the opposition—most notably, here, conservative Christians—began to organize.[28] To such groups, *Roe* provided the ultimate evidence of a godless nation, but it did so quietly. In 1973 abortion had not yet become *the* issue; it had not yet become *the* cause. Indeed, it was not even headline news in all media markets. The supporters of women's and abortion rights assumed the battle had been won when in reality, as their opposition was organizing, it had really only just begun. As the dozen major cases that followed in its footsteps demonstrate, *Roe* set in motion a complex network of legal, political, and group-based efforts designed to close the window of rights that had barely been opened.

While it is true that *Roe* served as a catalyst for Christian conservative interest group activity, we must also acknowledge the growing presence of such groups in American life, government, and media. Since the 1960s, prominent evangelicals found willing and responsive audiences both in office and over the airwaves. The 1960s and especially the 1970s saw a rapid rise in televangelism. The new and dominant media platform enabled leading figures to brand themselves and their messages to millions of viewers instead of hundreds of parishioners. Prominent among the new media pioneers was Billy Graham, who had become the informal advisor to presidents dating back to Nixon. Phyllis Schlafly led a faith- and-family-based conservative crusade against feminism and the Equal Rights Amendment. Jerry Falwell organized the Moral Majority largely in response to the court's prayer in school decisions and *Roe v. Wade*, and the Christian Coalition picked up where the Moral Majority left off. And then the Internet emerged. Groups could now use a single platform to share content, enlist new members, reach out to existing ones, research even passing interests, link to existing sites, and essentially create a virtual world for members to congregate. On any given day—today in fact—one can visit a Christian site and find messages and merchandise encouraging members and visitors: "Let's Take America Back."[29]

Linkages to faith were also prevalent in the White House and in Capitol Hill. In what has become known as his "Crisis of Confidence" speech, Jimmy Carter, on July 15, 1979, took to the airwaves to share with the public the bleak state of the economy, public confidence, morality, and the world.[30] On several occasions he called on Americans to restore their faith; faith in themselves, in one another, in government, and in God. And while he could not move beyond the malaise he defined, Reagan promised the voters he could. As is well documented in the next chapter, Reagan boldly crafted a God and country campaign that sought to restore the United States to its Judeo-Christian foundation.

Importantly, the Christian cause was not exclusively the domain of the religious right. In fact, one of the most salient cases of the 2013–2014 term of the U.S. Supreme Court has its origin in a Democrat-sponsored bill that passed by a unanimous vote in the House and a near-unanimous vote in the Senate and was signed into law by President Clinton in 1993: the Religious Freedom Restoration Act (RFRA). In a strictly legal sense, the Act was designed to restrict laws from substantially burdening a person's free exercise of religion. The bill's name was politically brilliant—who, then or now, would like to be on record in opposition to religious freedom? More important is the third word, *restoration*. The word clearly conveys the message that something—religious freedom—has been missing from American life. And this returns us to our myth. Recall that myths are stories about our past, and the myth of the RFRA is that religious freedom was present, that it vanished (or was banished), and now—thanks to Congress—it will be restored. And as with so many myths involving religion and politics, the court plays the role of the villain. In the 1997 case of *City of Boerne v. Flores*,[31] the U.S. Supreme Court effectively ruled that the RFRA does not provide a remedy for all perceived threats to individual and organizational religious liberty. Specifically, the court held that there are limits to Congress' enforcement powers and in reversing the Fifth Circuit of Appeals decision permitting Archbishop Flores to use the RFRA to circumvent local authority limiting construction and expansion of his church, ruled that Congress had overstepped its enforcement powers in the states. In short, and absent enforcement authority under the RFRA, religious liberty was not compromised by the City's action to deny the construction permit.

Although *Flores* is clearly a religion case, it must be understood in the context of both the separation of powers and federalism. Congress has the power to enforce the law, but not to alter its meaning, especially when the law is a fixed constellation of the Fourteenth Amendment. Similarly, the extension of Congressional authority into the states ultimately rendered, in Justice Kennedy's opinion, the RFRA unconstitutional and inapplicable in the states. However, it remains controversial and applicable to federal law, as seen most recently with the U.S. Supreme Court's *Hobby Lobby* decision. On June 30, 2014, the U.S. Supreme Court in *Burwell v. Hobby Lobby Stores* and *Conestoga Wood Products v. Burwell* struck down a provision of President Obama's Affordable Care Act requiring employers to cover free contraceptive services on their employees' health-care plans. The court ruled that small, closely held companies are protected under the RFRA and, as such, may object to and be exempt from mandates based on their religious beliefs. The political game, therefore, is one of protections, exceptions, and exemptions. In the former case, the RFRA was limited due to the blurry line Congress applied with regard to enforcement in general and in the states in particular. The upshot was that religious organizations –Flores's church, for example—could not find a safe harbor under a presumed blanket of RFRA protection. In the present case the court created a religious right and upheld corresponding legal exemptions for corporate entities, which begs the question of whether advocates of the ruling should be cheering a victory for religious liberty or, as with *Citizens United*, corporate rights.[32]

It's cultural

This chapter has dispelled a number of legal, political, and constitutional myths of the Christian nation. But do myths need to be codified? Surely not.

Indeed, most myths are cultural, not legal, and codifying a principle would remove its mythical standing. The Christian nation myth remains a myth in no small measure because attempts to breathe life into it, to make it real, have failed. So what of culture?

David Sehat argues that

> these myths have a purpose. They are civic myths that politicians, legal theorists, and cultural critics draw upon to advance their aims. They are stories used to explain how the United States as a political community came into being and what its values are. . . . They are in many respects false, resting as they do upon the slimmest of historical evidence. Yet irrespective of their factual inadequacies, they provide the foundation of the civic identity of the American people. At their very best they are inclusive, offering a means by which the many kinds of people who live in the United States can be understood to be part of the American polity. At their worst they are tools to justify exclusion and oppression.[33]

At their best, we have seen how components of Christian myths have yielded great intellectual and political profits, especially with regard to morality. Consider Jefferson and Paine: To each, if religions were stripped away of their tendencies toward corruption and their supernaturalism, one would find a reasonable foundation from which to function as a society and as a member of it. At their worst, there's the corruption, power, and culture wars rooted in divisiveness rather than democracy. At their very worst, the Christian nation myth stigmatizes individuals and polarizes the democratic process. We have seen evidence of this in the recent flag salute cases from Massachusetts and New Jersey. These laws beg the question of where, precisely, the law lies in terms of our ability to think and act according to our own minds, free of coercion. The myth is damaging when we critically assess how causes and groups latch onto and push a message that is more popular and profitable than it is true. No prayer in school, abortion on demand, opposition to same-sex marriage, the corrupting influence of LGBT issues, anti-Islamic sentiment—they all represent a stubborn commitment to a myth, and a Christian nation myth, articulated as a goal, a cause, a virtue, is dangerous precisely because it requires someone else to be demonized. But there is hope. "Americans will never agree on a common religion; but this is not necessary for constructing a healthy society in which various religious traditions can live together in peace and with mutual respect."[34]

Conclusion

"In short, not a molecule of ink on a molecule of paper reproducing the Constitution and the Establishment Clause will give anyone warrant to call the United States a Christian America."[35] In terms of constitutional text and judicial decisions, Martin Marty is correct; there is positively no codified principle, rule, or evidence to substantiate the Christian nation myth. In fact, this chapter demonstrates quite the opposite—that from its earliest days and at its most critical and opportunistic moments, the republic has resisted the trappings of theocracy in general and overt support for its most dominant religion in particular. It has resisted public pressure to fall back on faith and to establish a preference for Christianity despite the Christianity's efforts, through organized interests, to establish the republic as a Christian nation. In the court of public opinion, many cling to the notion that we are a Christian nation, but in the courts of law, and despite some perilous flirtations (decisions upholding the Pledge of Allegiance), we are not. Statistically, we are, as William Douglas indicated in his decision in *Zorach v. Clausen*, "a *religious* people whose institutions presuppose a Supreme Being."[36] As a nation "[w]e guarantee the freedom to worship as one chooses. We make room for as wide a variety of beliefs and creeds as the spiritual needs of man deem necessary."[37] But this acknowledgment of spirituality among the citizenry is not to be confused with our national identity.

Notes

1. http://www.oxforddictionaries.com/us/definition/american_english/myth (accessed December 1, 2014).

2. Article VII, The Constitution of the United States, available at http://www.archives.gov/exhibits/charters/constitution_transcript.html (accessed on December 1, 2014).

3. See, for example, Charles A. Beard, *An Economic Interpretation of the Constitution of the United* States (New York: The Free Press, 1913).

4. Thomas Paine, *The Age of Reason; Being an Investigation of True and Fabulous Theology*.

5. As noted in Jill Lepore, "The Sharpened Quill," *The New Yorker*, October 16, 2006, available at http://www.newyorker.com/magazine/2006/10/16/the-sharpened-quill (accessed on September 4, 2014).

6. Richard K. Matthews, *The Radical Politics of Thomas Jefferson* (Lawrence: University of Kansas Press, 1984).

7. The letters and their primary source citations are available at http://www.monticello.org/site/research-and-collections/jeffersons-religious-beliefs (accessed on December 1, 2014).

8. David Sehat, *The Myth of American Religious Freedom* (Oxford: Oxford University Press, 2011).

9. Martin Marty, "Getting Beyond the Myth of Christian America," In *No Establishment of Religion: America's Original Contribution to Religious Liberty*, eds. Gunn and Witte (Oxford: Oxford University Press, 2012).

10. Frank Lambert, *Religion in American Politics: A Short History* (Princeton: Princeton University Press, 2008, p. 2).

11. The quote is from a speech given by Ezra Stiles Ely, *The Duty of Christian Freemen to Elect Christian Rulers*, delivered in the Seventh Presbyterian Church in Philadelphia in 18287, and is cited in Lambert, Religion in American Politics, p. 3.

12. Derek H. Davis, "Religious Pluralism as the Essential Foundation of America's Quest for Unity and Order," *The Oxford Handbook of Church and State in the United States* (Oxford: Oxford University Press, 2010, p. 3). See also, Derek H. Davis, "Religious Pluralism and the Quest for Unity in American Life," *Journal of Church and State* 36 (Spring 1994): 245–259.

13. See Akhil Reed Amar, *The Bill of Rights* (New Haven: Yale University Press, 1998).

14. 381 U.S. 479 (1965).

15. 410 U.S. 113 (1973).

16. 389 U.S. 347 (1967).

17. 143 U.S. 457 (1892).

18. Ibid. See also Marty, "Getting Beyond the Myth of Christian America," 372.

19. Naturalization Act as cited in *Macintosh*, 283 U.S. 605 (1931).

20. Ibid.

21. Marty, "Getting Beyond the Myth of Christian America," 372. See also 283 U.S. 605 (1931).

22. *Minersville School District* v. *Gobitis*, 310 U.S. 586 (1940).

23. As quoted in Lee Epstein and Thomas G. Walker, *Constitutional Law for a Changing America: Rights, Liberties, and Justice*, 7th ed. (Washington, DC: CQ Press, 2010).

24. 542 U.S. 1 (2004).

25. *Jane Doe v. Action-Boxborough Regional School District*. 468 Mass. 64 (2014).

26. 491 U.S. 397 (1989).

27. Lambert, *Religion in American Politics*, 5.

28. Barbara Hinkson Craig and David M. O'Brien, *Abortion and American Politics* (Washington, DC: CQ Press, 1993).

29. http://www.cc.org/ (accessed on August 27, 2014).

30. Primary Resources: Crisis of Confidence. Available at http://www.pbs.org/wgbh/americanexperience/features/primary-resources/carter-crisis/ (accessed on December 7, 2014).
31. 521 U.S. 507 (1997).
32. *Citizens United v. Federal Elections Commission.* 558 U.S. 310 (2010).
33. Sehat, *The Myth of American Religious Freedom,* 7.
34. Davis, *The Oxford Handbook of Church and State in the United States,* p. 13.
35. Marty, "Getting Beyond the Myth of Christian America," 364.
36. 343 U.S. 306 (1952), emphasis added.
37. Ibid.

Chapter 6

The Establishment Clause: Misreading or Myth?

Congress shall make no law respecting an establishment of religion ... thus building a wall of separation between Church and State.

—Thomas Jefferson, Letter to the Danbury Baptist Association[1]

Arguably the most enduring myth about the Bill of Rights is that the First Amendment constructs a wall of separation between church and state. However, this myth is less attributable to a misreading of the Bill of Rights than it is to a wholesale substitution of constitutional text for an accessible metaphor. The first ten words of the First Amendment to the U.S. Constitution, the first part of the epigraph, comprise what has commonly become known as *the establishment clause.* The second part, penned by Thomas Jefferson scarcely a decade after the amendment's ratification, represents what the author took those words to mean. And from there, most Americans took him at his word.

While many of Jefferson's writings were crafted with political objectives in mind, his imagery of a wall separating church and state came not from a political treatise but from a letter to representatives of the Danbury Baptist Association. Writing to his audience in the wake of his election as president, Jefferson—inadvertently or cleverly—wove a rather intricate tapestry of religion, liberty, and democracy in a scant 134 words:

> Believing with you that religion is a matter which lies solely between Man & his God, that he owes account to none other for his faith or his worship, that the legitimate powers of government reach actions only, & not opinions, I contemplate with sovereign reverence that act of the whole American

people which declared that their legislature should "make no law respecting an establishment of religion, or prohibiting the free exercise thereof," thus building a wall of separation between Church & State. Adhering to this expression of the supreme will of the nation in behalf of the rights of conscience, I shall see with sincere satisfaction the progress of those sentiments which tend to restore to man all his natural rights, convinced he has no natural right in opposition to his social duties.

The letter in general and this second paragraph in particular, is not merely a testament to a compact between man and god, but also between citizens and government.[2] His "sovereign reverence" for the willful "act of the whole American people which declared that their legislature should 'make no law respecting an establishment of religion' " clearly communicates (1) that the people have spoken, and in so doing, have (2) applied a brake to the power of government, (3) proscribing its authority to establish a religion, (4) limiting its ability to disestablish religion, and (5) protecting the rights of the people to believe what they will.

By contrast, the entirety of the establishment clause is captured in a mere ten words. This begs the question: Why have we chosen Jefferson over the Constitution? Why *have* we chosen "a wall of separation between Church and State" over "Congress shall make no law respecting an establishment of religion"? And finally, what are the implications of this choice?

Into the Abyss

Answering these questions requires a dip into a jurisprudential abyss. Had there been a history of judicial decisions defining *establishment*, we would certainly find ourselves relying more on rulings and legal reasoning than external commentary. Absent that (it would be another 76 years before the court would address the establishment clause, in the case of *Reynolds v. United States*), we filled in our collective cognitive gap with something easy and authoritative: an example proffered by one of our nation's most prominent Founding Fathers. Jefferson's letter first appeared in February 1802, one month after he wrote it, but it reappears at defining moments of the nineteenth century: in an edition of his writing published in 1853, and recirculated during Reconstruction (specifically, in 1868, the year the Fourteenth Amendment was ratified), and 1871 (shortly before the court's first establishment clause case, *Reynolds v. United States*, decided in 1878). As the establishment clause lay dormant and as state tolerance of religious liberty gradually expanded, the metaphor remained a silent constant. While colonies were transforming into states and as new states joined the union, constitution writers looked to one another for inspiration and Jefferson's wall seemingly satiated the bounded rationality of the citizenry. Then, as now, the populace was less concerned with semantics than with heuristics. We latch onto what helps us make sense of the world around us, right or wrong, for better or for worse. Akhil Reed Amar argues that we have done this with our understanding of the Bill of Rights itself—by carving it up into its constituent parts and studying it accordingly, we have simplified our analysis but lost the big picture. Consequently, and until the publication of *The Bill of Rights*, we lacked a unified analytical framework and understanding of one of our most cherished historical, legal, and aspirational artifacts. Our understanding of the first ten amendments, filtered through the sieve of the Fourteenth Amendment's due process clause, shifted our attention away from structure and toward individual rights. A consequence of this is that we have created a false dichotomy, a binary world in which the Constitution laid out the structure, function, and operation of the government—a document that empowers a political system—while the Bill of Rights emerged as an expression of the public and political will to limit the authority of government. Misreading the Bill of Rights, writ large (as a sum of its parts and in unison with our national charter) or small (amendment by amendment), had become our tradition. In the space between misreading and not reading our national charter, myths about meaning took root and flourished.

Clearly, with regard to the establishment clause, the myth of its meaning is in no small part attributable to the fact that "[i]n the minds of many, [Jefferson's] words have even displaced those of the U.S. Constitution, which, by contrast, seem neither so apt nor so clear."[3] A wall of separation is easy to envision. It lends itself to the task of compartmentalizing rights and responsibilities into one of two mutually exclusive bins: church and state. The property and province of each bin is clear: All things ecclesiastical fall into the church bin; all things secular fall into the state bin. Just as it is the right and responsibility of the church to write and require of its members the recitation of prayers, it is the right and responsibility of the state to write and maintain fidelity laws. Within each realm, and within reason, the scope of authority is clear and the basic rule is that neither should breach the wall and control the other. Or so goes the myth.

Establishment, Disestablishment, and the Myth of Dormancy

The myth unravels when we recall that words define and that the document was a product of the political realities of its time. "Establishment," though previously not routinely associated with religion, is, however, used with intentionality throughout the Constitution to convey responsibility. As Gunn and Witte note, establishment was commonly understood to mean "to settle firmly," "to fix unalterably," "to enact," and politically— in the Constitution—to "establish justice," to "establish this Constitution," and to establish post offices and inferior courts.[4] Such practices and institutions were deliberately established to perform a particular service, often consistent with the enumerated powers of the Constitution. Thus, as the First Amendment—indeed, the entire Bill of Rights, pre–Fourteenth Amendment—applies exclusively to the national government, the establishment clause can be interpreted in relatively absolute terms, barring the *Congress* (but not the states) from establishing a religion. But the First Amendment is not so direct in its prohibition. Proscribed are laws *respecting* an establishment of religion. This subtle note intimates a nod of deference to state and municipal laws. As Amar argues, "Congress could make 'no law respecting [state] establishment [policy]'—that is, no law either establishing a national church or disestablishing a state church."[5] Accordingly, the limited application of the establishment clause to the states is not exclusively a pre–Fourteenth Amendment or pre-selective incorporation phenomenon; it is a deliberate limitation on the authority of the Congress to interfere with churches established at the state and local levels.[6] Indeed, as Daniel Conkle put it, "what united the legislatures was a much more narrow purpose: to make plain that *Congress* was not to legislate on the subject of religion, thereby leaving the matter of church-state relations to the individual states."[7] Conceived this way, the establishment clause is a double-edged sword that protects states and limits the power of the federal government.

This represents a pivotal point in our understanding of the establishment clause, for it compels us to shift our analytical prism from establishment to *dis*establishment. One of our enduring myths is that our forefathers set sail for the new world in search of, or to establish, a territory of religious tolerance. To the extent that this is true, religious liberty was extended to the practitioners of dominant (established) religions in specific colonies, but the portability of this right across religious lines was entirely less secure. At the time of ratification, as many as 11 of the original

13 states maintained restrictive laws (for example, religious qualifications for office holders), and several had officially established religions. The Puritan-led Congregational Church flourished in the Massachusetts Bay Colony while the Church of England took hold in southern states including Virginia, and the full rights of citizenship were conditioned (and often denied) accordingly. The effect of establishment, then, was "liberty for us, but not for you," and a federalism-based interpretation of the establishment clause generally preserved this status quo.

During the colonial period, including the transitional period under the Articles of Confederation, the colonies-turned-states were themselves sovereign. Settlers and citizens populated different states based, inter alia, on shared heritage and religious identity. To preserve their religious autonomy was to defend their constitution. But as the United States began to take shape, disestablishment gradually occurred through the volition of the various states, and often in the form of tolerance toward other (albeit Christian) religious groups. Rooted in liberty and conscience, states gradually expanded their bases of religious participation. Delaware's constitution proclaimed that "[t]here shall be no establishment of any religious sect in this State in preference to another." North Carolina articulated a right of the people to worship "according to the dictates of their own consciences," in tones that resonated with Jefferson's letter to the Danbury Baptist Association. In the space of only 15 years, from 1775, when about three-quarters of all states maintained established churches with religious qualifications for office holders and related legal restrictions, to 1790, when 11 of 14 states effectively abandoned tax assessments supporting established religions, the wall of separation had compartmentalized the affairs of church and state according to the growing consensus that such practices were "inconsistent with rights of conscience and beyond the authority of government."[8] This was the first wave of religious disestablishment.

The second wave of disestablishment occurred during the nineteenth century, a time period characterized by civil war, reconstruction, and a reconsideration of constitutional federalism brought about with the passage of the Fourteenth Amendment. Many constitutional law students and scholars alike gloss over the *second disestablishment* in favor of the reconstruction era amendments, only to define the era as one of relative civil liberties inactivity, that the Fourteenth Amendment's due process clause was a sleeping giant waiting to be awakened. Our understanding of constitutional law was and is, therefore, segmented, focusing on the ratification of the Constitution in 1789, the Bill of Rights in 1791, the Fourteenth Amendment in 1868, the doctrine of selective incorporation in 1947, and judicial incoherence thereafter. There are peaks and valleys in the history of legal and political change to be sure, but when attention is focused on the peaks alone, we miss what brought us there.

The second wave of disestablishment is characterized by changes in law and society associated with the growth of the nation and diversity of its citizens. During the first one-third of the nineteenth century, all state constitutions included language protecting the right to worship according to one's own conscience—a parallel to a free exercise clause—and by 1833, every state had removed provisions establishing denominational preference. By 1860, newly organized state constitutions commonly included language specifically prohibiting an establishment of religion, echoing the U.S. Constitution. The twist of that era, of the second wave of disestablishment, was the refutation of government support for public worship and clergy. Based in part on the anticlericalism of the first wave (captured in part in Thomas Paine's *Age of Reason*), but mostly on the growing consensus that no person should be compelled to support religion as a matter of conscience, state constitutions prohibited laws requiring citizens to "pay tithes, taxes or other rates for building or repairing places of worship, or the maintenance of any minister or ministry," and even declared that "[n]o money shall be drawn from the treasury for the benefit of religious societies, or theological or religious seminaries."[9] As Steven Green observes in his analysis of the second disestablishment, the middle of the nineteenth century is characterized by responses not only to the growth and diversity of the nation but also to the lateral diffusion of constitutional innovation. The temporal dynamic—change over time—is augmented by a spatial dynamic—change from state to state. The constitution of Michigan laid the "no public funding" foundation for those of Wisconsin (1848), Indiana (1851), Ohio (1851), and Minnesota (1857); Ohio, in turn, provided a model for Kansas (1858), while Indiana did the same for Oregon (1857).[10] These events culminated philosophically, if not legally, in the Blaine Amendment of 1875, which stipulated that

> [n]o State shall make any law respecting an establishment of religion, or prohibiting the free exercise thereof; and no money raised by taxation in any State for the support of public schools, or derived from any public fund therefore, nor any public lands devoted thereto, shall ever be under the

control of any religious sect; nor shall any money so raised or lands so devoted be divided between religious sects or denominations.[11]

Although the proposed amendment passed the House with only seven votes against it, it failed to secure the two-thirds vote required in the Senate. The Blaine Amendment nevertheless merits attention because it demonstrates an upward push for constitutional change from the people and from the states, and the fact that a considerable point of contention during the early part of the nineteenth century involved the lingering effects of religion in education.[12] The myth of dormancy is inaccurate and certainly not constitutional or political—change was occurring rapidly within and across the states and creating upward pressure. While the U.S. Supreme Court was rather silent on the establishment clause during this time period, the key ingredients for legal change were brewing. As we shall see later in text, the court's first establishment clause case repudiates the public funding principle central to the states. Additionally, the burst of judicial activity in the twentieth century and one of its chief battlegrounds—the schools—have their roots in these waves of disestablishment.

Enter the Court

It is tempting to portray the U.S. Supreme Court as the knight in shining armor, uniquely capable of righting wrongs through the authority of its rulings and the persuasiveness of its reasoning. Indeed, the beginning of this chapter alluded to the fact that if the court had decided cases early in its history, our attention would probably be more focused on the articulation and application of precedent than on the historical events and comments that filled the judicial abyss. However, as the late-developing history of judicial involvement with the establishment clause demonstrates, decisions do not always clarify. As Frank Guliuzza notes, in "the church-state debate the Court generates controversy as much from the inconsistency of its decisions as from their policy consequences."[13] The myth that the court will correct the problem and provide clarity is easily dismissed, but the consequences remain.

The court's foray into establishment clause jurisprudence came quietly on the heels of the Reconstruction Amendments. Indeed, it can plausibly be argued that the court's role began inadvertently but potently through a single line that had the legal effect of a time-released drug. The *Reynolds v.*

United States (1879) case is traditionally examined under the rubric of the free exercise clause, yet it is critical to our understanding of the myths of the Bill of Rights in general and the establishment clause in particular. Writing for a unanimous court, Chief Justice Morrison R. Waite proclaimed that Jefferson's wall of separation between church and state "may be accepted almost as an authoritative declaration of the scope and effect of the [first] amendment."[14] Perhaps because it was not entirely central to the free exercise claim, the court seemingly declared as common sense Jefferson's metaphor as imprimatur of the establishment clause side of the religious liberty coin. Regardless, the metaphor and the myth resurfaced, complicating the path to a lucid jurisprudence.

Twenty years later, in *Bradfield v. Roberts*,[15] the court's first and only establishment clause case until the middle of the twentieth century, the justices unanimously carved out the first exception to the wall of separation embraced in *Reynolds*. Despite the efforts of several states to codify rules barring the collection and application of public funds for religious purposes during the second wave of disestablishment, the court in *Bradfield* held that $30,000 in funding to support construction of a hospital operated by Roman Catholic nuns did not violate the establishment clause of the Constitution. The court reasoned that while the recipients of the funds were religiously affiliated, the purpose—caring for indigent patients—was secular, not religious. Thus, the court formally begins its establishment clause experience with an accommodationist posture, focusing on purpose, not receivership of funds, and clearly not as a matter of a formal *establishment* of religion. From the start, the court nuanced the meaning of the establishment clause to include questions about the relationship between church and state, not strictly a separation of them or a rigidly defined establishment of a national church.

Separation or Accommodation?

Perhaps the most enduring impact of the original myth of the establishment clause—that it requires a wall of separation dividing church and state—is that it has created two rival constitutional law camps: separationists and accommodationists. Separationists generally interpret establishment to include, and the Constitution to prohibit, government support for religion. It represents the *hard line* of the Jefferson mantra and an effort to guard against cross-contamination. Accommodationists, on the other hand, view the wall of separation as a picket fence or a blurry line, permitting varying degrees of comingling between church and state. The line in the accommodationist sand involves the literal establishment of an official church or preferential treatment of one denomination over others. For both, Jefferson's metaphor takes precedent over the words of the clause itself, and despite the ebb and flow of politics, it remains the analytical framework for jurists and laypersons alike. Problematically, as the court vacillates between these two diametrically opposed positions, it provides little guidance in our effort to understand what the Constitution means. This point is most pronounced in the first pair of cases decided by the U.S. Supreme Court in the twentieth century: *Everson v. Board of Education*[16] and *McCollum v. Board of Education*.[17]

Decided almost exactly a year apart—*Everson* in February of 1947 and *McCollum* in March of 1948—the court reached opposite conclusions about the establishment clause's meaning. Indeed, in that brief span of time, the court shifted from a 5–4 accommodationist position in *Everson* to an 8–1 separationist position in *McCollum*. Complicating matters, in what is commonly regarded as the first major case in establishment clause jurisprudence, it was not simply a divided court that revealed opposite positions, but the decision's author. As Joseph Kobylka so eloquently put it, "Four dissenting justices could not square Black's separationist language with his accommodationist decision."[18] Justice Black wrote,

> The "establishment of religion" clause of the First Amendment means at least this: Neither a state nor the Federal Government can set up a church. Neither can pass laws which aid one religion, aid all religions or prefer one religion over another. Neither can force nor influence a person to go to or to remain away from church against his will or force him to profess a belief or disbelief in any religion. No person can be punished for entertaining or professing religious beliefs or disbeliefs, for church attendance or nonattendance. No tax in any amount, large or small, can be levied to support any religious activities or institutions, whatever they may be called, or whatever form they may adopt to teach or practice religion. Neither a state nor the Federal Government can, openly or secretly, participate in the affairs of any religious organizations or groups and vice versa. In the words of Jefferson, the clause against establishment of religion by law was intended to erect "a wall of separation between Church and State."[19]

Despite the rigid, clear, and separationist argument central to his opinion, Black decided that the Illinois statute permitting transportation reimbursement for children to attend both public and private schools did not violate the establishment clause of the Constitution. A number of important implications stem from this ruling. First, as with its decision in *Bradfield*, the court reasoned that the law accomplished a valid secular purpose: providing the means for children to attain an education. Whereas *Bradfield* identified indigent patients as the primary consumer population of the law permitting funding of a religiously affiliated hospital, *Everson* identified children, not religious schools, as the benefactors of the law. The notion of a secular purpose was taking root. Second, and unlike *Bradfield*, this case found the court applying the establishment clause to the states, indeed, for the first time, thus incorporating the right under the authority of the Fourteenth Amendment's due process clause. Third, it raised the possibility—or the impossibility—of balancing separation with neutrality. Fourth, like *Reynolds*, it gave credence, if not primacy, to Jefferson's metaphor, yet abandoned its strictest application. This is the functional equivalent of the court saying, "we know what the constitution means, but we don't want to go that far." The consequence of this— "the crux of the matter," to quote Epstein and Walker—is that the court applied the metaphor as construct to reach an incompatible conclusion,[20] a tactic that undermined a generally shared separationist platform. And there is the rub that explains the apparent drift in *McCollum*. Separationism was not repudiated; it was watered down. Also, because *McCollum* centered around religious groups coming into the public schools to provide religious instruction during school hours, the court found religious causes and not students to be the primary recipients of state policy. The distinction seems clear until four years later, when the court decided *Zorach v. Clausen*.[21]

While the core similarity between *Zorach* and *McCollum* is that both involve time otherwise dedicated to the standard curriculum to be modified to accommodate religious instruction, the distinction is that, like transportation support, it is the students who are doing the moving—here, participating in a release-time program in order to obtain religious instruction. Is that distinction enough to usher in a doctrinal change in establishment clause jurisprudence? The answer is, partly. Writing for the majority, Douglas reasoned that "this 'released time program involves neither religious instruction in public school classrooms nor the expenditure of public funds" and therefore concluded that the case is "unlike *McCollum v. Board of Education*."[22] By upholding the New York policy, the court departed radically from the separationist mooring assembled but squandered in *Everson* and reinforced in *McCollum*. Indeed, with the same Supreme Court membership that decided *McCollum* one year earlier, and N-1 of the *Everson* lineup, the court, through the voice of one of the members of the majority in both prior cases, boldly asserted what Kobylka accurately describes as the "accommodationist creed":

> We are a religious people whose institutions presuppose a Supreme Being. . . . When the State encourages religious instruction or cooperates with religious authorities by adjusting the schedule of public events to sectarian needs, it follows the best of our traditions. . . . We cannot read into the Bill of Rights . . . a hostility to religion.[23]

1962

The year 1962 stands out mythologically for a number of reasons, not the least of which involves news drawn from the New York headlines. First, it featured the debut of the New York Mets and the team's stellar 40–120 season that shattered a loss record set in 1899 and remains to this day. (There is something to be said for the art of the possible.) Second, it featured a case—*the* case—that trumps all others in terms of establishment clause mythology: *Engel v. Vitale*.[24] Indeed, in all of constitutional law there are few rivals to the *prayer in school* case. Abortion jurisprudence comes close, for the public routinely inserts its own attitudes in place of empirical wisdom. The Second Amendment comes close on a textual front, given the public's penchant for interpreting it for the court. (With only one major case under its belt, the public has filled the void with a peculiar combination of fear and desire.) But few, if any, genuinely rival *Engel*.

According to the myth, this is the case in which the U.S. Supreme Court struck down prayer in school. In so doing, it erected an atheistic wall of hostility between church and state and signaled the beginning of the end for religious liberty, identity, and expression in schools. The Vinson Court, which ended on an accommodationist note, was over and done and the *liberal* Warren Court (1953–1969) was now well established. Such is the myth.

When discussing the mythological foundations of constitutional law and their implications, it is easy to be flippant; that is not the intention. With this case and time period in particular, the times had genuinely changed, and so did the composition of the court and its agenda. All that remained of the Vinson Court in 1962 were Justices Black, Clark, Douglas, and Frankfurter. In the court of public opinion, the U.S. Supreme Court had become a liberal political institution. It dismantled segregation in

Brown v. Board of Education,[25] ushered in a slate of rights for the criminally accused in *Gideon v. Wainright*[26] and *Miranda v. Arizona*,[27] and made districting a justifiable dispute in *Reynolds v. Simms*.[28] Certainly, a large cross-section of the citizenry approved of the court's behavior and the evolving civil rights agenda, but a vocal and expressive minority also countered with violent opposition, white flight, and efforts to impeach Earl Warren. Even on the bench, amidst the push for unanimity there were questions about whether the court should address *Brown*, and if so, how, given the state of race relations up to and including 1953/1954.[29] This time period, this slate of cases, and the application of ideological labels genuinely set the Warren Court apart, and while its decisions clearly had a liberating effect on individual rights, to others, they had a contaminating effect on the role of the court in a democratic society. To many, the pendulum of activism was swung too far to the left and the court drifted from a decision-making body to a counter-majoritarian law-making body. The popular perception was that the court was making policy, and beginning with *Engel*, the mix of establishment clause cases decided between 1962 and 1968 did not help its reputation.

Writ large, in the four major establishment clause cases heard by the U.S. Supreme Court, 1962–1968, three were separationist landslides: *Engel v. Vitale* and *School District of Abbington Township v. Schempp* (1963)[30] were both decided by 8–1 margins, while *Epperson v. Arkansas* (1968)[31] was decided by a 9–0 margin. *Board of Education v. Allen* (1968)[32] was the only accommodationist ruling, decided by a 6–3 margin. Unlike its counterparts, the lone accommodationist ruling did not involve *prima facie* controversial content. *Engel* and *Abbington* both involved (and rejected) school prayer laws and *Epperson* struck down a law barring the teaching of evolution in public schools. *Allen* asked whether public schools may loan secular textbooks to students attending private schools. Arguing that the primary purpose of the law was to further education, the court upheld the New York law.

Writ small, the decision in *Engel* ignited a powder keg of controversy because it was immediately and forever branded as the *no prayer in school* case. Like a pebble in the water, the ripples of controversy grew exponentially as a result of the mistaken assumption that prayer was heretofore prohibited in public schools. But what did the court really decide? Did the court really outlaw prayer in school? No, it did not. The real issue in *Engel* involves state-authored and state-led prayer. The Board of Regents for the State of New York composed and authorized the daily recitation of a nondenominational prayer. While some might see the nondenominational attribute as a sign of neutrality and the *opting out* privilege as a tolerable conscience- and participation-based choice, the court focuses mainly on the authority of the state to (a) compose a prayer and (b) lead students in its daily recitation. Despite the controversy surrounding the case—mostly in its aftermath and as a result of its misunderstanding—the first question is rather easily dispatched. Throughout our nation's history, the smallest step from officially setting up a religion is acting like one by composing prayers. Using the bin example discussed earlier in text, it is generally agreed that governments have the authority to write laws and churches have the authority to compose prayers. In this case an extension of the government—the Board of Regents—breached the wall and commenced the work of the church. And despite its nondenominational tone, it nevertheless appeals to an *Almighty God*. On the second question, it is generally agreed that the place for recitation of prayers is church, not an agency or extension of the state. It is further assumed that such prayers ought to be led by members of the clergy, not employees of the state. Thus, the court decided that state-led prayer is unconstitutional.

Had the case been understood as a question of whether a state can write and require the recitation of prayers, public opinion would surely have been less vehemently opposed to the court's ruling. Indeed, the faithful would no doubt agree that this is a job best left to organized religion. But cast in terms of the *no prayer in school* myth, the results are dramatically different. Virtually all of the modern world's ill—school shootings, drug abuse, teen pregnancies—can be and have been linked to a ruling that never was. And the implications of abiding by this myth are far reaching.

Implications: Political, Social, and Legal

In the decades following the Warren Court rulings in general and the *Engel* case in particular, church–state relations came to occupy a center stage in American politics. On the judicial front, the court sought to develop a disciplined approach to deciding establishment clause cases through the Lemon test. The test, derived from its namesake, *Lemon v. Kurtzman* (1971),[33] provides a three-pronged approach to determining the constitutionality of laws claimed to have violated the establishment clause:

1. A law must have a secular legislative purpose;
2. Its primary effect must neither advance nor inhibit religion; and
3. It must not foster excessive governmental entanglement with religion.

The first prong questions the purpose of the law and requires that it must have a secular purpose, which is reasonable and straightforward enough. Throughout its history, and as this chapter has demonstrated, the saving grace of many a case—even among more separationist courts—has been its secular purpose. But the reliance on legislative purpose invites investigations into legislative history, and politicians know how to play this game. Consider Justice Antonin Scalia's dissent in *Edwards v. Aguillard*.[34] Using the legislative history of the case, Scalia essentially argued that the testimony offered in defense of Louisiana's Balanced Treatment for Creation-Science and Evolution-Science in Public School Instruction Act—a law designed to require teaching creationism—placed the Act on solid ground. The majority ruled, 7–2, otherwise.

The second prong, which requires that a law's primary effect must neither advance nor inhibit religion, essentially asks, "[R]egardless of the purpose, what is the law's effect?" Even a well-intentioned, neutral, and secular law might nevertheless primarily affect religion in a way that establishes a preference for or against religion in general or of one over another. Should a law possess these attributes, regardless of the ruling on the first prong, it would fail.

The third prong, which has fallen by the judicial wayside is a safety net designed to catch laws that have a secular purpose and neutral primary effect but nevertheless blur the line between church and state. This prong is inherently problematic due to the vagueness of *entanglement* and then the point at which it is *excessive*.

In the years since *Lemon* was decided, Epstein and Walker have identified 16 cases that have applied the Lemon test to constitutional questions involving aid to religious schools. Of those cases, eight resulted in accommodationist rulings, six were separationist, and two were mixed. Since 1980, all but two of the cases were accommodationist. This is not to suggest that the court's newest members beginning with the Reagan appointees successfully stemmed the tide of separationism. Nor does it suggest that contemporary justices have embraced the Lemon test; quite the opposite is true, in fact. What the data do indicate is the beginning of a period of heightened self-awareness about the foundations of the court's own rulings amidst heightened political and social awareness about the relationship between church and state.

Just as abortion jurisprudence experienced its greatest surge in attention, litigation, politicization, and social movements in the decades after the court's landmark ruling in *Roe v. Wade*,[35] the impact of the Warren

Court's establishment decisions and the myths associated with them built through the 1970, into the 1980s, and persist today. During his campaign for the White House in 1980, Ronald Reagan sought to capitalize on the public's discontent in general and its appetite for American uniqueness —real or romanticized—in particular. To Reagan, few things were more American than its love of God and country.

Reagan's "God and country" campaign tapped into and drew from two separate wells: first, the idea that the country lost its moral compass but was capable of greatness once again, and second, that the court was largely responsible for the country's moral decline. Both in pursuit of office and in office, he advocated the vague promise of restoring the nation to its Judeo-Christian traditions, submitting to the Senate annually during his second term an amendment stipulating that "[n]othing in this Constitution shall be construed to prohibit individual or group prayer in public schools or other public institutions. No person shall be required by the United States or by any State to participate in prayer."[36] Like proposing a constitutional amendment prohibiting flag desecration in the month of July, the goal is not realistically to secure passage but to strike a chord with the electorate. On the legislative front, he was more successful, laying the foundation for vouchers to fund private school educational choice and equal access for student religious groups.

Part of Reagan's political calculus involved an assessment of public opinion. Shortly after taking office, a 1983 Gallup Poll reported that 81 percent of respondents supported a constitutional amendment permitting prayer in public schools.[37] In 2005, shortly after the Reagan and Bush appointees formed majorities in a pair of accommodationist establishment clause rulings, the level of support for such an amendment dropped slightly to 76 percent, and 60 percent believed that religion had too little of a presence in public education.[38] When combined with research findings about the level of knowledge and evaluations of the Supreme Court, the data work to the advantage of Republican candidates like Reagan, who sought to blame the court for shifting constitutional protection from freedom of religion to freedom from it. Of course this, too, is a myth, but political rhetoric does not require fidelity to law or facts—it just has to work. And for the most part it has, raising further implications for our love affair with myths. As Franklin and Kosaki demonstrate, most Americans operate in a low-information environment when it comes to the Supreme Court, and as a consequence, and as with Jefferson's metaphor, they substitute what is easy and comfortable for what is empirically true.[39]

Tellingly, they find that high-information respondents tend to formulate relatively accurate assessments of judicial affairs and that the least informed reveal the most off-base attitudes about the court. Relying on latent ideological convictions, liberals view the court as guardians of individual rights while conservatives view it as an activist institution, despite the factual information (decisions) to the contrary. Disturbingly, this suggests that our misreading of the Constitution is rivaled by our misreading of the court, and that political rhetoric has the potential to alter and influence our perceptions of reality.

Judicially, Reagan's appointments to the federal courts remained in close ideological proximity to their appointer.[40] Aside from the failed nomination of Robert Bork and a near miss of a similar outcome with Douglas Ginsburg, who withdrew prior to the formal nomination in light of accusations of smoking marijuana while a student and an assistant professor at Harvard, Reagan succeeded in appointing four justices to the U.S. Supreme Court: Sandra Day O'Connor, Chief Justice William Rehnquist, Antonin Scalia, and Anthony Kennedy. In 1993, 2001, and 2002, his appointees formed the nucleus in majorities upholding a cluster of establishment clause cases inspired by his legislative agenda.

In *Lamb's Chapel v. Center Moriches Union Free School District* (1993)[41] and *Good News Club v. Milford Central School* (2001),[42] Reagan's four appointees plus Clarence Thomas (appointed by his successor, George Bush) comprised majorities holding in each case that the exclusion of religious groups—by virtue of their religious identity—in school programs constituted viewpoint discrimination in violation of the establishment clause.[43]

In *Zelman v. Simmons-Harris* (2002),[44] the same bloc upheld by a 5–4 majority the constitutionality of an Ohio school voucher program, a centerpiece of the Reagan presidential platform. The new Reagan–Bush Justices also articulated a legal standard that tailored the Lemon test to the specific question at hand, moving the test one step closer to obsolescence.[45] Pertinent to the valid secular purpose prong, the court required that aid must go to parents and not schools and that potential beneficiaries must be broadly represented. Pertinent to the primary effect prong, the court required neutrality with respect to religion and the availability of nonreligious options. There was no excessive governmental entanglement prong. In the final analysis, although 86 percent of beneficiaries professed a religious identity, and although 96 percent of the schools attended by students receiving vouchers were religiously affiliated, the court upheld the constitutionality of the law.

Perspective

Much has been made of Reagan's direct and indirect influence on law, society, and politics in the modern era. Even more has been made of the public schools as a battleground for the establishment clause. The convergence of these two themes is important for his bid for and tenure as president link the past to the present. He politicized religion in a way that other modern presidents had not. He actively sought to influence the composition and conduct of the federal judiciary according to principles (real and romanticized) of religious liberty. The agenda of the court in this millennium continues (with decreasing frequency) to address a line of constitutional inquiry punctuated by the decisions of the Rehnquist Court. This does not mean that the court has done Reagan's bidding; it has not. Kobylka and others have shown that radical change and the *tyranny of absolutes* has been largely avoided. But the myths remain. From Jefferson's wall to prayer in school, our reliance on myths imperils legal and democratic progress. Scrambling to find exceptions to the rule, constitutional law becomes a cat–and-mouse game with the court chasing down and trying to corner new and often slightly different iterations of similar questions and controversies. Given the relative impossibility of rotely applying precedents to cases that exploit the gaps between them, the court finds it admittedly frustrating to establish and apply consistent and coherent legal doctrines. As a result, judicial behavior and judicial decisions appear fragmented. Yet there are patterns and occasionally even explicit attempts to resolve establishment clause myths and their consequences.

The Wall's Impact

The wall: Myth and metaphor

Reliance on non-constitutional text by constitutional courts is not, as this chapter has shown, inconsequential. Returning to 1962, Justice Potter Stewart, legendary for his "I know it when I see it" standard in *Jacobellis v. Ohio*,[46] famously remarked with equal wit that American jurisprudence has not been "aided by the uncritical invocation of metaphors like the 'wall of separation', a phrase nowhere to be found in the Constitution."[47] A year later, in the *Abbington* case, his frustration was even more apparent when he argued that "[t]he short of the matter is simply that the two relevant clauses of the First Amendment cannot accurately be reflected in a sterile metaphor which by its very nature may distort rather than illuminate the problem in a particular case."[48] Almost 25 years later, Chief Justice William Rehnquist lamented the court's reliance on the metaphor, arguing in *Wallace v. Jaffree* (1985) that "[w]hether due to its lack of historical support or its practical unworkability the *Everson* 'wall' has proved all but useless as a guide to sound constitutional adjudication."[49] He continued, observing—indeed warning—that "[i]t is impossible to build a constitutional doctrine upon a mistaken understanding of constitutional history, but unfortunately the establishment clause has been expressly freighted with Jefferson's misleading metaphor."[50] Now, almost 30 years after Rehnquist's remark, we are no closer to the Constitution or to an understanding of the establishment clause uncontaminated by Jefferson's enduring metaphor.

The Engel myth

By seemingly closing the door on God and faith in the public schools in 1962, the court opened the door to decades of new legal challenges, all in an effort to "put god back in the classroom." From moments of silence in the classroom[51] to broadcasting student-led prayer at football games;[52] from efforts to insert creationism in the curriculum[53] to public funding for private school attendance,[54] the court has had to address a host of tactics introduced by states to accommodate church and state in the schools. In the court of public opinion, *Engel*'s effects continue to reverberate as well: More than 50 years after the landmark ruling and 22 years after subsequent restrictions were put in place by the court,[55] political attitudes remain focused on "prayer in school" and political behavior still episodically challenges the authority of those rulings.

In June of 2013, headlines were made when a South Carolina valedictorian dramatically ripped up his approved graduation speech and recited the Lord's Prayer instead.[56] In an interview with CNN, the valedictorian argued that "taking prayer out of the schools is the worst thing we could do."[57] A 2012 Pew Research Center poll indicates that most Americans share this view, with 57 percent of respondents disapproving of the court's decision to prohibit recitation of the prayer and Bible verses in public schools.[58] However, by focusing on the controversial separatist decisions, the data mask a silent support for and growth emanating from the court's more recent accommodationist rulings. Despite the drama of the South Carolina incident, within the schools there has been a steady but quiet surge in religious activity. Indeed, a recent article in *The Christian Science*

Monitor reports that as a result of the opportunities for groups to organize and meet on school campuses, "God and faith [are] more present than ever."[59] As result of *Zelman*, "about 250,000 students [presently] take advantage of vouchers and tax-credit scholarship," costing the taxpayers of 14 states $1 billion.[60] Perhaps, as a 2012 report by the First Amendment Center suggests, "most public school officials have begun to get religion—and prayer—right. They (finally) understand the difference between government speech promoting religion—which the establishment clause prohibits—and student religious speech, which the free-exercise and free-speech clauses protect."[61]

Notes

1. Letter to Messrs. Nehemiah Dodge, Ephraim Robbins, and Stephen S. Nelson, a committee of the Danbury Baptist Association in the state of Connecticut, January 1, 1802, available at http://www.loc.gov/loc/lcib/9806/danpre.html (accessed November 12, 2014). See also James H. Hutson, "Thomas Jefferson's Letter to the Danbury Baptists: A Controversy Rejoined," *William and Mary Quarterly* 56, 4 (3d ser., October 1999): 779.

2. One may note with interest the tacit philosophical concurrence between Thomas Jefferson and Chief Justice John Marshall. While Jefferson is often credited for his Anti-Federalist posture and states' rights advocacy, on the question of democratic principles, he is championing a compact between the people and their government in a manner consistent with John Marshall's argument in "A Friend to the Union," which challenges the *Amphyction* thesis that the Constitution is a compact between the states and the federal government. See Gerald Gunther, *John Marshall's Defense of McCulloch v. Maryland* (Stanford, CA: Stanford University Press, 1969, pp. 84–91). See also Akhil Reed Amar's argument that "Thomas Jefferson, often invoked as a strong opponent of religious establishment, appears to have understood the states' rights aspects of the original establishment clause." *The Bill of Rights* (New Haven, CT: Yale University Press, 1998, p. 34).

3. Philip Hamburger, *Separation of Church and State* (Cambridge, MA: Harvard University Press, 2002, p. 1).

4. T. Jeremy Gunn and John Witte, Jr., *No Establishment of Religion: America's Original Contribution to Religious Liberty* (Oxford: Oxford University Press, 2012, p. 6).

5. Amar, *The Bill of Rights*, 246.

6. Joseph Story, *Commentaries on the Constitution of the United States* (Boston: Hilliard Gray, 1833).

7. Daniel O. Conkle, "Toward a General Theory of the Establishment Clause," *Northwestern Law Review* 82 (1988): 1113.

8. Steven K. Green. "The Second Disestablishment: The Evolution of Nineteenth-Century Understandings of Separation of Church and State," In *No Establishment of Religion: America's Original Contribution to Religious Liberty*, eds. T. Jeremy Gunn and John Witte, Jr. (Oxford: Oxford University Press, 2012, p. 281).

9. Iowa constitution of 1846 and Michigan constitution of 1835, respectively. See also, Green, "The Second Disestablishment," 288.

10. Green, "The Second Disestablishment," 288.

11. 4 Cong. Rec. 205 (1875).

12. Among the great constitutional ironies is that the very year the establishment clause was adopted, Congress created its first law providing land grants to sectarian schools. Thus, the *religion in schools* debate is as old as the Constitution itself.

13. Frank Guliuzza, "The Supreme Court, the Establishment Clause, and Incoherence," In *Religion, Public Life, and the American Polity*, ed. Luis E. Lugo (Knoxville, TN: University of Tennessee Press, 1994, p. 115).

14. 98 U.S. 145 (1879).

15. 175 U.S. 291 (1899).

16. 330 U.S. 1 (1947).

17. 333 U.S. 203 (1948).

18. Joseph F. Kobylka, "The Mysterious Case of Establishment Clause Litigation: How Organized Litigants Foiled Legal Change," In *Contemplating Courts*, ed. Lee Epstein (Washington, DC: CQ Press, 1995, p. 95).

19. 330 U.S. 1 (1947), 15–16.

20. Lee Epstein and Thomas G. Walker, *Constitutional Law for a Changing America: Rights, Liberties, and Justice* (Washington, DC: CQ Press, 2010, p. 135).

21. 343 U.S. 306 (1952).

22. Ibid., 309. See also http://www.law.cornell.edu/supremecourt/text/343/306 (accessed on August 26, 2014).

23. Kobylka, "The Mysterious Case of Establishment Clause Litigation," 95.

24. 370 U.S. 421 (1962).

25. 347 U.S. 483 (1954).

26. 372 U.S. 335 (1963).

27. 384 U.S. 436 (1966).

28. 377 U.S. 533 (1964).

29. John David Fassett, Earl E. Pollock, E. Barrett Prettyman, Jr., Frank E. A. Sander, and John Q. Barrett, "Supreme Court Law Clerks Recollections of *Brown v. Board of Education*," *St. John's Law Review* 78, 3 (2004): Article 8, available at http://scholarship.law.stjohns.edu/lawreview/vol78/iss3/8 (accessed on November 12, 2014).

30. 374 U.S. 203 (1963).

31. 393 U.S. 97 (1968).

32. 392 U.S. 236 (1968).
33. 403 U.S. 602 (1971).
34. 482 U.S. 578 (1987).
35. 410 U.S. 113 (1973).
36. This is the wording of a Constitutional Amendment offered by President Ronald Reagan in 1981. Newt Gingrich offered a similar amendment in 1995. For full text, see John W. Vile, *Encyclopedia of Constitutional Amendments, Proposed Amendments, and Amending Issues* (Santa Barbara, CA: ABC-CLIO, 2003).
37. http://www.gallup.com/poll/18136/public-favors-voluntary-prayer-public-schools.aspx (accessed on November 12, 2014).
38. Ibid.
39. Charles H. Franklin and Liane C. Kosaki, "Media, Knowledge, and Public Evaluations of the Supreme Court," In *Contemplating Courts*, ed. Lee Epstein (Washington, DC: CQ Press, 1995).
40. Kevin Lyles, *The Gatekeepers: Federal District Courts in the Political Process* (Westport, CT: Praeger Publishers, 1997).
41. 508 U.S. 384 (1993).
42. 533 U.S. 98 (2001).
43. The court decided similarly in the 1995 case of *Rosenberger v. University of Virginia*, 515 U.S. 819 (1995). Because the central argument in the main body of the text pertains to the public schools (K–12) and not universities, it is addressed here.
44. 536 U.S. 639 (2002).
45. It is clear, especially from his famous opinion in *Lamb's Chapel*, that Scalia preferred the adoption of a new legal standard for adjudicating establishment clause cases but that the "docile and useful monster," that is, the Lemon test, would not, and perhaps should not, disappear so rapidly.
46. 378 U.S. 194 (1964).
47. *Engel v. Vitale*, 370 U.S. 421 (1962).
48. 374 U.S. 203 (1963).
49. 472 U.S. 38 (1985).
50. As quoted in Haig Bosmajian, *Metaphor and Reason in Judicial Opinions* (Carbondale: Southern Illinois University Press, 1992, pp. 76–77).
51. *Wallace v. Jaffree* (1985).
52. *Santa Fe Independent School District v. Doe* 530 U.S. 290 (2000).
53. *Edwards v. Aguillard* (1987).
54. *Zelman v. Simmons-Harris* 536 U.S. 639 (2002).
55. *Lee v. Weisemen* 505 U.S. 577 (1992).
56. "South Carolina Valedictorian Reignites Debate on Prayer in School," *Pew Research Center*, available at http://www.pewresearch.org/fact-tank/2013/06/13/south-carolina-valedictorian-reignites-debate-on-prayer-in-school/ (accessed on November 12, 2014).

57. Ibid.

58. Ibid. Interestingly, an almost equal number of respondents 18–29 (56 percent) approve of the court's ruling.

59. Lee Lawrence, "School Prayer: 50 Years After the Ban, God and Faith More Present Than Ever," *Christian Science Monitor*, June 16, 2013, available at http://www.csmonitor.com/The-Culture/Family/2013/0616/School-prayer-50-years-after-the-ban-God-and-faith-more-present-than-ever (accessed on November 12, 2014).

60. Stephanie Simon, "Special Report: Taxpayers Fund Creationism in the Classroom," *Politico*, March 24, 2014, available at http://www.politico.com/story/2014/03/education-creationism-104934.html (accessed on November 12, 2014).

61. http://www.firstamendmentcenter.org/50-years-later-how-school-prayer-ruling-changed-america (accessed on November 12, 2014).

Chapter 7

The Right to Bear Arms and the Myth of Gun Ownership: Guarding Against Tyranny, Not Your Neighbor

Introduction

Like much of the U.S. Constitution, the Second Amendment is written in vague, ill-defined language that is the subject of considerable dispute. Does it recognize the need for *a well-regulated militia* or the right of individual citizens to own guns as a mechanism for self-defense? The answer is not particularly satisfying to gun control advocates or Second Amendment defenders. The Second Amendment was written to assure protections against an overly intrusive federal government *and* likely extends to individual gun ownership. However, none of our rights are absolute, so there is little reason to believe that the Founders would recoil at limits on semi-automatic rifles or mandatory background checks for ownership. And there is little reason to connect the Second Amendment to protection from criminal behavior. The Second Amendment does not give a right to *stand your ground* and shoot an intruder. In this chapter, we address the myth that the Second Amendment was written to protect Americans against criminals.

The Debate Over Meaning

A well regulated Militia, being necessary to the security of a free State, the right of the people to keep and bear Arms, shall not be infringed.

Before we begin to consider the meaning of the Second Amendment, we should start with this important but often overlooked observation. The U.S. Constitution was created because of concerns over an armed rebellion. It was not the result of rebellion nor was its purpose to codify the liberties won in the American Revolution. It was created to stabilize an untenable and chaotic political environment. Before ratification, the states were governed by the Articles of Confederation, a weak and ineffective federal government that could not raise an army, pay off its debts, keep states from imposing tariffs on neighboring states, or negotiate foreign treaties. The obvious weaknesses led to the Annapolis Convention in September 1786, officially titled a Meeting of Commissioners to Remedy Defects of the Federal Government. The Annapolis Convention attracted only 12 delegates from five states and could only muster a call for second convention to be held in Philadelphia six months later. While the weaknesses of the federal government were well recognized at the time, there was no great sense of urgency for energizing or strengthening it. As is so often the case in American politics, in the absence of crisis the complacency of the status quo overwhelmed the call for change.

When Daniel Shays lead a group of Massachusetts farmers in revolt against foreclosures on their farmland, the need for a reconstituted federal government became much more apparent and urgent. Shays's initial target was an armory and the weapons stored inside, a necessary ingredient to any armed rebellion. The inability of state and national authorities to put down the uprising created the urgency necessary for a more radical restructuring of the federal government. Curiously, this bit of history is often missing in conversations about Second Amendment rights, which instead focus on the American Revolution, the struggle for independence against an oppressive British government, and the need for armed resistance. Adding in this bit of context, it is easier to see the Second Amendment as a tool for assuring states had the capability to maintain militias sufficient for putting down armed rebellions rather than as a tool for assuring individuals the capacity for armed rebellion should the federal government become unduly repressive. Indeed, George Washington used state militias to put down the Whiskey Rebellion in 1794, a tax rebellion led by Revolutionary War veterans, thus proving the newly constituted federal government was adequate to the task of maintaining stability and order.[1] The ability to collect the tax proved another matter as even after the Whiskey Rebellion many Americans simply refused to pay. Aside from putting down rebellion, state militias also served as an important check against a national military, helping to assure that a national army would not become a means of oppression.

Because this "states' right" interpretation is consistent with calls for gun control, it is often favored by legal scholars and political liberals.[2] Constitutional rights to possess guns are connected to the need for state governments to maintain militias, and not to individual rights to gun ownership. When it comes to debates over gun control, advocates on both sides often reason backward from contemporary political debates, showing preference for favorable evidence while ignoring contradictory or competing evidence.[3]

Yet, if gun control advocates prefer this *states' rights* view of the Second Amendment, they ignore a different and equally compelling piece of historical context. The alternative *individual rights* interpretation of the Second Amendment is well rooted in English common law and the need for self-defense to protect fundamental rights to life, liberty, and property. This conception of gun rights is also more akin to popular beliefs about gun ownership (that Americans have a right to own a handgun for protection or a hunting rifle), and fits more neatly into the broader constitutional history emphasizing the home as a *castle*, free of government intrusion. Individuals have a right to defend their home, separate and independent of any police power. This logic of the Second Amendment as an individual right serves as the basis for controversial *stand your ground* and *castle* laws, allowing the use of deadly force to protect life and property. Many of these laws extend the right to personal protection outside the home, allowing individuals to use deadly force whenever and wherever they feel threatened. George Zimmerman, for example, used *stand your ground* as a defense in the murder of Trayvon Martin, even though he initiated the altercation and even though the altercation occurred outside of his home.

For those who argue that the Second Amendment was primarily a collective right of states to maintain militias, the implication of the individual right to bear arms is contained within the collective need for state militias. If militias were to be maintained as a check against a standing army, the citizens who compromised these militias needed individual rights to gun ownership. Consider, for example, that the Second Militia Act of 1792 required that white males aged between 18 and 45 participate in local militias and in military training and own muskets or rifles, as well as the powder and bullets necessary to fire them. The states' right interpretation of the Second Amendment is thus dependent on an individual right to gun ownership. Or perhaps stated differently, the state militias envisioned by the Founding Fathers are unthinkable absent an individual right to gun ownership.

Buoyed by the National Rifle Association (NRA) and other gun rights organization, gun rights supporters often articulate a nearly unlimited right to carry firearms. Most recently, this has manifested itself in open-carry protests, in which supporters go to stores or appear in public places heavily armed. This particular position ignores a truism in debates over constitutional rights, that is, that no right is absolute. The First Amendment quite clearly states that "Congress shall make no law respecting an establishment of religion, or prohibiting the free exercise thereof; or abridging the freedom of speech, or of the press; or the right of the people peaceably to assemble, and to petition the government for a redress of grievances." Yet Congress has frequently made laws, subsequently upheld by the Supreme Court, limiting and punishing speech, prohibiting the free exercise of religion, and establishing religion via federal or state government supports. There is little reason to believe that an individual "right to bear arms" should be any more absolute than fundamental rights to free speech or the free exercise of religion. In fact, Justice Antonin Scalia acknowledges that the right to bear arms is not unlimited. Writing in support of an individual's right to bear arms, he equates free speech protection with the right to bear arms: "[W]e do not read the Second Amendment to protect the right of citizens to carry arms for any sort of confrontation, just as we do not read the First Amendment to protect the right of citizens to speak for any purpose."[4]

Constitutional Interpretation and the Importance of a Comma

Debates over constitutional meaning often begin by trying to discern the intent of the Founding Fathers in drafting the Bill of Rights. Such exercises are fraught with peril as the Founders often wrote in intentionally vague language and argued and disagreed over meaning. The open-ended nature of the Ninth Amendment protecting rights not enumerated in the Bill of Rights provides a particularly acute challenge to advocates who believe the meaning of the U.S. Constitution is limited to its text or its original meaning.

Perhaps nowhere is the search for original intent more narrowly focused than in Second Amendment debates where meaning often hinges on arguments over the placement of commas. Did the framers mean that the right a well-regulated militia shall not be infringed, or did the framers intend to protect the people's right to keep and bear arms? The placement of the second comma, advocates of an individual gun rights contend, makes the second clause, "the right of the people to keep and bear arms," the operative clause. Advocates of a states' rights interpretation, in contrast, contend that the Founders were reckless with punctuation and that the protected right was intended to be the well-regulated militia necessary in a federal system of government.

Scholars point to two different periods in history to support their arguments. For those that support an individual's right to bear arms, the English monarchy's history of disarming potential rabble-rousers illustrates the need for protection from the government. On the other hand, contemporaneous notes on the debate over the Second Amendment show the framers focused on the need to maintain state militias. The arguments are complicated by post–Civil War legislation. As former slaves joined local militias, Southern legislators fought against an individual's right to bear arms. After more than 150 years of dismissing Second Amendment claims, the Supreme Court addressed an individual's rights under the amendment in *United States v. Miller*.[5] The precedent from *Miller*—that the government could limit weapons unrelated to a militia—is used by those that support an individual's right to bear arms as well as those advocating firearm restrictions. In the past decade, the Supreme Court addressed the issue twice. Unfortunately, the decisions did little to settle the issue of an individual's right to possess a firearm. To gain a better perspective on the myths associated with the Second Amendment, it is best to start at the beginning—by looking at English law before the American Revolution.

English Bill of Rights

Firearm ownership was an essential part of an orderly English society.[6] The English did not maintain a standing army outside wartime until the seventeenth century. Most towns did not have an organized police force. An armed citizenry was an integral tool for maintaining order. In addition to maintaining firearms ready for militia service, English subjects were taxed for contributions to the militia. The Statute of Winchester and a series of later statutes mandated firearm ownership as well as practice sessions for firearms.[7] English law did limit certain firearms. Crossbows and handguns, which could easily be concealed, were prohibited for all but a few. In the 1620s, England moved to modernize its militias. The royal army disarmed local residents. On his return to England in 1660, Charles II worked to remove guns from his opponents. Parliament passed laws in 1661 and 1662, which allowed searches and seizures for anyone "dangerous to the Peace of the Kingdom."[8] In 1671, Parliament passed the Game Act, which significantly reduced Englishman's rights to keep weapons. Only landowners with significant income were allowed to hunt. Lawyers, merchants, and those without land or significant income had no right to keep a weapon. The effect of the Game Act was to legally remove firearms from 95 percent of the population, though it was not enforced uniformly across the country. A disproportionate number of weapons were seized from Protestants, effectively disarming opposition to the Catholic king. When James II fled England in the 1680s, Parliament moved to identify rights guaranteed to all Englishmen. Among those rights was the right to own a firearm for defense of one's person and property. Despite these rights, King George III attempted to limit the rights of gun ownership for colonists. Colonists who considered themselves Englishmen met those restrictions with hostility. As the Founding Fathers worked to articulate the fundamental rights of citizens in the United States, some argue that the Second Amendment was written to protect every citizen's right to have arms for personal defense.[9]

Drafting the Second Amendment

Between the Declaration of Independence and the Bill of Rights, four states adopted provisions similar to the Second Amendment. Pennsylvania's Declaration of Rights of 1776 gave people the right to bear arms for their own defense. Vermont's provisions were substantially similar to Pennsylvania's. North Carolina, on the other hand, gave people "the right to bear arms, for the defence of the State."[10] Similarly, the 1780 Massachusetts constitution gave people the right to keep and bear arms for the "common defence."[11] After the ratification of the Bill of Rights, four more states gave people the right to bear arms in defense of themselves and state.[12] Two other states used only the common defense language.[13]

James Madison was tasked with drafting the Second Amendment. He incorporated suggestions from a number of proposals from ratifying states. Some states, like Maryland, Pennsylvania, and Massachusetts, had no official proposals for the Second Amendment. There were, however, individual delegates from those states that advocated for conscientious objectors and against standing armies. New Hampshire's proposal advocated for the protection of the possession of weapons. Many states focused on the dangers posed by standing armies. Virginia, North Carolina, and New York all sent proposals seeking to limit the federal government's ability to maintain standing armies. Virginia's proposals may have had the most influence on the final version of the Second Amendment. One proposal focused on the right of people to bear arms. Another exempted people from compelled military service due to religious beliefs. Madison attempted to compile these suggestions into a single amendment in June of 1789:

> The right of the people to keep and bear arms shall not be infringed; a well armed and well regulated militia being the best security of a free country but no person religiously scrupulous of bearing arms shall be compelled to render military service in person.[14]

The proposed language was revised in July and August, paring words to accommodate the wishes of the select committee members reviewing the amendment. Congress debated at least four versions of the bill. Much of the debate on the amendment focused on the provisions relating to the militia. Britain's attempts to destroy local militias before the revolution remained fresh in the minds of the framers. Militias were viewed as a necessary check on the powers of the federal government. The House and Senate agreed to the final wording of the amendment in early September. The version passed by Congress provides "[a] well regulated Militia, being necessary to the security of a free State, the right of the people to keep and bear Arms, shall not be infringed."[15] The version ratified by the states is slightly different: "A well regulated militia being necessary to the security of a free state, the right of the people to keep and bear arms shall not be infringed."[16] The loss of two commas would have a dramatic effect on interpretations of the amendment more than 200 years later.

The Civil War

The rights of armed citizens in militias did not face significant challenge during the first century of the republic. After the Civil War, some Republican-led state legislatures created militias for black and white citizens. The inclusion of black citizens meant that most Southern whites refused to join the militias.[17] In South Carolina, opposition to arming black citizens led to fierce resistance. The Ku Klux Klan terrorized black citizens, beating or lynching militiamen and stealing their weapons.[18]

When black citizens attempted to vote in Colfax, Louisiana, armed militias of white Democrats used force to prevent Republican voters from casting ballots. Black citizens were disarmed. Black voters were jailed. More than 100 black citizens and three white citizens were killed in the massacre. "Cruikshank himself allegedly marched unarmed African-American prisoners through the streets and had them summarily executed."[19] Some white members of the mob were charged under a federal law that attempted to stop voter intimidation. The mobsters were charged with violating black citizen's constitutional rights.[20] The court in *US v. Cruikshank* refused to apply First and Second Amendment protections to actions initiated by local mobs. "The second amendment declares that it shall not be infringed; but this, as has been seen, means no more than it shall not be infringed by Congress."[21] Local mobs could deny black citizens the right to bear arms without running afoul of federal law. The decision in *Cruikshank* gave states the power to disarm citizens. Following *Cruikshank*, 10 of the 11 former Confederate states passed laws that instituted grandfather clauses or similar restrictions to disarm black citizens.[22] Eleven years later, the Supreme Court in *Presser v. Illinois*[23] reaffirmed its decision in *Cruikshank*. Members of a citizen militia group "Lehr und Wehr Verein" (Instruct and Defend Association) marched in the streets of Chicago. The militia was comprised of German-American citizens and was organized and certified under Illinois law. The socialist group was formed in opposition to the armed private armies retained by companies in Chicago. Herman Presser led the group of approximately 400 armed citizens in a parade and drill. He was arrested and fined $10 for his participation in the drill. Justice William B. Woods wrote, "[T]he right of the people to keep and bear arms 'is not a right granted by the constitution.' "[24] The city of Chicago could lawfully disarm citizens without violating the Second Amendment.

The post–Civil War history of Second Amendment challenges shows that an individual's right to bear arms was not consistently protected by states or courts. The decisions in *Cruikshank* and *Presser* may also reflect political pressures. Defending former slaves or socialists may not have been popular. The Supreme Court had yet to embrace the incorporation doctrine, which applies the Bill of Rights to any state actor, not just the federal government. Whatever the reason, the United States operated without recognizing citizens' unfettered right to bear arms for a significant part of American history. When the Supreme Court revisited the issue of the Second Amendment more than 50 years later, the court focused on the relation to militia service, not an individual's right to bear arms.

In *US v. Miller*,[25] two men were charged with violating the National Firearms Act of 1934 for transporting a short-barreled shotgun approximately 70 miles from Claremore, Oklahoma, to Siloam Springs, Arkansas. The defendants argued that the Firearm Act usurped the power reserved for states under the Second Amendment. Justice James McReynolds found that owning a short-barreled shotgun had no reasonable relationship to a well-regulated militia. Thus, the Second Amendment did not guarantee the right to possess the shotgun. McReynolds focused on the Second Amendment's reliance on a well-regulated militia, discussing "[t]he signification attributed to the term Militia appears from the debates in the Convention, the history and legislation of Colonies and States, and the writings of approved commentators."[26] Because the firearm was not a "part of the ordinary military equipment or that its use could contribute to the common defense,"[27] it was not entitled to any protection under the Second Amendment.

The holding in *Miller* was the Supreme Court's last word on Second Amendment protections for more than 40 years. The court in *Lewis v. US*[28] acknowledged in a footnote that the Second Amendment protected only those firearms that had some reasonable relationship to a militia. Gun rights activists argued that *Miller* protected an individual's right to possess a firearm. Gun control activists argued that *Miller* and its Circuit Court progeny supported restrictions on firearm possession. But the growing political power of the NRA began to shape public opinion about individual gun rights in the 1970s.

The NRA

For the first 100 years of its existence, the NRA worked to improve marksmanship and "promote and encourage rifle shooting on a scientific basis."[29] The organization was founded by two Union Army veterans who felt the Civil War dragged on because urban Northerners could not shoot as well as rural Southerners.[30] The organization championed marksmanship, supporting youth competitions and rifle clubs on college campuses. In the 1940s and 1950s, the group focused its efforts on hunter training. It developed hunter education programs throughout the country. The NRA developed its Legislative Affairs Division in 1934. The group worked with government officials on gun control legislation as late as 1968, when Congress passed the Gun Control Act of 1968. The legislation came in response to a decade of gun violence. Restrictions on mail order gun sales were proposed following President Kennedy's assassination. Lee Harvey Oswald purchased the rifle used to kill Kennedy through a mail order ad in the *National Rifleman*, the magazine of the NRA. The assassinations of Martin Luther King and Senator Robert F. Kennedy in 1968, as well as the rise of armed Black Panthers and race riots, led to the reauthorization of New Deal–era gun control laws. When dozens of armed Black Panther members protested gun control measures at the California legislature, then Governor Ronald Reagan noted, "There's no reason why on the street today a citizen should be carrying loaded weapons."[31] The NRA blocked some measures that included registration and licensing for all gun owners. But NRA leadership supported the passage of the amended bill, support that enraged a faction of the organization.

By the late 1970s, gun right supporters turned that anger into action. At the annual meeting of the NRA in 1977, the leadership of the organization changed dramatically. Known as the Revolt at Cincinnati, new leadership reoriented the NRA from a marksmanship group to a gun rights lobby. Membership in the organization swelled as the organization fought gun control legislation. The NRA pushed for the Firearm Owners Protection Act of 1986, which limited the federal government's ability to create a gun database. *Fortune* magazine ranked the NRA as the nation's most powerful lobbying group in 2001,[32] citing the group's influence over "gun-toting Democrats" in swing states during the 2000 presidential election.[33]

Supreme Court Interpretation in *Heller*

The 30-year swing in public opinion over gun rights culminated with the 5–4 Supreme Court decision in *District of Columbia v. Heller*. The District of Columbia generally prohibited the possession of handguns. The chief of police could issue one-year licenses for firearms. Dick Heller, a special police officer authorized to carry a weapon on duty, was denied a license for a handgun he wished to keep at home. Writing for the majority, Justice Scalia carefully parsed the language of the Second Amendment. He found that *the right of the people* was the operative clause of the amendment. The amendment was written, in his opinion, to protect the right of the people to keep and bear arms. He pointed to the Stuart kings of England and the 1671 Game Act in support of his argument for an individual right to bear arms. The dissenting justices, on the other hand, sharply criticized the majority for ignoring the history surrounding the passage

The Right to Bear Arms and the Myth of Gun Ownership 123

of the amendment as well as the two centuries of decisions that linked the right to bear arms to militias. Writing for the dissenting justices, Justice Stephen Breyer pointed to the court's decision in *Miller*, which clearly placed the right to bear arms within a military context. He focused on the preamble to the Second Amendment—"A well regulated Militia, being necessary to the security of a free State"—as an essential part of the amendment. The phrase "must not be treated as mere surplusage"; the preamble "sets forth the object of the Amendment and informs the meaning of the remainder of the test."[34]

The majority opinion that the Second Amendment guarantees an individual right to bear arms is tempered in *Heller* by Justice Scalia's acknowledgment that the Second Amendment does not protect the right "to carry arms for any sort of confrontation, just as we do not read the First Amendment to protect the right of citizens to speak for any purpose."[35] The right to bear arms is protected, but that protection has limits. Scholars hoped for more clarity on the limits of Second Amendment rights when the court ruled in *McDonald v. City of Chicago*,[36] but that case only raised more questions about Second Amendment rights. Chicago enacted a handgun ban in 1982 to protect residents from "injury or death from firearms."[37] Writing for the 5–4 majority in *McDonald*, Justice Samuel Alito affirmed that "self-defense is a basic right, recognized by many legal systems from ancient times to the present day."[38] Alito focused on the right to "self-defense within the home,"[39] which should receive the most protection. *McDonald* is a logical explanation of the right protected under *Heller*, bearing arms for self-defense in the home is a right protected under the Constitution. But what about the fears of then-governor Reagan in 1968? Does the Second Amendment give citizens the right to carry loaded weapons on the street?

Public Opinion and Guns

In the wake of the shooting at the University of California Santa Barbara (UCSB) that left six dead (three by stabbing and three by shooting), Samuel Wurzelbacher, aka Joe the Plumber, for his role during the 2008 presidential campaign offered this candid assessment of Second Amendment rights: "Your dead kids don't trump my constitutional rights."[40] The UCSB shootings followed just two years after the Newtown massacre in 2012, which left 20 schoolchildren dead and generated what appeared to be a critical mass in favor of imposing restrictions on gun ownership.

Yet, despite mass shootings that occur far too frequently, the United States' gun laws remain the most lenient of any advanced industrial democracy, making it is easier to get a gun in the United States than in any other country in the world. As a result, the United States has the most civilian firearms per capita of and the most gun-related deaths and highest rates for gun-related violence. Most of these deaths are not the result of a highly sensational and tragic mass shooting but are instead gang related and occur in high-crime inner-city neighborhoods.

Cause and effect is difficult to establish, and there are scholars who argue that more guns equate to less crime.[41] For present purposes, we are more interested in a slightly different question. Unlike other areas protected by the First Amendment, threats to security typically result in a shrinking of protected freedoms. The terrorist attacks on September 11, 2001, for example, resulted in the Patriot Act, a legislative effort to enhance national security by increasing the government's capacity for surveillance. Many of the provisions of the Patriot Act appear to violate the Fourth Amendment, a concern expressed at passage by civil libertarians but that only truly took form as politically viable opposition when the threat of 9/11 had faded. Indeed, the Patriot Act passed the U.S. Senate in 2001 with only one no vote.[42] After the Newtown tragedy, talk of gun control never yielded meaningful action. Indeed, since the shooting at Sandy Hook Elementary School, more states have loosened existing gun laws than tightened them.[43] The reason is quite simple: Public opinion on gun control favors gun rights activists, even during periods of crisis and even when a majority of Americans favor legislative action.

Properly understood, public opinion is not simply the aggregated preferences of American citizens but is instead multidimensional, reflecting the stability, intensity, and salience of opinion as well. Perhaps nowhere is this more apparent than in the politics of gun control where overwhelming majorities of Americans have favored limits on gun ownership, including background checks and registration requirements, but an intense and activist gun rights minority has consistently won the policy debate. For example, in an April 2013 Gallup Poll, 83 percent of Americans said they would vote for a law that would require background checks for all gun purchases, while 56 percent supported reinstating the assault weapons ban and 51 percent supported limiting the sale of ammunition.

For the majority of Americans, gun control is just one issue on the agenda, but for the minority of gun rights activists, it is *the* issue. For these activists, what might seem like a trivial limitation, for example, more extensive background checks and registration, is the first step down the slippery slope to government seizing their weapons and ultimately to a loss of freedom and oppression.

Gun rights advocates have been guided to this position by the NRA, one of the most successful and powerful interest groups in the United States. The success of the NRA to control the policy agenda is rooted in its ability to (1) withstand the immediate aftermath of gun-related tragedies when political elites, the media, and the public are reconsidering the role of guns in society; (2) use well-positioned elites to offer counter-frames, specifically by focusing on the mental health of the culprit; and (3) mobilize gun rights activists to engage not only in the political debate but also in the larger political process. In the United States uniquely individualistic political culture, citizens typically look at individual-level causes of behavior as opposed to large economic, political, or social forces. "Guns don't kill people, people kill people" may be cliché, but it also connects to deeper public sentiments about the causes of crime. Samuel Wurzelbacher's comments (noted earlier in text) are perhaps more crassly worded than many of the reactions, but they nevertheless capture much of the flavor of how the NRA frames gun-related tragedies. Consider, for example, the reactions to the following tragedies:

- *Columbine*: "If there had been even one armed guard in the school, he could have saved a lot of lives and perhaps ended the whole thing instantly," Charlton Heston.[44]
- *Sandy Hook*: "The only thing that stops a bad guy with a gun is a good guy with a gun," Wayne LaPierre.[45]

The NRA further plays into individual cynicism and distrust by framing gun control efforts as "feel good" laws that will have little real effect, arguing many of the necessary laws are already on the books but are not enforced, and connecting the issue back to Second Amendment rights.[46] While Democrats and gun control advocates often attempt to frame the issue as a problem of guns, Republicans have countered with concerns about the effect of popular culture (movies, music, and video games) on individual behavior. In the context of these framing contests, the NRA and gun rights advocates have time on their side.[47] The issue attention cycle is brief, leaving a fairly small window for serious policy reform. Finally, when it comes to the Second Amendment, the NRA has been critical in linking gun rights to personal safety.

Estimates vary but typically indicate that approximately four in ten Americans have a gun inside their home. The most common reasons for owning a gun is for personal safety followed hunting.[48] Interestingly, the percent of Americans saying they own a gun for personal safety has nearly doubled since 1999.[49] Bear in mind, this is a period without rising crime rates, suggesting that purchasing a gun for personal safety may be largely divorced from an objective indicator of personal safety. People fear crime even as crime rates are declining.

At the same time, opinion on whether gun laws should be more or less strict has shifted from overwhelming majorities favoring stricter laws to opinion that is nearly evenly divided. In 1990, 78 percent of Americans wanted stricter gun laws. By 2013, only 49 percent wanted stricter laws while 37 percent wanted more lenient laws, and 13 percent were unsure or did not know. Similarly, Americans do not want to see a ban on handguns, and have grown less supportive of the idea over time. In 1990, 41 percent of Americans supported a ban on handguns compared to only 25 percent in 2013, a 16-point drop. Overall, these shifts indicate the effectiveness of the NRA in linking handguns to personal safety as well as making the case that the problem is not with existing law but with its enforcement and implementation. They have also successfully made the case that the problem with school shootings is not with guns but with lax school security. In a January 2013 Gallup Poll, 65 percent of Americans said the key to preventing school shootings was not to change laws on guns and ammunition but to change school security measures and the mental health system.

Myths are created and persist when they serve a useful purpose. The myth that the Second Amendment exists to allow individuals to shoot an intruder or to use deadly force to protect life and property is one such example. First, it fits within a common law tradition defining the home as a castle. While some scholars argue that the Second Amendment was *only* to allow for state militias, the historical evidence suggests otherwise. However, given the context in which the Second Amendment was written, it is likely that the original intent was primarily to assure that states could tap into a militia adequate to putting down a local rebellion. Scholars who prefer to see the Second Amendment entirely through the prism of state militias must deal not only with the common law tradition but also with the reality of state militias. They were simply unthinkable in the absence of an individual right to own guns. This does not, however, mean that gun ownership was free of all limitations. Just as the right to free speech is not absolute, neither is the right to keep and bear arms. The Second Amendment almost certainly allows for reasonable restrictions.

Notes

1. The militias proved unnecessary as the rebellion had run its course before armed conflict was necessary.

2. Don Kates, Jr., "The Second Amendment: A Dialogue," *Law and Contemporary Problems* 49 (1986): 143–150.

3. Saul Cornell, "Mobs, Militias, and Magistrates: Popular Constitutionalism and the Whiskey Rebellion," *Chicago-Kent Law Review* 81 (2006): 883–903.

4. *Dist. of Columbia v. Heller*, 554 U.S. 570, 595 (2008).

5. *United States v. Miller*, 307 U.S. 174 (1939).

6. Joyce Malcolm, "The Right of the People to Keep and Bear Arms: The Common Law Tradition," *10 Hastings Constitutional Law Quarterly* 285 (1983): 290.

7. Ibid., 292.

8. Ibid., 301.

9. Ibid., 315.

10. *Dist. of Columbia v. Heller*, 554 U.S. 570, 601 (2008).

11. Ibid., 602.

12. Kentucky, Ohio, Indiana, and Missouri. Ibid., 603.

13. Tennessee and Maine. Ibid.

14. Annals of Congress, House of Representatives, 1st Congress, 1st Session: p. 451.

15. http://www.archives.gov/exhibits/charters/bill_of_rights_transcript.html (accessed on October 4, 2014).

16. http://memory.loc.gov/cgi-bin/ampage?collId=llsl&fileName=001/llsl001.db&recNum=220 (accessed on October 4, 2014).

17. *Dist. of Columbia v. Heller*, 554 U.S. 570, 671 (2008). citing Saul Cornell, *A Well-Regulated Militia: The Founding Fathers and the Origins of Gun Control in America* (New York: Oxford University Press, 2006, pp. 176–177).

18. Ibid.

19. *McDonald v. City of Chicago*, 130 S. Ct. 3020, 3030 (2010).

20. *United States v. Cruikshank*, 92 U.S. 542, 544-545 (1875).

21. Ibid., 553.

22. Joshua A. Chafetz, *Democracy's Privileged Few: Legislative Privilege and Democratic Norms in the British and American Constitutions* (New Haven: Yale University Press, 2007).

23. 116 U.S. 252 (1886).

24. Ibid., 265.

25. 307 U.S. 174 (1939).

26. Ibid., 178.
27. Ibid.
28. 445 U.S. 55, 65 n. 8 (1980).
29. https://www.nrahq.org/history.asp (accessed on October 4, 2014).
30. http://www.salon.com/2013/01/14/the_nra_once_supported_gun_control/ (accessed on October 4, 2014).
31. Ibid.
32. Jeffrey H Birnbaum, "Fat and Happy in DC Republicans Are Busting Out All Over, Not Just in Congress and The White House But Also on Fortune's Latest List of The Capital's Most Powerful Lobbyists," *Fortune*, May 28, 2001, available at http://archive.fortune.com/magazines/fortune/fortune_archive/2001/05/28/303880/index.htm (accessed on December 4, 2014).
33. Joel Achenbach, Scott Highham, and Sari Horwitz, "How NRA's True Believers Converted a Marksmanship Group into a Mighty Gun Lobby," *Washington Post*, January 12, 2013, available at http://www.washingtonpost.com/politics/how-nras-true-believers-converted-a-marksmanship-group-into-a-mighty-gun-lobby/2013/01/12/51c62288-59b9-11e2-88d0-c4cf65c3ad15_story.html (accessed on December 4, 2014).
34. *Heller*, 544 U.S. 643.
35. Ibid., 595.
36. 130 S. Ct. 3020 (2010).
37. Ibid., 3026.
38. Ibid., 3036.
39. Ibid., 3044.
40. Joe, "the Plumber," Wurzelbacher, "An Open Letter to the Parents of the Victims of Elliot Roger," Barbwire, May 27, 2014, available at http://barbwire.com/2014/05/27/open-letter-parents-victims-murdered-elliot-rodger/ (accessed on December 4, 2014).
41. John Lott, *More Guns, Less Crime: Understanding Crime and Gun Control Laws*, 3rd ed. (Chicago: University of Chicago Press, 2010); John Lott, *The Bias Against Guns: Why Almost Everything You've Heard About Gun Control Is Wrong* (Washington, DC: Regnery Publishing, 2003).
42. The one no vote was from Wisconsin Senator Russ Feingold (D). One of the more principled members of the U.S. Senate, Feingold was defeated in 2010 by a Republican Tea Party challenger, Ron Johnson.
43. Danny Franklin, "Framing the Danger of Guns as a Public Health Risk Will Change the Debate Over Gun Control," *Washington Post*, May 2, 2014, available at http://www.washingtonpost.com/opinions/framing-the-danger-of-guns-as-a-public-health-risk-will-change-the-debate-over-gun-control/2014/05/02/e4a73490-cf27-11e3-a6b1-45c4dffb85a6_story.html (accessed on September 19, 2014).

44. Ed Leibowitz, "Charlton Heston's Last Stand," *Los Angeles Magazine*, February 2001, available at http://www.lamag.com/longform/charlton-hestons-last-stand/4/ (accessed December 4, 2014).

45. Peter Overby, "NRA: 'The Only Thing That Stops a Bad Guy With A Gun Is A Good Guy With A Gun," *National Public Radio*, December 12, 2012, available at http://www.npr.org/2012/12/21/167824766/nra-only-thing-that-stops-a-bad-guy-with-a-gun-is-a-good-guy-with-a-gun (accessed December 4, 2014).

46. Karen Callaghan and Frauke Schnell, "Assessing the Democratic Debate: How the News Media Frame Elite Policy Discourse," *Political Communication* 18 (2001): 183–212.

47. Thomas Birkland and Regina Lawrence, "Media Framing and Policy Change After Columbine," *American Behavioral Scientist* 52 (2009): 1405–1425.

48. Unless noted otherwise, these numbers are from Gallup, which provides historical trends on selected issues, including guns. Specific question wording is as follows: *In general, do you feel that laws covering the sale of firearms should be made more strict, less strict, or kept as they are now?* Available at http://www.gallup.com/poll/1645/guns.aspx (accessed on September 14, 2014).

49. According to the Pew Center in 2009, 26 percent of Americans had guns for personal safety. By 2013, this had jumped to 48 percent. Bruce Drake, "5 Facts About the NRA and Guns in America," *FACTANK: News in the Numbers, Pew Research Center*, April 14, 2014, available at http://www.pewresearch.org/fact-tank/2014/04/24/5-facts-about-the-nra-and-guns-in-america/ (accessed on September 19, 2014).

Chapter 8

Procedural Due Process and the Myth of Constitutional Loopholes as Criminal Protection

We have watched this scene play out a million times. The rugged police officer, a maverick committed to justice but not process, tracks down the killer, the gang leader, or the terrorist only to watch helplessly as the paper-pushing bureaucrats in the district office let the killer go on the basis of some narrow technicality. The erstwhile cop, the sole defender of justice in a broken and corrupt system handcuffed by administrative incompetence, never waivers, stays on the chase, and saves the day by killing the killer. In doing so, he shows the inherent weakness of following rules rather than convictions, of pursuing legal doctrine at the expense of justice.

This theme is perhaps best characterized in the *Dirty Harry* movies popularized by Clint Eastwood,[1] in which Eastwood portrays a *dirty* cop willing to bend the rules in pursuit of justice. Yet the theme transcends *Dirty Harry* permeating the nightly crime dramas and news programs that define much of prime time television viewing. Indeed, it is one of our more pervasive and influential constitutional myths that criminals are routinely let go because of narrow technicalities.

Never mind that those technicalities are carefully constructed constitutional amendments designed to protect the innocent from political harassment. Or that the myth itself is almost entirely divorced from the truth. Federal prosecutors win 90–95 percent of their cases; state prosecutors win 60–85 percent.[2] Most of these convictions are not appealed, and those that are, are generally upheld by appellate courts. Despite the myth, our society is not full of criminals running amok because a police officer forgot to read them their Miranda rights, put the wrong address on the search warrant, or made some other *technical* error that had little bearing on guilt or innocence.

Yet, as with so many myths, anecdotes are powerful. The killer whose conviction is overturned is a more influential cultural narrative than the *truth* that—even with the protections provided for in the Bill of Rights—our criminal justice system is stacked against the accused,[3] particularly if the accused happens to be poor. Georgetown Law Professor Paul Butler offers this assessment:

> In criminal cases poor people lose most of the time, not because indigent defense is inadequately funded, although it is, and not because defense attorneys for poor people are ineffective, although some are. Poor people lose, most of the time, because in American criminal justice, poor people are losers.[4]

Court-protected rights of the accused have not, Butler contends, protected the poor from wrongful convictions, and, indeed, may have made matters worse. Incarceration rates are higher than they were prior to the courts decisions establishing the exclusionary rule, Miranda rights, and the right to attorney, and disparities in income, race, and education have grown over time. Not all of these individuals are guilty. According to the Innocence Project, more than 300 individuals convicted of crimes have been exonerated based on DNA evidence. While most of these convictions were based on eyewitness misidentification, approximately 27 percent involved incriminating statements made by the defendant.[5] Given the limited resources of the Innocence Project to conduct DNA testing, the actual number of individuals wrongfully convicted is likely much higher.

This reality belies what we are taught (and teach) about our constitutional rights. "In the United States," we often proclaim, "we let the guilty go free to protect the innocent." Indeed, this is one of the central pillars of individual liberty and freedom. It is also a myth that persists because of media norms that favor sensationalistic news stories,[6] the dramatic narratives that attract television viewers and movie audiences, a political process that favors "tough on crime" candidates, and a public that is woefully ignorant of the how the criminal justice system actually functions.[7] Myths step into the empty space created by public ignorance and elite manipulation.

Much of the academic research focuses on the social and political consequences of crime-related news and entertainment programs, emphasizing that heavy viewers perceive more crime in the real world than light viewers.[8] They subsequently overestimate the probability that they could be a victim of crime; are more likely to believe crime is violent, perpetrators are black, and the accused are guilty; and support harsher penalties and longer sentences.[9] While there is some question about whether (and how) local context mitigates these effects—especially the amount of crime in local neighborhoods[10]—there is little question that exposure to news, entertainment, and reality crime programs shapes individual perceptions of the world.

If we turn the question on its head, however, we can also see that the theme of justice denied has deep cultural resonance. That is, it may well be that watching *Dirty Harry* and other crime-related programs shapes our view of the criminal justice system, but these programs work because they tap into deeper cultural beliefs. Or perhaps stated differently, they do not simply create their audience; they find their audience, ready to believe that we are too lenient on individuals accused of a crime.

Curiously, the cultural resonance is at odds with our historical experience. The technical protections provided for in the Bill of Rights are deeply rooted in the American colonial experience in which criminal law was used to minimize political opposition and dissent. General searches of homes by British authorities to find evidence of any wrongdoing or simply as a tool for political harassment were common and invasive.[11] Authoritarian governments similarly and routinely use criminal proceeding to silence political opponents. Criminal law is one of the most effective tools of despotic governments. The importance of political considerations in the definition of civil liberties, however, is poorly understood and generally unappreciated. As a result, Americans show a willingness to scale back individual protections against self-incrimination, search and seizure, and trial by jury if it means putting more criminals behind bars. In this chapter, we examine this myth that too many criminals get off on technicalities, and find it lacking in evidence and reasoning. Perhaps more troubling, in a "flat" world where threats are more immediate and real,[12] our willingness to scale back on these protections opens the door to the potential of abuse in pursuit of order and security.

The Origins of Due Process

Procedural due process is simple enough to define but far more difficult to understand. In its simplest forms it involves procedural protections against government taking of life, liberty, or property. The principle was well rooted in English common law and the Magna Carta (1215) long before the Bill of Rights was drafted, proposed, or ratified. The Magna Carta specifically provided for procedural protections, noting that

> [n]o free man shall be taken, imprisoned, disseised, outlawed, banished, or in any way destroyed, nor will we proceed against or prosecute him, except by lawful judgment of his peers and by the law of the land.

The phrase *due process*—as opposed to law of the land—can be traced to Edward the Third, who in 1354 declared that

> no man of what Estate or Condition that he be, shall be put out of land or Tenement, nor taken, nor imprisoned, nor disinherited, nor put to death, without being brought in answer by due process of law.[13]

Due process was later used by English jurist Edward Coke in the fourth article of the Petition of Right (1628)[14] and was adopted in U.S. common law, even though it is not clear that "due process of the law" meant the same thing in England as it did in the United States. In England, "due process of law" and the "law of the land" were conceptually distinct (though related) while in the United States these concepts were merged into a single set of procedural protections against government action. Regardless, American colonists largely believed they were protected as free Englishmen by the procedural protections spelled out in the Magna Carta and codified in English common law, and early colonial assemblies generally reaffirmed these rights and protections.[15] In 1761, for example, James Otis challenged the general "writ of assistance" allowing authorities to search the home of anyone thought to be involved in smuggling. Though he lost, his challenge reflected the prevailing view that general searches were an affront to individual liberty.

In drafting the Bill of Rights and specifically the Fifth Amendment, James Madison used the term *due process of the law* largely to connect to widely supported and embraced procedural freedoms. It is worth recalling that Madison's goal in writing the Bill of Rights was not to establish new rights but rather to protect the institutional structure of the U.S. Constitution while codifying shared principles of governance and undermining Anti-Federalist opposition. While the specific phrase "due process of law" appeared in the Fifth Amendment, the principle also underlies the procedural safeguards provided in Fourth and Sixth Amendments. Collectively, we may think of due process as including the following:

- Fourth Amendment protections against unreasonable search and seizure.
- Fifth Amendment protections providing protections against double jeopardy (being tried twice for the same offense) and self-incrimination, as well as requiring indictments by a grand jury and compensation for taking property.
- Sixth Amendment provisions for trial by jury, the right to an attorney, the right to confront and present witnesses and to compel them to appear before the court, and to know the specific nature of the charges.
- Eight Amendment providing against excessive bail and cruel or unusual punishment.

Until the ratification of the Fourteenth Amendment, these protections applied only against federal government action. Protections against state government action were left to state constitutions and state courts. As noted in Chapter Two, the Fourteenth Amendment seemingly provided blanket protection against state action in a very clear and indisputable language: No state shall "deprive any person of life, liberty, or property, without due process of law; nor deny to any person within its jurisdiction the equal protection of the laws." The application of the Bill of Rights to state action, however, happened not at once but on case-by-case and selective basis. To scholars like Akhil Reed Amar, whose study of the Bill of Rights transcends specific clauses, provisions, and amendments, this process has become known as "refined incorporation," and is based on the assertion that all of the Constitution's privileges and immunities—all of the rights belonging to citizens and not the states themselves—have become fully incorporated under the authority and application of the Fourteenth Amendment.[16] The case-by-case approach to incorporating individual rights, however, reveals the court's selectivity, protecting fundamental rights in piece-meal fashion as opposed to a full incorporation of the Bill of Rights in one fell swoop. In constitutional law this is commonly referred to as the process or doctrine of selective incorporation. In this process, the consensual procedural protections outlined in the Bill of Rights have been gradually but with notable exceptions, as with state grand jury requirements discussed later in text, expanded by the court. And as our history has shown, the expansion of liberties, though seemingly compatible with our democratic ethos, has tended to usher in controversy.

Incorporation and the Rights of the Criminally Accused

In March of 1882, Joseph Hurtado was arrested for the murder of Jose Antonio Estuardo. Hurtado's indictment was issued in the form of an *information for murder* document produced to a judge by the prosecuting attorney listing the accusations, charges, and evidence against the defendant. Information indictments did not require grand jury hearings under existing California law and Hurtado was tried, convicted, and sentenced to death accordingly. He appealed to the U.S. Supreme Court on the grounds that the U.S. Constitution's Fourteenth Amendment guarantees the right to a grand jury hearing. The court in the case of *Hurtado v. California* (1884)[17] disagreed, arguing that the existing procedure provided a satisfactory substitution for a grand jury hearing, creating an exception to the myth of full incorporation that exists to this day.

The case is important to our understanding of constitutional law as well because it represents the first major (albeit, failed) case that sought to apply the Fourteenth Amendment's protections of life and liberty to the states. In the case's lone dissent, Justice Harlan acknowledged the majority's recognition of the due process clause's applicability to core principles of liberty at the state and federal levels but challenged its conclusion that the grand jury requirement constitutes an exception to the rule. Thirteen years later, in *Chicago, Burlington and Quincy Railroad v. Chicago* (1897), Harlan's dissenting voice in Hurtado became the majority and seemingly moved the court a step closer to incorporation and a tethering of the Fourteenth Amendment to the Bill of Rights.[18] The case involved government takings, here in the form of the state of Illinois taking private property (railroad property) for public use (street improvements) without just compensation ($1 for railroad companies versus $13,000 for individual property owners). On the matter of eminent domain and compensation, Harlan wrote:

> If compensation for private property taken for public use is an essential element of due process of law as ordained by the fourteenth amendment, then the final judgment of a state court, under the authority of which the property is in fact taken, is to be deemed the act of the state, within the meaning of that amendment.... In our opinion, a judgment of a state court, even if it be authorized by statute, whereby private property is taken for the state or under its direction for public use, without compensation made or secured to the owner, is, upon principle and authority, wanting in the due process of law required by the fourteenth amendment of the constitution

of the United States, and the affirmance of such judgment by the highest court of the state is a denial by that state of a right secured to the owner by that instrument.[19]

Three years later, the court proved that its perceived progress was an illusion. In a case that returns the due process clause to criminal law matters, the court ruled in *Maxwell v. Dow* (1900) that Utah's laws permitting eight-person juries (as opposed to the customary 12) and omitting grand jury hearings were constitutionally permissible and that as a broad legal principle, "[t]rial by jury has never been affirmed to be a necessary requisite of due process of law."[20] As with other areas of law that have witnessed the court operating in the absence of a clear legal standard (consider, for example, the evolution of establishment clause jurisprudence and speech rights), turn-of-the-century (nineteenth to twentieth) jurisprudence found the court operating in piece-meal fashion, addressing specific issues instead of overarching concepts. Despite arguing in Hurtado that "[l]aw is something more than mere will extended as an act of power. It must not be a special rule for a particular person or a particular case," the court asserted in Twining that it "has always declined to give a comprehensive definition of [due process], and has preferred that its full meaning should be gradually ascertained by the process of inclusion and exclusion in the course of the decisions of cases as they arise."[21] Consequently, from year to year and from case to case, the court neither followed nor established a linear and coherent path to due process. This returns us to a more general theme: Constitutional rights, as interpreted by the courts, are not static but are constantly changing as they are reinterpreted and reevaluated in light of new evidence and changing social, political, and economic conditions.

In *Twining v. New Jersey* (1908), despite the piece-meal approach adopted by the court, noted earlier in text, the path to incorporation began to straighten. Although it is tempting to cluster *Twining v. New Jersey* (1908) together with *Maxwell* on the basis of rejected claims of constitutional protection—exempting jury trials in the former and self-incrimination in the latter—the lasting impact of the case involves the emergence of a limited legal standard, framed as and in response to a rhetorical question:

> Is it a fundamental principle of liberty and justice which inheres in the very idea of a free government and is the unalienable right of a citizen of such a government? If it is, and if it is of a nature that pertains to process of law, this court has declared it to be essential to due process of law.[22]

This is a curious and important statement. Fundamental rights spelled out in the Bill of Rights were to be protected, while less fundamental rights were not, but the decision as to what was fundamental was left to the Supreme Court. Capitalizing on the "fundamental" and "unalienable" currency of *Twining*, the court decided in *Gitlow v. New York* (1925) that the freedoms of speech and press are "among the fundamental rights and 'liberties' protected by the due process clause of the Fourteenth Amendment from impairment by the states."[23] In the double jeopardy case of *Palko v. Connecticut* (1937), the court indicated that the Fourteenth Amendment absorbs rights that are so important that "neither liberty nor justice would exist if they were sacrificed."[24] In this case, the court added the double jeopardy claim to other rights of the criminally accused, noting that while they may carry "value and importance," they are not "of the very essence of a scheme of ordered liberty." Elaborating on its emerging standard, the court asked:

> Is that kind of double jeopardy to which the statute has subjected him [Palka[25]] a hardship so acute and shocking that our polity will not endure it? Does it violate those "fundamental principles of liberty and justice which lie at the base of all our civil and political institutions"? The answer surely must be "no."[26]

While criminal law lies at the heart of the doctrine of selective incorporation, the rights of the criminally accused were more often eschewed than championed by the court. To tie into an earlier theme (see Chapter One), the court was, at least until the 1960s, no more protective of the rights of the accused than legislatures. Change occurred incrementally as the court incorporated the Fourteenth Amendment into Fourth Amendment jurisprudence in *Mapp v. Ohio* (1961); the Fifth Amendment's double jeopardy provision in *Benton v. Maryland* (1969), which effectively overruled *Palko*, and protections against self-incrimination in *Miranda v. Arizona* (1966); and the Sixth Amendment right to counsel in *Gideon v. Wainright* (1963)—cases that expanded and protected the rights of the accused but also kicked the hornet's nest of controversy.[27]

From Gideon to Miranda to the Myth

In Chapter Six we traced the myth and resulting misperceptions about religious liberty in general, and school prayer in particular, to the case of *Engel v. Vitale* (1962). In much the same way that *Engel* ignited a powder keg of controversy and public backlash for church–state relations, *Miranda v. Arizona* (1966) triggered public outrage for freeing an admitted violent criminal." In March of 1963, Ernesto Miranda was arrested for kidnapping and raping an 18-year-old woman. Ten days after the crime was committed, he was identified by his victim and taken into custody in Phoenix, Arizona. While in custody, and after two hours of questioning, the barely literate and indigent suspect confessed to the crime. He was subsequently tried and convicted.

To the average American, this is a textbook example of the way the criminal justice system operates: A crime is committed, it is investigated, an arrest is made, a confession is provided, a trial is held, and the suspect is found guilty. Overturning a conviction on the narrow grounds that a guilty defendant was not read his rights appears to be a striking and gross miscarriage of justice. Where is *Dirty Harry* when we need him? But there is a vitally important procedural side to due process; indeed, as the preeminent constitutional scholar John Hart Ely observes in his classic book *Democracy and Distrust*, "it all sounds quite straight-forward, and more than a few commentators have concluded that it is crystal clear that the framers of the Fourteenth Amendment intended their Due Process Clause to reach only procedural questions."[28] In the present case, the process that is so vital involves police conduct. Law enforcement officers are required to abide by the law as much as they are empowered to enforce it and here we discover that Miranda is an intervening variable, nestled in-between and stemming from *Gideon v. Wainright* (1963) and the articulation of one of the most widely known legal standards in American history: the Miranda Rights, listed as follows:

> You have the right to remain silent. Anything you say can and will be used against you in a court of law. You have the right to an attorney. If you cannot afford an attorney, one will be provided for you. Do you understand the rights I have just read to you? With these rights in mind, do you wish to speak to me?[29]

In the court of public opinion, the unforgivable tragedy of Miranda is that a confessed rapist was set free. In the nation's high court, this was the necessary consequence of the failure of law enforcement officials to abide by the law while enforcing it. Since *Gideon v. Wainright*, indigent right to legal counsel has been expressly protected as a fundamental right of the criminally accused.[30] Noting the high value the framers of the Constitution placed on the rights of the criminally accused, the justices unanimously ruled that the right to counsel is not a privilege reserved for those with the means to afford it. Indeed, the court proclaimed that the combination of precedent, reason, and reflection

> require us to recognize that in our adversary system of criminal justice, any person haled into court, who is too poor to hire a lawyer, cannot be assured a fair trial unless counsel is provided for him. This seems to us to ne an obvious truth. ... From the beginning, our state and national constitutions and laws have laid great emphasis on procedural and substantive safeguards designed to assure fair trials before impartial tribunals in which every defendant stands equal before the law. This noble ideal cannot be realized if the poor man charged with crime has to face his accusers without a lawyer to assist him.[31]

In the 1964 case of *Escobedo v. Illinois*,[32] a narrowly divided Supreme Court expanded this legal principle into the realm of interrogation, making clear that the right to counsel applies not only to judicial proceedings but to the implementation of procedures necessary for the prosecution to develop a case against a defendant. Specifically, the court ruled that when the focus of police conduct shifts from investigation to accusation—"when its focus is on the accused and its purpose is to elicit a confession"—"the accused must be permitted to consult with his lawyer."[33] Thus, by the time the court decided *Miranda* in 1966, two relevant precedents were available, but instead of exercising compliance with controlling judicial precedence, the state of Arizona exercised defiance and avoidance, depriving Ernesto Miranda of a recently but clearly established legal right. Absent the fidelity to the law essential for the operation of a fair and just criminal law system, the only constitutionally permissible alternative was to free him.

Over the course of time the details of the case have faded and what remain are *the Miranda Rights* and the myths surrounding them. Citizens and suspects alike believe that we must all be *read our rights*, that lawyers must be present prior to and during criminal trials, and that we must know our rights, including those against self-incrimination, beginning at the moment of first contact. While there is truth to certain of these claims, like all constitutional rights, they are not absolute. Over the course of time Miranda has endured but the court has created exceptions. Epstein and Walker[34] identify ten key cases decided between 1971 and 2010 in which the U.S. Supreme Court has limited a blanket application of what is commonly expected of Miranda. In cases involving perjury,[35] the public safety,[36] willfully waiving the right to an attorney,[37] providing voluntary statements to undercover officers,[38] evidence obtained from voluntary information provided in the absence of full Miranda warnings,[39] and even confessions elicited as a result of police unlawfully entering a suspect's house,[40] the court has refined and limited the scope and applicability of *Miranda*, exposing the myth of the blanket protection of our rights and how well we know them.

Misreading the Fourth Amendment Through the Prism of the Fourteenth

The Fourth Amendment to the U.S. Constitution reads:

> The right of the people to be secure in their persons, houses, papers, and effects, against unreasonable searches and seizures, shall not be violated, and no Warrants shall issue, but upon probable cause, supported by an Oath or affirmation, and particularly describing the place to be searched, and the persons or things to be seized.

To the Founders, the Fourth Amendment was an essential bulwark against an intrusive government, a clear signal that nothing tantamount to English writs of assistance—the equivalent of search warrants, minus the places to be searched and the evidence sought and gathered—would stand in our newly formed republic. The amendment echoes the prevailing wisdom that citizens have a general right to be left alone and, especially in the confines of one's person and property, a fundamental right to be free from government intrusion. The important modifier, however, is the word *unreasonable*. The amendment does not prohibit searches and seizures of property, only *unreasonable* searches and seizures. Misread, the amendment draws a line in the sand, forbidding the government from searches and seizures without a lawful warrant. As the following cases indicates, this is far from the truth.

The history of civil liberties jurisprudence has been defined by incrementalism and segmentation: taking on specific questions and seeking to answer them in a clear and limited way. In its refusal to bite off more than it can chew, the court has traditionally, and at first, relied on a combination of literalism and original intent, believing that it was closing the door on issues as they arose rather than opening them like Pandora's box. With regard to the Fourth Amendment, this was clear in the 1928 case of *Olmstead v. United States*.[41] At issue in this case was the government's use of electronic eavesdropping equipment in surveillance activities of Roy

Olmstead, who was suspected of distributing alcohol in violation of the National Prohibition Act. Conversations of illegal activities were overheard and submitted as evidence against him. The government's response was that because they had not physically trespassed, their conduct was not in violation of the Fourth Amendment. The court agreed, noting that "[t]here was no searching. There was no seizure. . . . There was no entry of the houses or offices of the defendant." Based on the strictest of literal readings, the "physical penetration" rule was thus established, barring only physical trespasses into a person's property. "Unreasonable" means did not enter into the equation, but they were at the heart of Justice Brandeis's famous dissent, in which he argued that the framers "conferred, as against the Government, the right to be let alone—the most comprehensive of rights and the right most valued by civilized men. To protect that right, every unjustifiable intrusion by the Government upon the privacy of the individual, whatever the means employed, must be deemed a violation of the Fourth Amendment."[42]

Seventy-three years later, in the case of *Kyllo v. United States* (2001), the court addressed a similar question. In both cases, the police used what was then the height of technology to gather evidence of illegal activity without physically penetrating a suspect's property. Whereas Olmstead was suspected of trafficking illegal alcohol, Kyllo was suspected of growing—with the intent to distribute—marijuana. Whereas the police used listening devices in *Olmstead*, they used thermal imaging devices designed to register heat signals inside Kyllo's home. Whereas the words recorded constituted evidence against Olmstead, the heat in Kyllo's home provided evidence of a growing operation. Whereas Olmstead's conviction was upheld by the Supreme Court, Kyllo's was not. Reversing the Olmstead precedent and relying on the privacy rights advanced and upheld in *Katz v. United States* (1967),[43] the court ruled that citizens have a reasonable expectation of privacy, the violation of which—absent a warrant—is prohibited by the Fourth Amendment.

This logic was reiterated in the 2014 case of *Riley v. California*, when a unanimous court ruled that cell phones and other mobile devices are protected against government intrusion by the Fourth Amendment. Chief Justice Roberts wrote, "The fact that technology now allows an individual to carry such information in his hand does not make the information any less worthy of the protection for which the Founders fought." He further opined:

> It is true that this decision will have some impact on the ability of law enforcement to combat crime. But the Court's holding is not that the

information on a cell phone is immune from search it is that a warrant is generally required before a search. The warrant requirement is an important component of the Court's Fourth Amendment jurisprudence, and warrants may be obtained with increasing efficiency. In addition, although the search incident to arrest exception does not apply to cell phones, the continued availability of the exigent circumstances exception may give law enforcement a justification for a warrantless search in particular cases.[44]

The preceding cases all point to the significance of a search warrant, but the opening argument in this section has been that the second clause of the Fourth Amendment—regarding warrants—does not control the first. Indeed, a prevailing myth is that lawful searches and seizures cannot be commenced without a warrant. Roberts's decision, discussed earlier in text, provides a hint that there are exceptions. While cases such as *Illinois v. Gates*[45] clearly establish the centrality of a warrant in cases for which probable cause has been established as well as the rules for a lawful search—the warrant must specifically identify the property to be searched and the items to be searched for, and the investigation must be constrained by the parameters of said warrant—a series of exceptions to the rule exist. Epstein and Walker[46] present these exceptions clearly and concisely as follows:

1. *Searches incident to a valid arrest*, which occur when, in the course of a lawful arrest, officers search persons and property for evidence related to a crime;
2. *Loss of evidence searches*, which occur when time literally is of the essence, as when evidence that must be obtained and preserved can easily be destroyed or removed;[47]
3. *Consent searches*, which occur when consent is provided voluntarily by a criminal suspect;
4. *Safety searches*, which occur when a law enforcement officer believes a person poses a danger to the public or the police;
5. *Hot pursuit*, which occurs when law enforcement agents, fearing they will be evaded, pursue a fleeing suspect into other properties; and
6. *The plain view doctrine*, which grants law enforcement agents the authority to gather evidence in plain view of, but not listed in, the original warrant.

The sixth exception is the most controversial for it brings to light something that is actually less an exception *to* a warrant than an exception to the faithful enforcement *of* a warrant. *Mapp v. Ohio* is the landmark Supreme Court ruling that applied a key principle of Fourth Amendment law—the exclusionary rule—to the states.[48] Simply stated, the exclusionary rule bars the use of illegally obtained evidence against defendants in a criminal trial. In what amounts to one of the most fascinating cases in criminal law history, Dollree Mapp was suspected of a variety of unlawful activities including illegal gambling. In May 1957, Cleveland police had reason to belief she was harboring a fugitive wanted for bombing the home of racketeer-turned-boxing promoter Don King. When the police arrived at her house, she refused to let them in absent a warrant. Sergeant Carl Delau allegedly called in a warrant. Three hours later, additional law enforcement officers arrived, presumably with said warrant. Police forced open the door and entered, producing what appeared to be and was presented as a search warrant.[49] Mapp wrestled the document away from Delau. She was promptly restrained and the document in question was retrieved. The officers searched the house but found no evidence of the alleged crimes. They did, however, find a number of artifacts deemed obscene under Ohio law. These materials were seized and Mapp was arrested, tried, and convicted for felony possession of obscene material.

Originally, the case before the court was designed to challenge the Ohio obscenity law, but as is their right, the justices of the U.S. Supreme Court instead focused on the search and seizure aspect of the case, emphasizing the centrality of the exclusionary rule to state as well as federal Fourth Amendment jurisprudence. In a synthesis of due process jurisprudence, privacy rights interests, and political insight and foresight, Justice Clark proclaimed that in criminal law,

> [t]he criminal goes free, if he must, but it is the law that sets him free. Nothing can destroy a government more quickly than its failure to observe its own laws, or worse, its disregard of the character of its own existence. Nor can it lightly be assumed that, as a practical matter, adoption of the exclusionary rule fetters law enforcement. . . . The ignoble shortcut to conviction left open to the State tends to destroy the entire system of constitutional restraints on which the liberties of the people rest. Having once recognized that the right to privacy embodied in the Fourth Amendment is enforceable against the States, and that the right to be sure against rude invasions of privacy by state officers is, therefore, constitutional in origin, we can no longer permit that right to remain an empty promise. Because it is enforceable in the same manner and to like effect as other basic rights secured in the Due Process Clause, we can no longer permit it to be revocable at the whim of any police officer who, in the name of law enforcement itself, chooses to suspend its enjoyment. Our decision, founded on reason and truth, gives to the individual no more than that which the Constitution guarantees him, to the police officer no less than that to which

honest law enforcement is entitled, and, to the courts, that judicial integrity so necessary in the true administration of justice.[50]

Of all modern criminal court cases, *Mapp* stands virtually unrivaled as the fulcrum where the court tilted from protecting the rights of law-abiding citizens to endangering them by setting free criminals on the basis of a flaw in the administration of justice. To the public, law enforcement took a back seat to the rights of the accused. To this day the myth persists, despite decisions like *Hudson v. Michigan*[51] and *Herring v. United States*[52] that limited the application of the exclusionary rule. While Epstein and Walker note that "[t]hose who favor law enforcement interests believe that the Court's current view is a reasonable one that balances individual protections with the need to combat crime,"[53] public opinion remains fixed on the myth that too many criminals get off on technicalities. Even as the composition of the Supreme Court was transformed during the Reagan administration and even as their decisions scaled back on the expansive interpretations of the Warren Court, the public continued to believe in the myth that the court was more interested in protecting the rights of the accused than in assuring justice.

Public Opinion and the Myth of Technicalities

Not all myths are rooted in misinformation; some are sustained because they provide a narrative that reinforces our social, political, and economic values. Myths about procedural due process, however, are more often rooted in misperception and fear of crime than in shared cultural values.[54] The myth that criminals are let go on technicalities persist because it reinforces fears of crime and victimization. The fear is reinforced through local television news with its relentless focus on crime; entertain programs like *Law and Order*, which claim story lines *ripped from the headlines*; and news magazines and 24-hour news channels that gravitate to the most sensational crimes of the day. When the jury in the O. J. Simpson trial returned with a *not guilty* verdict or when Casey Anthony was acquitted, perceptions that the American criminal justice system does too much to protect the rights of the accused are confirmed. Despite the verdict, nearly two-thirds of Americans believed Casey Anthony was definitely (20 percent) or probably (44 percent) guilty of killing Caylee, her two-year-old daughter.[55] Public opinion was equally tilted toward guilt in the O. J. Simpson case with 66 percent of Americans believing it was definitely or probably true that

Simpson murdered Nicole Brown Simpson and Ronald Goldman. In these high-profile (but unique) cases, large majorities of Americans believe not only that justice is being denied but also that this is symptomatic of a broken criminal justice system.

True or not, sensational cases overwhelm the more mundane realities of American criminal justice, fueling distrust and cynicism about a criminal system that appears to protect the guilty.[56] Stories detailing convictions overturned on the basis of DNA evidence, for example, may sustain a moment of interest but are generally less compelling and less capable of holding our long-term interest than individuals convicted in the court of public opinion but acquitted by a judge and jury. They subsequently have fewer lasting effects on public beliefs. Henry McCollum, intellectually disabled but freed after 30 years on death row by new DNA evidence, hardly seems as outrageous in the public mind as O. J. Simpson or Casey Anthony walking free. Indeed, it is unlikely that many Americans could name Henry McCollum but most could name Casey Anthony and offer an opinion on her trial and her guilt.

This is possible, in part, because Americans have little factual understanding or knowledge about the processes or institutions that comprise the criminal justice system,[57] but also because the image they do have in their heads of the criminal justice system is distorted. One consequence is that Americans often perceive crime as increasing (even when it is not) and are supportive of *tough on crime* policies. In early 1990s, for example, concern about crime increased and state governments adopted tough-on-crime policies even as crime rates were falling. More generally, in any given year, more Americans believe crime is increasing than decreasing regardless of actual crime rates.

This is possible because most of what the public knows about crime comes from local television news and entertainment programming. Local television news is heavy on crime but lacks context. Entertainment programming, including news magazines, provides regular and heavy doses of simplified crime-related content. *Law and Order*, for example, advertises that its programs are *ripped from the headlines*, suggesting the television drama is representative of the real world. News magazines like *20/20* and *Prime Time*, often focus on the crime of the day, attracting viewers with fear-inducing promotions "could this happen to you?" where *this* is any number of unpleasant outcomes from adduction to carjacking to home invasion to identity theft.

Where individual rights are simply a product of constitutional text, public fears of crime would have no bearing on individual rights. We know, however, that a public frightened by external events (e.g., crime or terrorism) often results in a shrinking of individual rights, and that such context plays an important role in how the courts interpret individual freedom.

When asked if the "criminal justice system is capable of dealing with terrorism" or if "it allows terrorist suspects too many rights," 53 percent said the system allowed too many rights, 35 percent said the system was capable of dealing with terrorism, and 13 percent were unsure or did not know. Perhaps the more revealing piece of evidence is this: Americans typically have little confidence in the criminal justice system but great confidence in the police. The percent saying they have a great deal or quite a lot of confidence in the criminal justice system ranged from 15 percent in 1994 to 34 percent in 2004.[58] The system, Americans believe, is broken. Confidence in the police runs much higher, particularly among white Americans, hovering near 60 percent. While confidence in the police is lower for racial minorities, it still outpaces confidence in the criminal justice system. White-Black differences in confidence are reflected in the racial divide over allegations of police misconduct in the Michael Brown shooting in Ferguson, Missouri, and in the death of Eric Garner in New York. In both instances, White police officers were accused of killing Black suspects. Neither officer was indicted. An NBC News/Marist poll conducted in December 2014 found that 79 percent of White Americans had "a great deal" or "a fair amount" that police officers would not use excessive force compared to 43 percent of Black Americans.[59]

For many Americans, again especially white Americans, protections of due process of rights are not associated with the individual freedoms protected by the Bill of Rights but by courts that have expanded these rights beyond their original meaning and lawyers who have manipulated the rights to free criminals. If there is a door open for limiting individual freedom in the future, it is most likely found here. Luckily, at least at the present time, more informed and better educated citizens, particularly lawyers, are more supportive and defensive of these freedoms, reflecting the role of elite opinion leadership on public opinion.[60] But as long as we are more concerned about O. J. Simpson's acquittal than the 30 years Henry McCollum spent behind bars for a crime he did not commit, we are all potentially vulnerable to the myth that our criminal justice system is too lenient and that too many criminals get off on technicalities.

Notes

1. Michael Stokes Paulsen, "Dirty Harry and the Real Constitution," *University of Chicago Law Review* 64 (1997): 1457–1491.

2. Radley Balko, "Myths of the Criminal Justice System: Part 2," *Huffington Post*, June 22, 2011, available at http://www.huffingtonpost.com/2011/06/22/myths-of-the-criminal-justice-system-part-two_n_881975.html (accessed on September 3, 2014).

3. This may be overstated, but if the deck is stacked, it is stacked in favor of convictions rather than acquittals.

4. Paul Butler, "Poor People Lose: Gideon and the Critique of Rights," *Yale Law Journal* 122 (2013): 2176–2204, especially 2178.

5. See the Innocence Project at http://www.innocenceproject.org/ (accessed on September 6, 2014).

6. Daniel Romer, Kathleen Hall Jamieson, and Sean Aday, "Television News and the Cultivation of Fear of Crime," *Journal of Communication* 53 (2003): 88–104.

7. Julian Roberts, "Public Opinion, Crime, and Criminal Justice," *Crime and Justice* 16 (1992): 99–180.

8. The cultivation hypothesis was first articulated by Gerbner and Gross in 1976, and has been the subject of considerable research over time. See George Gerbner and Larry Gross, "Living with Television: The Violence Profile," *Journal of Communication* 26 (1976): 172–199.

9. Frank Gilliam and Shanto Iyengar, "Prime Suspects: The Influence of Local Television News on the Viewing Public," *American Journal of Political Science* 44 (2000): 560–573.

10. See, for example, P. Hirsch, "The 'Scary World' of the Nonviewer and Other Anomalies of Gerbner et al.'s Findings of Cultivation Analysis," *Communication Research* 7 (1980): 403–456.

11. William Cuddihy, *The Fourth Amendment: Origins and Original Meaning* (New York: Oxford University Press, 2009, pp. 602–1791).

12. Thomas Friedman, *The World Is Flat: A Brief History of the Twenty-first Century* (New York: Farrar, Straus and Giroux, 2005).

13. Keith Jurow, "Untimely Thoughts: A Reconsideration of the Origins of Due Process of Law," *The American Journal of Legal History* 19 (1975): 265–279, especially 266.

14. George Carey, *Due Process, First Principles*, available at http://www.firstprinciplesjournal.com/articles.aspx?article=867 (accessed on September 2, 2014).

15. James W. Ely, "The Oxymoron Reconsidered: Myth and Reality in the Origins of Substantive Due Process," *Constitutional Commentary* 16 (1999): 315–346.

16. Akhil Reed Amar, *The Bill of Rights* (New Haven: Yale University Press, 1998).
17. 110 U.S. 516 (1884).
18. *Chicago, Burlington & Quincy Railroad Co. v. City of Chicago*, 166 U.S. 226 (1897).
19. Ibid.
20. *Maxwell v. Dow*, 176 U.S. 581 (1900).
21. *Twining v. New Jersey*, 211 U.S. 78 (1908).
22. Ibid.
23. *Gitlow v. New York*, 268 U.S. 652 (1925).
24. *Palko v. Connecticut*, 302 U.S. 319 (1937).
25. Note that the plaintiff's name was typed incorrectly in the record of the court and thus has been thereafter referred to as *Palko* instead of *Palka*.
26. Ibid.
27. *Mapp v. Ohio*, 367 U.S. 643 (1961); *Benton v. Maryland*, 395 U.S. 784 (1969); *Miranda v. Arizona*, 384 U.S. 436 (1966); *Gideon v. Wainwright*, 372 U.S. 335 (1963).
28. John Hart Ely, *Democracy and Distrust: A Theory of Judicial Review* (Cambridge: Harvard University Press, 1980, p. 15). For his classic commentary on procedural and substantive due process, see p. 18.
29. These rights were articulated in *Miranda v. Arizona*, 384 U.S. 436 (1966), though Miranda set forth protected right, the case did not specify the exact language which has developed over time.
30. For an excellent account of the landmark case, see Anthony Lewis, *Gideon's Trumpet* (New York: Vintage Books/Random House, 1964).
31. *Gideon v. Wainright*, 372 U.S. 335 (1963).
32. 378 U.S. 478 (1964).
33. Ibid.
34. Lee Epstein and Thomas G. Walker, *Constitutional Law for a Changing America: Rights, Liberties and Justice*, 7th ed. (Washington, DC: CQ Press, 2010, pp. 512–513).
35. *Harris v. New York*, 401 U.S. 222 (1971).
36. *New York v. Quarles*, 467 U.S. 649 (1984).
37. *Moran v. Burbine*, 475 U.S. 412 (1986).
38. *Illinois v. Perkins*, 496 U.S. 292 (1990).
39. *United States v. Patone*, 542 US 630.
40. Harris v. *New York*, 401 U.S. 222 (1971).
41. *Olmstead v. United States*, 277 U.S. 438 (1928).
42. Ibid.
43. 389 U.S. 347 (1967).
44. For an interesting contrast, but on a subject more central to the next chapter, consider *McNeely v. United States* (2013), which involved warrantless and involuntary blood drawing in a driving-while-intoxicated case.

45. 462 U.S. 213 (1983).

46. Epstein and Walker, *Constitutional Law for a Changing America*, 460–464 specifically and 460–477 generally.

47. Note that in *McNeely* the court created an exception to the exception, holding that the warrantless and nonconsensual blood evidence drawn from a suspect is not permissible under the loss of evidence exception.

48. 367 U.S. 643 (1961).

49. It remains unclear whether a warrant was issued and enforced or not in the case.

50. *Mapp v. Ohio*, 367 U.S. 643 (1961

51. 547 U.S. 586 (2006).

52. 555 U.S. 135 (2009).

53. Epstein and Walker, *Constitutional Law for a Changing America*, 497.

54. Unless one wants to argue, fear of crime is shared value.

55. Lydia Saad, "Americans Express Mixed Confidence in Criminal Justice System," *Gallup Politics*, July 11, 2011, available athttp://www.gallup.com/poll/148433/americans-express-mixed-confidence-criminal-justice-system.aspx (accessed on September 8, 2014).

56. Nicholas Battaglia, "The Casey Anthony Trial and Wrongful Exonerations: How 'Trial by Media' Cases Diminish Public Confidence in the Criminal Justice System," *Albany Law Review* 75 (2012): 1579–1611.

57. Julian Roberts, "Public Opinion, Crime, and Criminal Justice," *Crime and Justice* 16 (1992): 99–180.

58. Saad, "Americans Express Mixed Confidence in Criminal Justice System."

59. Carrie Dann, "Poll Shows Deep Racial Divide in Confidence in Law Enforcement," *NBC News*, December 7, 2014, available at http://www.nbcnews.com/meet-the-press/poll-shows-deep-racial-divide-confidence-law-enforcement-n263041 (accessed on December 8, 2014).

60. Shmuel Lock, *Crime, Public Opinion, and Civil Liberties: The Tolerant Public* (Westport, CT: Praeger, 1999).

Chapter 9

The Right to Privacy and the Myth of Government Surveillance: Why We Believe in Privacy but Let Government into Our Homes

Introduction

The right to privacy is not mentioned in the U.S. Constitution. The right emerged more than a century later, when advertisers used the image of a child without her family's permission. The body of law has grown to include the right to protect one's body, likeness, reputation, and even emotional state. Some protections are firmly rooted in sections of the Fourth Amendment, which limit police search and seizures. As the branch of privacy rights have developed, we shed light on the rights covered under the penumbra of privacy protection. In doing so, we return to an earlier point: The Founding Fathers never intended for our rights to be limited to those protections specifically spelled out in the U.S. Constitution. We also address our ninth myth "if you haven't done anything, you shouldn't care if government searches your house or monitors your emails." Privacy protections exist not to protect the guilty but to protect the innocent from unnecessary government intrusion. In the chapter, we impugn broad notions of a constitutional right to privacy. We also show the limited protections from governmental intrusions on privacy and reveal the broad areas left unprotected by the constitution.

The Collective Yawn: Government Surveillance, the NSA, and Public Opinion

Edward Snowden serves as a Rorschach test on American politics. How we perceive him reflects our own beliefs about where the line should be drawn between personal privacy and government intrusion. In 2013, Snowden leaked thousands of documents to journalist Glen Greenwald revealing the massive amount of surveillance being conducted by the U.S. government, including the monitoring of telephone calls and online activities of American citizens without search warrants or, in many cases, even reason to believe there was the possibility of wrongdoing.[1] In the age of big data, analysts scour through the nearly infinite interactions looking for hidden security risks. They often do so with the cooperation of online media giants like Microsoft, Google, and Facebook and telephone companies AT&T and Verizon. "Big Brother," the name given to an omnipresent government in George Orwell's *1984*, was alive, well, and watching.

Edward Snowden's massive leak of government documents generated mixed reactions with some lauding his service as heroic (mostly in the news media) and others lamenting his acts as criminal (mostly in government). Daniel Ellsberg, the leaker at the center of the *Pentagon Papers* case, called the Snowden leak the most significant in American political history.[2] The *New York Times* attempted to find nuance between the hero versus traitor rhetoric by describing the leaks as unfortunate but necessary; and, on balance, a public service.[3] The American public was similarly split on whether Snowden's actions served or harmed the public interest. In a Pew Center for the People & the Press Poll conducted in January 2014, 45 percent of respondents said Snowden's leaks served the public interest while 43 percent said they harmed the public interest.[4] Even so, a majority of Americans—56 percent—believed the government should pursue a criminal case against Snowden, suggesting that at least some Americans believed that his leak was, at once, criminal and a public service. Perhaps a more telling indicator of public ambivalence, asked whether they supported or opposed Snowden releasing the documents, 24 percent of Americans supported the leak and 34 percent were opposed, but the plurality—40 percent—said they had no opinion either way.[5] In the same survey, roughly a third of respondents described Snowden as a traitor while 57 percent described him more favorably as a "whistleblower."

In these public reactions to Snowden, we see the inherent contradiction in American beliefs about privacy. Americans, at once, gladly value privacy but are relatively nonplussed by revelations of government surveillance. Or perhaps stated differently, we believe in the right to privacy but gladly surrender it. For some, this surrender is a matter of balancing the right to be left alone against national (or personal) security. If government surveillance is necessary to keep us safe, it is worth the price we pay in terms of a loss of privacy. For others, surrendering privacy is justified under the pretense that "if you have nothing to hide, you have nothing to fear" from government surveillance. These views are, of course, related and reinforcing. Who can possibly be concerned about violations of personal privacy in the aftermath of a security threat? Obviously, only someone with something to hide. We discuss this misguided belief as one of the myths surrounding the Bill of Rights and its consequences for contemporary debates over government surveillance. Before doing so, however, we begin by discussing the creation of an explicit right to privacy.

The Creation of a Right

Nowhere in the U.S. Constitution can you find the word "privacy." Yet the principle that Americans have a right to be left alone is deeply ingrained in the American mythology. Indeed, one might fairly argue that this general principle underlies the entire Bill of Rights, the U.S. Constitution and its institutional safeguards, and provides the foundation for much of our civic discourse. Even before a "right to privacy" was explicitly developed or recognized, the law protected individuals within the home from government surveillance as well as their personal correspondence transmitted via the U.S. Postal Service.[6] Long before "stand your ground" became a controversy, the notion that "a man's house is his castle" allowed individuals the right to use force to protect personal property or their personal safety, and individuals expected personal information to be kept private even when transmitted outside of the home.

Recent court rulings protecting cell phones from searches upon arrest reaffirm this fundamental belief:[7] Government should not go looking where there is no expectation of wrongdoing, nor should government eavesdrop where individuals have a reasonable expectation of privacy.

Even in the case when an individual has been arrested for one offense (e.g., a traffic violation), the police do not have carte blanche to search a cell phone or other mobile or digital device for evidence of other wrongdoing. Or perhaps stated differently, the police have no more leeway to conduct a general search of a cell phone than they would to conduct a general search of one's home. The information stored on a digital device is no less protected because it is mobile than words written on paper and stored in a desk drawer. In making the ruling, the Supreme Court largely adhered to the historical development of the law on search and seizure, prohibiting general searches as "unreasonable."

To understand why this is so, it is worth recalling why these protections were included in the Bill of Rights in the first place (see Chapter Eight). During the colonial era, British authorities routinely used general searches as a tool for harassment and for finding evidence of wrongdoing. The simple logic is that if the authorities look hard enough, they can find something wrong, even if it is very minor or unintentional. In a digital age, imagine the search of a cell phone for music, video, or images that have been illegally downloaded. Outside of illegal activity, consider activity that might be personally embarrassing (nude photos) or harmful (evidence of an extramarital affair) if made public. Placed in this context, protections against "unreasonable" search and seizure were seen as a mechanism for protecting individuals within their homes from harassment. While this falls short of an explicit right to privacy, it lays the foundation for a broader and more encompassing right, that is, there are certain areas of our lives that should remain outside of the view of government officials. This is not to protect the guilty by allowing them to operate in the shadows but rather to protect the innocent from undue and unnecessary intrusions into their private space.

The Constitution worked to prevent the federal government from interfering with property rights, but ignored protection for less tangible rights. Intellectual property rights were generally ignored. The only protection for intellectual property is found in Article I, Section 8, which gives Congress the power to give authors and inventors the exclusive right to their writings and discoveries.[8] The laws of the new republic mirrored English law, which worked to provide limited protection for inventors, authors, and map makers, but gave printers great latitude in reproducing interesting ideas. Over the next century, however, English law developed for privacy and intellectual property.

The Right to Privacy and the Myth of Government Surveillance

The articulation of an express right to privacy did not fully take shape in America until Samuel Warren and Louis Brandeis developed the argument in an 1890 *Harvard Law Review* article.[9] Curiously, and particularly relevant for contemporary conversations, Warren and Brandeis were concerned less with government intrusion than with an increasingly intrusive mass media circulating private photographs and gossip into the public domain. "The press is overstepping in every direction the obvious bounds of propriety and of decency," they wrote. Technology, the ability to take photographs of individual private lives without their consent, challenged their understanding of privacy. Individuals, Warren and Brandeis argued, should have the right to control how they were presented in public domain. "The common law," they argued, "secures to each individual the right of determining, ordinarily, to what extent his thoughts, sentiments, and emotions shall be communicated to others." Americans deserved the right to remain private individuals, to prevent the public display of their likeness, and to prevent the public discussion of their private affairs. The scholars pointed to England and France, which already affirmed a right to privacy.

This was notably not an argument against government infringement of privacy but against the press or any other individual, organization, or entity that might violate an individual's right to be left alone by communicating their "thoughts, sentiments, or emotions" via gossip pages in the local newspaper or personal and private photographs. Such gossip may be titillating but it did little to advance public discourse. For Warren and Brandeis, violations of privacy of this sort should be treated in a manner akin to libel or slander but with an even higher level of protection. Unlike libel or slander, the truth would not be a defense against violations of privacy, nor did injured parties need to show malice on the part of the publication. In this respect, the right to privacy was broader, more encompassing and more fundamental to protecting individual freedom than libel or slander laws. Warren and Brandeis further argued that the right to privacy extended beyond copyright or ownership as privacy was not simply a property right to control images or words but a more far-reaching right covering personal space and the private sphere. Under this framework, which has notably never been adopted, individuals would be able to choose what to keep private about their lives (and what to make public).

Their complaints went unheeded until ten years later, when a flour company produced unauthorized photographs of a young girl.[10] Franklin Mills Flour placed Abigail Roberson's picture on boxes of flour with the tagline "Flour of Family." The Rochester Folding Box Company produced more than 25,000 boxes for the Franklin Mills. Little Abigail was humiliated by the scoffs and jeers of people that recognized her face from the box cover. She suffered a "nervous shock," was confined to her bed, and required medical assistance. The lower court in New York recognized her claim for a right of privacy. The appellate court rejected the claim. Citing Brandeis and Warren's law review, as well as many of the cases discussed in the law review, the court found that New York did not recognize a cause of action for the right to be left alone. Without action by the New York legislature, citizens had no right to privacy. The legislature in New York and many other jurisdictions acted quickly to close this gap in the law. Today, most jurisdictions recognize causes of action for false light, publication of private embarrassing facts, and appropriation or commercialization. The overwhelming majority of privacy cases rely on state causes of action.

Federal courts moved in a different direction, working without express protection from congress, federal courts have occasionally identified fundamental privacy rights by incorporating provisions of the Fourteenth Amendment.[11] Traces of the right to privacy may be found in a variety of Amendments. The right to believe in a religion (or no religion) receives protection in a number of ways under the First Amendment. Citizens have the right to freely exercise their religious beliefs. The Amendment also protects the right to share private beliefs publically (freedom of speech). The Third Amendment protects the privacy of the home, forbidding soldiers from trampling on the privacy rights of homeowners. The Fourth Amendment protects against illegal searches and seizures. The Fifth protects against self-incrimination. In theory, the Ninth Amendment also provides protection for other rights. Though not specifically addressing privacy, the Amendment protects "certain rights . . . retained by the people." In an early case, *Barron v. Baltimore*,[12] the Court found that the Ninth Amendment only applied to the federal government. Following the addition of the Fourteenth Amendment, state governments had to consider the effects of the Bill of Rights, including the Ninth Amendment. But courts didn't raise the issue of a constitutional right to privacy until 1923.

In *Meyer v. Nebraska*,[13] the Court used the Fourteenth Amendment to strike down a state statute that prevented schools from teaching foreign languages to children before ninth grade. The rationale for the state statute was to prevent "foreigners . . . [from educating] their children in the language of their native land." Nebraska legislators reasoned that small children learning foreign languages might not become fully "American" in their thinking and beliefs. The Supreme Court disagreed, finding that the Fourteenth Amendment protected citizens against states that attempted to deprive them of "life, liberty or property without due process of law." The liberty interests guaranteed by the constitution extended beyond physical liberty:

> Without doubt, it denotes not merely freedom from bodily restraint but also the right of the individual to contract, to engage in any of the common occupations of life, to acquire useful knowledge, to marry, establish a home and bring up children, to worship God according to the dictates of his own conscience, and generally to enjoy those privileges long recognized at common law as essential to the orderly pursuit of happiness by free men.[14]

Meyer quietly ushered in a new right of privacy recognized by the Supreme Court. The *Meyer* Court found that there is at least a liberty interest that protects citizens from arbitrary state laws. A parent's right to educate a child falls within the rights protected by a federal right to be left alone. Two years later, in *Pierce v. Society of Sisters*,[15] the Court again recognized a fundamental right for a parent to set an educational path for their children. Pierce involved an Oregon statute that required parents to enroll their children in public schools. Religious and private schools objected, arguing that the statute "unreasonably interfere[d] with the liberty of parents and guardians to direct the upbringing and education of children."[16] Thus, the Court introduces a "liberty interest" that is constitutionally protected. In both *Meyers* and *Pierce*, the court mentioned constitutional protection for fundamental rights of marriage, establishing a home, and raising children. The government may not interfere with an individual's right to make those choices.

In 1928, then Supreme Court Justice Louis Brandeis attempted to extend the right to privacy in a dissenting opinion in *Olmstead v. United States* (1928) to include taped conversations. The case involved the question of whether taping a phone call should be protected as a private conversation or whether its transmission through telephone wires located outside the home gave the government the right to listen in. In his dissent, Brandeis made the case that private conversations should be protected from government invasion, and that the creation of new technologies should not afford the government an unrestrained ability to wiretap private conversations. The Founding Fathers, Brandeis argued, "conferred, as against the Government, the right to be let alone—the most comprehensive of rights and the right most valued by civilized men. To protect that right, every unjustifiable intrusion by the Government upon the privacy of the individual, whatever the means employed, must be deemed a violation of the Fourth Amendment." For Brandeis, it was immaterial that the wiretap occurred on lines located outside the home or that the purpose of the wiretap was to further a legitimate government interest.

Constitutionally protected liberty interests were raised once more in the 1940s. The Court touched briefly on basic rights of individual autonomy in *Skinner v. Oklahoma*.[17] Oklahoma's Habitual Criminal Sterilization Act mandated sterilization for "habitual criminals"—people with two or more convictions for "felonies involving moral turpitude." Skinner stole chickens in the 1920s and was convicted twice for armed robbery in the 1930s. The Court found that the rights of marriage and procreation were basic civil rights. The court warned against the "subtle, farreaching and devastating" effects of this policy: "[i]n evil or reckless hands it can cause races or types which are inimical to the dominant group to wither and disappear." State actors could not deprive citizens of these basic liberty interests absent an essential state interest. These liberty interests were used decades later to establish a fundamental right of individual autonomy in the 1960s.

In *Katz v. United States* (1967), the theories championed by Brandeis in the early part of the century finally gained a majority on the Court. The Court held the Fourth Amendment should apply where there is a reasonable expectation of privacy. In this case, Katz used a pay phone to place bets (an illegal activity) that had been wired with listening devices. Though the listening devices were intentionally placed outside the phone booth, the Court ruled that by entering a telephone booth and shutting the door, Katz was entitled to a reasonable expectation that his conversation would not be public. This is yet another example of one of this book's central themes: Our rights are not static but change with the larger social, economic, and political context. As our technological capacity expands, the nature of our rights must also shift. The ability of contemporary government to track digital communications to determine who we are communicating with and what we are saying (or texting or emailing) has expanded. Should the Bill of Rights protect your email? What about Facebook postings or Google searches?

Privacy in the context of wiretapping referred to protection against government intrusion, most often as part of the delicate balance between maintaining security and not violating personal privacy. While the definition of privacy extends beyond the home, this specific notion of privacy is generally physically based and can be thought of primarily as the protection of private space. The privacy right articulated by Warren and Brandeis offered a very different definition of privacy, the right to control private information as it entered into the public domain. As they articulated this right, it extended even to information or images obtained in public.

The most controversial definition of privacy involves yet another domain—the right to personal autonomy over one's private life.[18] This right to privacy was "created" in *Griswold v. Connecticut* (1965) in which the Court overturned a state law banning doctors from providing contraceptives. Writing for the Court, Justice Douglas argued that while there is no explicit right to privacy in the U.S. Constitution, it can easily be constructed out of the First, Third, Fourth, and Fifth Amendments. The *Griswold* decision was itself less controversial than the fact that it later became the precedent for *Roe v. Wade* (1973) and *Lawrence v. Kansas* (2003).

In *Roe v. Wade*, the courts provided for a legal right to an abortion up through the first trimester of pregnancy when the fetus was not yet fully formed. The decision, and the extension of the right to privacy into the abortion debate, has made the "right to privacy" more controversial than it would otherwise be, and has subjected it to the criticism that the courts should not "create" rights despite the Ninth Amendment's clear language. Consider that most conservatives, even some who claim to adhere to an "originalist" approach to constitutional interpretation, embrace the idea of limited government and an individual's right to be left alone. Most believe this right extends beyond the narrow language of the Bill of Rights. "Government exists not to confer rights but to 'secure' preexisting rights," writes conservative columnist George Will,[19] meaning those "unalienable rights" of life, liberty, and the pursuit of happiness "endowed" by a creator and provided for in the *Declaration of Independence*. The Bill of Rights, Will contends, must be interpreted in the context of the *Declaration* and its clarion call to protect individual liberty against democratic majorities. Whether privacy should be protected is less the question than whether it should be extended to protect a women's right to choose in the case of abortion. It is the application and not the principle that is at issue.

One might think protecting private sexual relations under the umbrella of privacy rights would be a natural extension of an evolving right to privacy, but this was not—at least initially—the case. For much of American history, sodomy, including oral and anal sex and often (but not always) applicable to same-sex and heterosexual couples, has been outlawed but not widely enforced. In the 1960s and 1970s states began to repeal these laws though they remained on the books in a number of states, including Georgia. In *Stanley v. Georgia* (1969), the Supreme Court set the stage for overturning sodomy laws by extending the right to privacy to include the right to possess and view pornography in one's own home. "If the First Amendment means anything," Justice Marshall observed, "it means that a State has no business telling a man, sitting alone in his own house, what books he may read or what films he may watch." In this case, it included having pornographic materials that were illegal to manufacture or distribute as long as possession occurred within the privacy of one's home.

Against this backdrop, a challenge to state sodomy laws seemed overdue. The opportunity presented itself when a police officer went to Michael Hardwick's home to deliver an arrest warrant and caught Hardwick and another man engaged in sexual relations. They were subsequently arrested but not charged for sodomy. Hardwick sued claiming the arrest and the sodomy laws which criminalized homosexual relations were violations of his constitutional rights. Perhaps surprisingly, the Supreme Court upheld the Georgia law and opted to not extend constitutional protection to private sexual relations within one's home. Writing for the majority, Justice Bryon White declared that the Constitution did not confer "a fundamental right to engage in homosexual sodomy."

Once again, a dissenting opinion served to create the foundation for a future ruling. Justice Blackmun, joined in his dissent by Justices Brennan, Marshall, and Stevens, argued powerfully that the case was no more about a right to engage in sodomy than *Stanley v. Georgia* was about a right to view pornography. *Bowers v. Hardwick*, Justice Blackmun argued, was about the "right most valued by civilized men, namely 'the right to be let alone.'" Blackmun concluded with the hope that the Court would "reconsider its analysis and conclude that depriving individuals of the right to choose for themselves how to conduct their intimate relationships poses a far greater threat to the values most deeply rooted in our Nation's history than tolerance of nonconformity could ever do."

Seventeen years later, Blackmun's hope was fulfilled when the court overturned the *Bowers v. Hardwick* striking down sodomy laws in Texas. Much like *Bowers v. Hardwick*, John Geddes Lawrence and Tyron Garner were caught in sexual relations and arrested for sodomy after the police were called in response to a reported weapons disturbance. In writing for the majority, Justice Kennedy offered this concise assessment:

> *Liberty protects the person from unwarranted government intrusions into a dwelling or other private places. In our tradition the State is not omnipresent in the home. And there are other spheres of our lives and existence, outside the home, where the State should not be a dominant presence. Freedom extends beyond spatial bounds. Liberty presumes an autonomy of self that includes freedom of thought, belief, expression, and certain intimate conduct. The instant case involves liberty of the person both in its spatial and more transcendent dimensions.*

In overturning Bowers, Justice Kennedy also rebuilt the foundation for privacy rights. Instead of justifying the creation of a right to privacy as a penumbra formed from various amendments, Kennedy turned to the due process clause of the Fourteenth Amendment. With due process as its constitutional foundation, the right to privacy protects individual decisions over raising children, having children, family, and private sexual behavior.[20]

The Patriot Act and Its Challenge to the Right to be Left Alone

The actions of terrorists on September 11, 2001 reversed the 30-year trend toward a federal right to be left alone. Forty-five days after the terrorist attacks, Congress passed the Uniting and Strengthening America by Providing Appropriate Tools Acquired to Intercept and Obstruct Terrorism Act of 2001 (the "USA/Patriot Act"). Ostensibly designed to prevent future terrorist attacks, the Patriot Act gave government officials substantial access into the private lives of citizens. Civil liberties groups criticized the increased power for government surveillance under the Patriot Act. Groups were concerned with the government's ability to search an individual's records held by third parties, searches without notice to owners, and an expansion in the government's ability to search for intelligence purposes.

Section 215 of the Patriot Act received the most attention and litigation. The section changed existing law, which allowed the government to review "records" for foreign intelligence purposes. The Patriot Act expanded the scope of the law to include more businesses, and lower the threshold for obtaining the records. In the past, the government needed to show the target was "a foreign power or an agent of a foreign power." The Patriot Act allowed the government to obtain anyone's records as long as they were "relevant" to an investigation of foreign powers or agents. A law created to prevent foreign spying was amended to provide government access to essentially any information held by third parties. The American Civil Liberties Union (ACLU) argued that, on a daily basis, the government obtained call detail records or "telephony metadata" for every Verizon customer. Section 215 also prevented third parties like Verizon from disclosing that an individual's records were handed over to the government. The ACLU argued that the broad scope of the requests and the secrecy associated with the requests would have a chilling effect on speech. People would be less likely to call the ACLU for assistance, check out controversial books from the library or communicate dissatisfaction with the government if they believed the government was monitoring their actions. District court judges had sharply differing opinions on the constitutionality of the Act. In Washington, D.C., Judge Richard Leon found that the Act was likely to be unconstitutional.[21] He thought Madison "would be aghast" at the privacy invasion. A day later, New York federal district Judge William Pauley III found that there was no significant privacy interest in telephone metadata.[22] The Supreme Court may ultimately weigh in on the matter. Until then, clarification on federal protection for privacy may be on hold. As with our other constitutional rights, the definition of privacy remains amorphous and subject to reinterpretation as the political, social, and economic context shifts.

What the Right to Privacy Does Not Cover

Throughout this text, we have noted an important qualification to the Bill of Rights. It only protects us from government not from private individuals or business. There are certain qualifications. Businesses are not allowed to release personal financial or health data but this is protected through statute and not the Bill of Rights. If your employer releases your health information, for example, there are penalties in place to address violations but this is not a constitutional issue. Personal financial information can similarly not be shared without disclosure and consent but again these are rights protected via statute and are not constitutionally protected. It is perhaps worth noting in this context that not all rights are rooted in the U.S. Constitution, and indeed some of the rights we view as "fundamental" to our individual privacy are protected by statute. This returns us to an earlier theme: Constitutionally protected rights are less critical to individual liberty than the public's commitment to individual freedom, broadly construed, and to specific individual rights.

Even with these qualifications, technology allows private business to collect and share massive amounts of personal data, including purchasing habits, online activities, and even physical location within a store. Bar codes, discount cards, and credit and debit cards allow stores to track individual purchases. These data are collected and analyzed to better understand consumer behavior and more effectively target advertising. This is easy to see in the online world where advertising follows recent search histories. If you have recently searched for shoes online, for example, your Facebook ads will quickly follow suit, often advertising the specific brands and type of shoes you viewed.

Just as in the area of national security, the public expresses concerns about violations of privacy but does very little to protect it. For some consumers, targeted advertising is a blessing as it assures the advertisements they receive actually reflect their interests and desires. Others express more alarm but almost regardless of their opinion, a 10 percent discount on purchased goods is enough to reveal purchasing behaviors to national grocery chains or retail outlets. Online media companies, Google and Facebook, are able to use search behaviors and likes to develop more detailed psychological profiles that provide even greater insight into purchasing behavior. Embedded experiments then test the effectiveness of advertising to see which versions lead to more clicks. Many of these companies then sell the data, often making more profit on personal information than the products they sell. As consumers, Americans may express concern that this personal data is being collected, sold, and used; but they are simultaneously giving the data away, often for discounted purchases or special offers.

The television news magazine, *60 Minutes* profiled Acxiom, one of the corporations that collects, analyzes, and sells personal data, in a segment that aired in March 2014. Correspondent Steve Kroft noted that while we are worried about government intrusion, businesses collecting personal data may be an even bigger threat. There is an irony at play here as journalists also routinely invade individual privacy in pursuit of "public interest" stories. *60 Minutes* reporting with alarm at businesses collecting personal data will show up at individual homes, places of work, or any public place in efforts to ambush people involved in leading stories into an interview. Protected by the First Amendment, journalists are often persistent invaders of personal privacy.

Most of these intrusions have been protected by the courts under the First Amendment. Reporters cannot trespass on private property but if they have "clear view" inside a home they can take photographs or video. More generally, what happens in public is generally seen as fair game for journalists or photographers, and public figures are provided less privacy protection than private individuals. Famous celebrities may decry the gaggle of reporters and photographers who follow them but their celebrity status affords them little privacy when in public places. The privacy of public figures will be further challenged as news organizations deploy drones for photographs and video further threatening individual privacy.

While reporters cannot publish false statements, especially when statements are made with malicious intent, they are generally protected when what they are publishing is factually accurate and in the public interest. Because public interest has been broadly defined, much of what reporters uncover can be published without running afoul of privacy law. In *Sidis v. F-R Publishing Corp*, for example, the court ruled that story on a child prodigy who was living his later life in seclusion and isolation did not violate his privacy because there was a public interest in his story. On the other hand, the publication of the name of a reformed convict, in this case a hijacker, was deemed not protected given that the public had little "need to know" and that the publication could potentially inflict significant harm on the subject of the story. In these cases, the courts have tried to balance the privacy rights of individuals against freedom of the press. In Europe, individual citizens have an established "right to be forgotten" allowing them to request that information (videos, news stories) be removed from search engines when it is no longer relevant.

It is less clear what is protected when the press engages in undercover operations secretly videotaping or audiotaping for news stories. Limitations are often set by state law requiring one, both, or all party consent. Massachusetts, for example, requires all party consent, making taping of police officers a potential crime, though the Court has not upheld individual convictions. While the right to privacy protects much of what occurs inside your home, it does not protect your garbage. Police may freely search garbage without a warrant or even probable cause. Credit card receipts, prescription medications, and personal notes or letters indicating religious or political affiliations are all fair game under the Supreme Court's current interpretation provided they are first thrown away.[23]

Context and the Right to Privacy

Americans often pride themselves as a nation of rights, deeply individualistic, and committed to the right to be left alone. Indeed, one might fairly argue that this general right—the right to be left alone—is the cornerstone upon which all of the other rights enumerated in the Bill of Rights reside. Perhaps surprisingly then, the right to privacy has been embedded in controversy over whether courts should have the power to "create rights." The existence of the controversy is itself revealing: As Americans, we are often more concerned about specific applications of rights than general principles. Or perhaps stated differently, we are practitioners rather than theorists. The application of the right to privacy first to birth control and later to abortion generates a controversy over a "right to privacy," which otherwise enjoys widespread public support.

Public support for privacy in the abstract, however, does not mean that we are unwilling to give away personal data and information. We routinely share personal information with private companies and cast suspicion on individuals or groups who are unwilling to open their doors and their homes to government surveillance. Right or not, there is the expectation that only the guilty protect their privacy from government surveillance.

Perhaps because of our ambivalence about privacy, we lag other advanced democracies in protecting an individual right to privacy. As early as 1953, Europe worked to protect an individual's right to privacy. The Convention for the Protection of Human Rights and Fundamental Freedoms mandates respect for one's "private and family life, his home and his correspondence."[24] Courts have given broad protection for the "private and family life" provisions of the Convention. For example, in the case of *von Hannover v. Germany*,[25] Caroline von Hannover (also known as Princess Caroline of Monaco), filed suit against a number of German magazines for printing photographs of her and her family. While European law recognizes that photograph of public figures may have some public interest, the court in *von Hannover* found that Princess Caroline was entitled to a level of privacy when she was not engaged in acts related to her public life. The court tried to balance freedom of expression with the right to be left alone. In this case, the court found that the privacy interest in Princess Caroline eating with friends or swimming with family outweighed any public interest in her activities. The *von Hannover* case is just one example of how European courts support an individual's right to privacy. Despite a rabid interest in a public figure's activity, European courts fight to protect private and family life in way that is hard to imagine in the United States where lines between public and private are increasingly blurred.

As the difference across continents reveals, a Bill of Rights is less necessary than a public committed to protecting individual freedom. This is especially true in the larger context of the digital revolution, which makes it possible to transmit information quickly and to wide audiences. Private information captured legally (or illegally) can quickly attract millions of views on Facebook or Twitter. When nude photos of Jennifer Lawrence, Kate Upton, and others were illegally obtained and shared online, they attracted millions of views. If the right to privacy is to be maintained, our commitment to privacy must outweigh our collective voyeurism. The Bill of Rights, in this instance, provides little protection.

Notes

1. The U.S. Government wasn't alone as Britain, Australia, and Canada also participated.

2. Daniel Ellsberg, "Edward Snowden: Saving Us from the United Stasi of America," *The Guardian*, June, 10, 2013, available at http://www.theguardian.com/commentisfree/2013/jun/10/edward-snowden-united-stasi-america (accessed on August 29, 2014).

3. David Carr, "Whistle-Blowers in Limbo, Neither Hero Nor Traitor," *New York Times*, July 31, 2013, available at http://www.nytimes.com/2013/08/01/business/media/whistle-blowers-in-limbo-neither-hero-nor-traitor.html?_r=0 (accessed on August 31, 2014).

4. "Obama's NSA Speech Has Little Impact on Skeptical Public," *Pew Center for the People & the Press*, January 20, 2014, available at http://www.people-press.org/2014/01/20/obamas-nsa-speech-has-little-impact-on-skeptical-public/ (accessed on August 27, 2014).

5. From an NBS News Poll conducted May 27–29, 2014 with 800 respondents. The relevant topline data are available at http://www.pollingreport.com/terror.htm (accessed on August 29, 2014).

6. "The Right to Privacy in the Nineteenth Century America," *Harvard Law Review* 94 (1981): 1892–1910.

7. The cases are *Riley v. California*, in which the individual was initially stopped for a routine traffic offense but police found evidence of gang-related activity on a cell phone, and *United States v. Wurie* in which an individual was arrested for a drug-related offense and cell phone calls were used to identify the caller and to pursue a subsequent search and conviction.

8. *Article I, Section 8, Clause 8:* "The Congress shall have Power To ... promote the Progress of Science and useful Arts, by securing for limited Times to Authors and Inventors the exclusive Right to their respective Writings and Discoveries. ... "

9. Samuel Warren and Louis Brandeis, "The Right to Privacy," *Harvard Law Review* 4 (1890):193–220. One can easily argue that the idea of a right to privacy developed much earlier, but Warren and Brandeis are the first to lay out a legal argument for a much broader right.

10. *Roberson v. Rochester Folding Box Co*, 64 N.E. 442 (NY 1902).

11. John M. Devlin, "State Constitutional Autonomy Rights in an Age of Federal Retrenchment: Some Thoughts on the Interpretation of State Rights Derived from Federal Sources," *EMERGING ISSUES IN ST. CONST. L.* 3 (1990): 195, 197.

12. 32 U.S. 243 (1833).

13. 262 U.S. 390 (1923).

14. Ibid., 400.

15. 268 U.S. 510 (1925).

16. Ibid., 534.

17. 316 U.S. 535 (1942).

18. Erwin Chemerinsky, "Rediscovering Brandeis' Right to Privacy," *Brandeis Law Journal* 45 (2009): 643–657.

19. George Will, "The Constitutional Right to be Left Alone," *Washington Post*, April 18, 2012, available at http://www.washingtonpost.com/opinions/the-constitutional-right-to-be-left-alone/2012/04/18/gIQA8YrlRT_story.html (accessed on September 1, 2014).

20. William Musgrove, "Substantive Due Process: A History of Liberty in the Due Process Clause," *University of St. Thomas Journal of Law & Public Policy* 2 (2008): 125–140.

21. http://www.nytimes.com/2013/12/17/opinion/a-powerful-rebuke-of-mass-surveillance.html (accessed on September 18, 2014).

22. http://www.nytimes.com/2013/12/28/us/nsa-phone-surveillance-is-lawful-federal-judge-rules.html?ref=us&pagewanted=all&_r=0 (accessed on September 18, 2014).

23. Several states have provided protection under their state constitutions. In general, states may raise the floor but not lower the ceiling of federal constitutional protections.

24. Eur. Comm'n H.R. Art. 8.

25. *von Hannover v Germany* [2004] ECHR 294 (June 24, 2004), European Court of Human Rights.

Chapter 10

Protections Against Cruel and Unusual Punishment and the Myth That Killing Isn't Cruel (or Unusual)

Introduction

The language in the Eighth Amendment prohibits "cruel and unusual punishment," but most Americans are willing to let criminals rot in jails. Few Americans sympathize with criminals subject to hard labor, squalid conditions, and overcrowding. The penitentiary system did not exist at the drafting of the Bill of Rights. Punishments were often swift and public. Jails were reserved for those awaiting trial, not as a form of punishment for committing a crime. In this chapter, we examine how our notions of cruel and unusual punishment have changed over the last two centuries. Many of the swift and painful punishments doled out by our Founding Fathers would not be socially acceptable today. Alternatively, many of our contemporary practices would fail colonial definitions of cruel and unusual punishment. In doing so, we address our tenth myth that "killing isn't cruel or unusual, but torture is" by critically examining the cruelty of executions. We also challenge conventional thinking about our current plan to "throw away the key" for certain criminals.

Soft on Crime (and Punishment)

The true design of all punishments being to reform; not to exterminate mankind.[1]

Is the United States tough on crime but soft on criminals? The United States' rate of incarceration trails only the tiny island Republic of Seychelles.[2] We imprison more people than any other country in the world. We provide mandatory minimum sentences for a variety of crimes. We charge juvenile offenders as adults. Repeat offenders, even those that commit relatively minor crimes, can face a lifetime behind bars. We stopped executing people with mental disabilities only in the last decade. Despite fear that may be caused by overexposure to television violence,[3] the United States has become a very bad place to commit a crime.

Once we convict, are we treating criminals too well? We reserve our harshest punishment—the death penalty—for people who commit the most heinous crimes. Lethal injections, the most widely used method of administering the death penalty, may be too humane for some Americans. At least one member of the Supreme Court, Justice Antonin Scalia, publically declared that lethal injections for violent offenders might not be cruel enough. In *Callins v. Collins*,[4] Scalia lamented the timing, precision, and absence of pain associated with lethal injections. He compared it to the death of the victim murdered in *Callins*. He noted that death by lethal injection was far less brutal then the murder of a man shot and left to bleed to death on a tavern floor. He lamented the enviable, quiet death by lethal injection for men accused of raping an 11-year-old girl and killing her by stuffing her panties down her throat.[5] Reading Scalia's pointed barbs against a humane death penalty; one wonders whether society is providing mercy for violent offenders that refused to show mercy for their victims.

Scalia is not alone in thinking that we provide too many comforts for people we deem unfit to remain in society. In Louisiana's Angola State Penitentiary, the long-serving warden Burl Cain refuses to make prison life easy for the inmates under his watch. Convicts on death row stewed in cells that exceeded 125°F. It took lawsuits, a court order, and a special visit by a federal judge to finally end the slow roasting of inmates on death row.[6] Public support for Cain never wavered. Hundreds posted comments on social media to support the hard-nosed warden. When the same penitentiary came under fire for holding prisoners in solitary confinement for *decades*, supporters once again cheered the warden's attempts to make prison life uncomfortable.[7] Even in more moderate prisons, inmates have little choice but to work long hours for tiny sums. Every year, state legislators around the country introduce bills to add stiffer penalties for criminal conduct. State legislatures question whether prisoners need access to television.[8] Judges, especially judges facing reelection, hand down longer sentences to prove that they're tough on crime.[9]

One way to ratchet up punishment would be to let victims mete out justice. Instead of a cold and calculating prison employee delivering justice, some commentators suggest a role for victims or their families in the criminal justice system. Victims have a right in many states to testify during the sentencing phase of a trial, but American jurisprudence seems hostile to giving victims more than a voice. As a world power, we tend to look with disdain upon societies that allow citizens to take justice into their own hands. While most societies have moved beyond an "eye for an eye and a tooth for tooth," there are still places in the world that allow citizens to extract their own forms of justice. Stoning, honor killings, and other forms of justice exist in modern society, but Americans frown upon systems that allow aggrieved parties to deliver justice.

As we move more toward a society that provides few means of returning to society for prisoners, have we lost sight of constitutional prohibitions against cruel and unusual punishment? In this chapter, we examine the myths surrounding cruel and unusual punishment in the United States. How did we move away from the swift but brutal punishments of our budding nation? In the late eighteenth century, courts employed the ducking stool, the pillory, and various forms of amputation to punish criminals. How could a punishment that consisted of nailing one's ear to a pillory not be considered cruel and unusual? What would the Founding Fathers think of lifetime sentences for drug dealers or repeat criminals? How would a "throw away the key" mentality be viewed by Hamilton, Adams, and Madison? As mores have changed over the years, have we reached a consensus on what constitutes cruel and unusual punishment?

A Brief History of Cruel and Unusual Punishment

Justice requires some form of punishment for those that break society's rules. The Old Testament Book of Leviticus commanded an eye for an eye and a tooth for a tooth. While interesting in theory, the practice would leave everyone blind.[10] The sources of colonial law attempted to balance crime and punishment. Section 20 of the Magna Carta[11] provided that "a free man shall be amerced for a trivial offense, except in accordance with the degree of the offense; and for a serious offence he shall be amerced according to its gravity saving his livelihood." This section attempted to provide some form of proportionality for crime and punishment.

In the first millennium, the rich could essentially buy their way out of crimes. The poor, on the other hand, were subject to the whims of the people entrusted to dole out justice. By guarding against arbitrary and capricious penalties and fines, the Magna Carta tried to protect citizens. By protecting a man's livelihood, the Magna Carta gave the working class a level of protection that allowed them to keep producing. The Magna Carta adopted laws of Edward the Confessor of the eleventh century. He tried to provide standards for crimes and punishment. While the laws on the books were pretty severe, in practice they were far more moderate. The pillory, notching nostrils, and branding allowed swift justice while protecting a man's livelihood.

English law established a set of norms for crime and punishment by the time colonists began enacting their own codes in the seventeenth century. In 1583, Robert Beale, Clerk of the Privacy Council, wrote a book that condemned the racking of offenders as cruel, barbarous, and contrary to the liberty of English subjects. English law established a difference between excessive and cruel. In 1615, the Court of King's Bench, England's highest criminal court, censured as extreme and unlawful the punishment of a man thrown into a dungeon for criticizing an officer of the crown. The court noted that imprisonment "ought always to be according to the quality of the offence."[12]

Punishment from English courts would probably still shock sensibilities of most Americans. Particularly gruesome were the punishments handed out by Lord Chief Justice George Jeffreys of the Kings Bench in the 1680s. Jeffries, known as the "hanging judge," presided over the "Bloody Assizes" following an aborted rebellion in 1685. A special commission led by Jeffreys tried, convicted, and executed hundreds.[13] In one instance, Jeffreys ordered the hanging of 144 convicts, and had their remains displayed as a reminder of the consequences of rebelling against the king. The penalties drew harsh criticism from the public. But it was not the drawing and quartering, burning of women, beheading or disemboweling that drew the most ire. Rather, it was Jeffreys's sentencing of a Protestant cleric that had the greatest effect on English law and early American rights.

The strange case of Titus Oates became a tipping point for cruel and unusual punishment under English law. He was the author of the infamous Popish Plot hoax, which claimed Catholics intended to assassinate Charles II. At least 20 people were disemboweled, quartered, and beheaded for high treason. Hundreds were imprisoned and/or tortured. The accused vigorously denied the charges. Their declarations, coupled with inaccuracies in Oates' accusations, led to charges against Oates for perjury.

Historically, people bearing false witness leading to execution were treated as murderers and punished by death. But at the time of Oates' trial, death was no longer an available penalty. Incensed, Jeffreys complained that "a proportionable punishment of that crime can scarce by our law, as it now stands, be inflicted upon him."[14] The judges were left with options that several of them found inadequate. They met and decided to punish Oates as much as possible without killing him. Oates was ultimately defrocked, fined, whipped, pilloried, and imprisoned for life.

The public was outraged and concerned about excessive punishment. The outcry led to the Declaration of Rights, which protected against cruel and unusual punishments (albeit too late to protect Oates). Four months after the passage of the Declaration of Rights, Oates petitioned the House of Lords to set aside his conviction. The Lords affirmed the punishment, which lead to more protests. The House of Commons passed a bill to annul the sentence. The main arguments against the punishment did not seem to focus on the physical punishment. The greatest objection was that a cleric was divested of his Canonical Habit. The House of Commons also objected to the life sentence and the barbarous manner of punishment, which they felt was likely to result in death. The House of Lords stood by the punishment, imprisoning Oates and whipping him publicly for more than four years. Finally when William III and Mary II ascended to the throne, Oates was pardoned. He lived the rest of his life quietly, receiving a modest pension from the crown. Jeffreys on the other hand, was imprisoned "for his own safety." As an ally of the deposed king, Jeffreys became a wanted man. Jeffreys died in the Tower of London less than five years after sentencing Oates. Justice was swift for the punisher and the punished in seventeenth century England.

Oates' treatment led to the English Declaration of Rights of 1689, which prohibited the arbitrary application of punishment.[15] English law stated that "excessive bail ought not be required, nor excessive fines imposed, nor cruel or unusual punishments inflicted." The Declaration still provided ample power for courts to punish wrongdoers. Courts could seize property or an inheritance, prevent people from holding office or prevent employment. Mutilating or dismembering an offender, slitting nostrils, branding, and even life imprisonment were acceptable penalties for serious crimes. Punishments that might be considered torture today, including breaking backs on the rack, being tied to wild horses, and being buried alive were allowable in certain courts under special warrants. Quartering was authorized until 1870 under English law.[16]

The majority of colonies had provisions similar to the English Bill of Rights' prohibition against cruel or unusual punishment. The colonies definition of cruel and unusual was interpreted as broadly as the law in England. For example, Massachusetts prohibited punishments that were inhumane, barbarous or cruel. The law didn't stop Massachusetts from burning at the stake, beheading or imprisoning for life. Horse thieves were branded and flogged. Mutilations were rarer in the colonies. The practice may have something to do with the limited number of able-bodied workers. Permanently disabling a colonist would deprive the community of the full fruits of their labor. Criminals were more likely to face public penalties like the ducking stool, pillory or scarlet letters.[17] Similar prohibitions against cruel and unusual punishment were included in Virginia's Constitution and the constitutions of seven other states.[18] Virginia and Pennsylvania said punishment had to be moderate. Maryland prohibited sanguinary laws.

The prohibition against cruel and unusual punishment was subject to little debate during the passage of the Bill of Rights. James Madison is credited with drafting the language for the Eighth Amendment.[19] Prohibitions against cruel and unusual punishment existed under the Articles of Confederation.[20] There was little debate on its inclusion in the Bill of Rights. Madison presented the language for the amendment. Two delegates protested. O'Brien Smith of South Carolina opined that the term 'cruel and unusual' was too indefinite.[21] Samuel Livermore of New Hampshire also questioned the vagueness of the words. He noted that "villains often deserve whipping, and perhaps having their ears cut off." He worried that these punishments might be limited under the Bill of Rights, and argued "we ought not be restrained from making necessary laws by any declaration of this kind."[22] The amendment passed without amendment, despite these two objections.

While the Founding Fathers toiled in Philadelphia on the Bill of Rights, another group of citizens met blocks away at the home of Benjamin Franklin to address issues of crime and punishment.[23] At the time, jails were often used to hold the accused before meting out punishment. Men, women, and children were often locked up together. Reformers insisted that United States needed radical changes to the prison system. The Pennsylvania Prison Society worked to change the model for punishment. The religious beliefs of the Pennsylvania Quakers affected the reformers. The nonviolent Quakers frowned on the physical penalties involved in the post-colonial justice system. They believed prayer and reflection would cure criminal behavior. In the early part of the nineteenth century, they convinced the Pennsylvania legislature to adopt their suggested reforms. Many of the reforms centered on the use of penitentiaries. This new form of prison isolated convicts so that they could reflect on their crimes and reform. Prisoners were essentially held in solitary confinement for the duration of their sentences. Communication among prisoners was prohibited. Prisoners' sole possession was a Bible. By the time the Eastern State Penitentiary was completed in 1829, it had become a model for penal institutions. Hundreds of dignitaries from around the world came to observe practices at the prison. Within years, the Pennsylvania model was adopted across the growing country. In theory, the new model shifted the focus of the justice system from punishing the accused to reforming criminals. In practice, punishment shifted from swift, painful physical injury to slow psychological reform.

The adoption of the post–Civil War amendments also contributed to changes for crime and punishment in the United States. The passage of the Fourteenth Amendment forced all states to refrain from cruel and unusual punishment. Congressman John Bingham, credited with crafting the Fourteenth Amendment, noted, " 'cruel and unusual punishments' have been inflicted under State laws within this Union upon citizens, not only for crimes committed, but for sacred duty done, for which and against which the Government of the United States had provided no remedy and could provide none."[24] Following the passage of the Fourteenth Amendment, states had to worry about Constitutional problems with sentencing.

Those concerns were quickly ignored in the South, where local sheriffs used criminal statutes to replace lost slave labor. Douglas Blackmon's insightful book *Slavery by Another Name: the Re-Enslavement of Black Americans from the Civil War to World War II*[25] sheds light on Black Codes and peonage practices that started in the Deep South after the Civil War. The Thirteenth Amendment explicitly prohibited slavery or involuntary servitude. But the Amendment left a large loophole for those duly convicted of a crime. Twenty-seven states ratified the Amendment in 1865. Several Southern states enacted Black Codes that same year, which essentially criminalized black life.[26] African-Americans could be convicted of crimes that included vagrancy, "illegal" sales, or using obscene language. Perhaps one of the most interesting crimes was vagrancy, which forced former slaves to enter contracts with white farmers each year. African-Americans without contracts were arrested as vagrants and quickly convicted by local officials.

Those convictions allowed county officials to levy court costs and prison charges on the convicts. To pay off their debt, convicts were sold to farms, factories, and other enterprises that needed cheap labor. Blackmon describes one Black citizen's encounter with vagrancy laws. After a dispute with a landowner over wages, the man abandoned his job on a farm. He was quickly arrested by the local sheriff and brought before a local judge on vagrancy charges. He was convicted, charged with costs, and sold to a steel mill within 72 hours of leaving the farm. The convict would work at the mill during the day and return to the county jail or the mill's sleeping quarters at night. Each night he incurred additional debt for food and shelter. The debt always outpaced the wages "earned" by the former slave. In theory, the sinister plot could ensure years of labor at a minimal cost. In practice, job hazards meant the vagrancy conviction was a life sentence. Most died within the first year of work at a mill or mine.

In addition to convictions for Black Code violations, former slaveholders established peonage systems to trap former slaves. A landowner might "loan" a former slave food and shelter in exchange for working on a plantation. The landowners could charge for food and shelter during the planting and harvest seasons. Former slaves were trapped in a spiral of escalating debt, which allowed former slaveholders to use debt to force labor. Former slaves might live in the same slave quarters they occupied before the war, receive food and water from their former slaveholder, and work on the same plantation where they served as slaves before the war. The cost of food and shelter always outpaced the wages earned by the former slaves. Each former slave's debt, and the obligation to repay that debt, meant that life after the Thirteenth Amendment differed little from life before the Civil War. A worker's debt could be bought and sold, forcing former slaves to continue to exist in a system of forced labor without much protection under the Constitution. African-Americans that tried to flee their debts were arrested as vagrants and sold as workers under the Black Code system.

The parallel systems of Black Codes and peonage allowed the country to become dependent on low cost prison labor. By the turn of the twentieth century, the model for punishment was radically different from punishment a century earlier. Public whippings, the pillory, and scarlet letters gave way to industrialized prisons with labor forces available for hire by local businesses. The ideals codified hundreds of years earlier in the Magna Carta—amercing only to the extent the punishment wouldn't interfere with a man's livelihood—were outweighed by the enticement of cheap labor. Protection against cruel and unusual punishment no longer protected a citizen's right to a livelihood. It became a last line of defense against especially egregious state action.

Federal courts were reluctant to use the Eighth Amendment to intervene in state criminal matters, even for white citizens. Federal challenges to state punishments based on the "cruel and unusual" provisions of the Eighth Amendment began at the turn of the twentieth century. One of the first involved an issue that would have been familiar to the framers of the Bill of Rights. *Graham v. West Virginia*[27] involved an incorrigible horse thief. James H. Graham, also known in Pocahontas County as John H. Ratliff and in Wood County as J. H. Gray, was convicted of stealing a mare valued at $50 in 1898. Three years later, he attempted to steal another horse valued at $100 dollars. Six years later, he was convicted of stealing yet another horse valued at $75. West Virginia Courts imposed a life sentence on Graham under its recidivist statute. He appealed, claiming that the sentence was cruel and unusual. The Supreme Court disagreed, holding that the West Virginia Legislature was best suited to determine the punishment for repeat offenders.

Long sentences for incorrigible horse thieves may seem to fit under the post-colonial Eighth Amendment standard for punishment. But the court's deference to state legislatures meant that even petty criminals were subject to virtually any Draconian punishment drafted by state legislatures. In *Rummel v. Estelle*,[28] William James Rummel appealed a life sentence imposed in Texas under its recidivist statute. Under the statute, people convicted of a felony three times could be imprisoned for life. Mr. Rummel argued that his three relatively minor offenses did not merit a lifetime in prison. In 1964, he was convicted of his first felony: fraudulent use of a credit card to obtain $80 worth of goods or services. The second charge was for passing a forged check in the amount of $28.36. In 1973, he was convicted of his third felony: obtaining $120.75 by false pretenses. Rummel was paid to fix an air conditioner. Depending on the source, he either did not fix the unit or did not even attempt the repair. Prosecutors charged him under the Texas recidivist statute. So for stealing a grand total of $229.11 over a ten year period, Mr. Rummel was sentenced to a life behind bars.

Rummel claimed his sentence was so disproportionate to his crimes that his sentence was cruel and unusual. In a five to four decision, the Supreme Court held that the sentence was not disproportionate. The court acknowledged that the Eighth Amendment did mandate some proportionality between the crime committed and the sentence, but found that Rummel's sentence was not disproportionate. The case sets an extremely high bar for disproportionality. If life behind bars for stealing $230 is not disproportionate, it's hard to determine a situation where any punishment would be excessive. In a more recent case, the court explained again that "excessive" punishments are not necessarily a violation of the Eighth Amendment. In *Ewing v. California*,[29] a parolee was convicted of felony grand theft after he tried to walk out of a golf pro shop with three $399 golf clubs stuffed down his pants. Under California's recidivist criminal statute, he was sentenced to life in prison. Writing for the 5-4 majority, Justice O'Connor wrote that the "Eighth Amendment does not require strict proportionality between crime and sentence [but] forbids only extreme sentences that are 'grossly disproportionate' to the crime." The grossly disproportionate standard gives state legislatures ample room to legislate "tough on crime" penalties for relatively minor infractions.

The Eighth Amendment provides little protection for sentencing. Once behind bars, the cruel and unusual punishment clause also does little to protect the incarcerated. The Supreme Court held that "the Eighth Amendment does not outlaw cruel and unusual 'conditions'; it outlaws cruel and unusual 'punishments.' "[30] Prisoners are protected against "the unnecessary and wanton infliction of pain" while incarcerated.[31] The Constitution "does not mandate comfortable prisons,"[32] but it does not allow inhumane ones.[33] Prison officials may not use excessive physical force against prisoners.[34] They must ensure that inmates receive adequate food, clothing, shelter, and medical care, and must "take reasonable measures to guarantee the safety of the inmates." [35] The standard the Supreme Court applies is one of "deliberate indifference" for prison officials. If officials are deliberately indifferent to the suffering of inmates, an inmate's confinement may be cruel and unusual. On the other hand, if an official is unaware of a situation, or takes reasonable measures to ensure inmate safety, a prison may comply with Eighth Amendment guarantees.

The Death Penalty: Neither Cruel Nor Unusual

The death penalty, on the other hand, mandates significant Constitutional protection. Death is not cruel unless the manner of execution is inhuman or barbarous.[36] Courts refused to fix the definition of inhuman or barbarous. "It is not fastened to the obsolete, but may acquire meaning as public opinion becomes enlightened by humane justice."[37] Interestingly, courts acknowledge that the definition "must draw its meaning from the evolving standards of decency that mark the progress of a maturing society."[38] The death penalty gives courts reason to tread very carefully. In cases that don't involve the death penalty, courts have been much more willing to impose harsh sentences on repeat offenders.

As Pennsylvania led the way for prison reform, it also moved to reform the imposition of the death penalty. The state moved executions out of the public and into the penitentiary in 1834. Executions were less of a public spectacle. Other states followed suit, with some completely abandoning the death penalty. Michigan restricted the death penalty to the crime of treason. Rhode Island and Wisconsin abolished the death penalty. Other states shifted the power of a death sentence to juries, passing laws against mandatory death sentences for most crimes. Constitutional challenges to the death penalty sprouted up after the passage of the Fourteenth Amendment. The earliest cases involving the death penalty emerged from novel state punishments. In *Wilkerson v. Utah*,[39] Wallace Wilkerson was convicted of first-degree murder in the territory of Utah. Utah law allowed multiple options for applying the death penalty, which included death by hanging, firing squad, beheading, or the choice of the defendant.[40] Wallace was sentenced to death by firing squad. He appealed; saying that death by any method other than hanging was a cruel and unusual punishment. The Supreme Court disagreed, citing a long history of death by firing squad in military tribunals. The court noted that the state legislature was free to prescribe the method for executing convicted murders, so long as the method did not involve torture. Wilkerson was later killed by firing squad in a manner that might cause some concern for modern day Justices. Wilkerson refused a blindfold at his execution.[41] When the sheriff ordered the squad to fire, "Wilkerson braced for the barrage." He was struck in the arm and torso. He shrieked, "My God, they have missed!" He died almost 30 minutes later from his wounds.

As new technology invited new methods for administering the death penalty, the Supreme Court addressed the issue of "unusual" in death penalty cases. The New York legislature authorized the use of the electric chair in 1888. William Kemmler was sentenced to death via the electric chair. He appealed. The Supreme Court found that "punishments are cruel when they involve torture or a lingering death, but the punishment of death is not cruel."[42] The new method might be unusual, the court wrote, but was not cruel. In fact, the New York legislature allowed the electric chair because it argued that electrocution was a more humane way of executing convicts. The legislature's theory proved wrong in Kemmler's case. He remained alive after the first shock of one thousand volts coursed through his body.[43] "Nauseated witnesses and a tearful sheriff fled the room as Kemmler's coat burst into flames." He died after executioners applied a second surge of electricity. Despite the problems in Kemmler's execution, many states adopted the electric chair as the preferred way of executing criminals.

In *Territory v. Ketchum*,[44] the Supreme Court of the Territory of New Mexico pledged great deference to the state legislature. Ketchum was convicted of robbing a train. The New Mexico Supreme Court said, "[i]t must be clear that legislative discretion in determining the severity of punishment for crime is not to be interfered with by the courts, so long as all forms of torture are avoided."[45] Courts should not interfere with the judgment of the legislature unless "the punishment proposed is so severe and out of proportion to the offense as to shock public sentiment and violate the judgment of reasonable people."[46] The U.S. Supreme Court did acknowledge that the judgment of reasonable people could change over time. "The clause of the Constitution ... may be therefore progressive, and is not fastened to the obsolete, but may acquire meaning as public opinion becomes enlightened by a humane justice."[47]

This boy really got a shock when they turned that machine on.[48]

The combination of the questionable efficacy of the electric chair, courts' reluctance to challenge legislative sentiment for administering the death penalty, and Constitutional prohibitions against torture met violently in the case of Willie Francis. Seventeen-year-old Francis was sentenced to death for murder in 1945. Less than a year later, he was strapped into the electric chair at Angola State Penitentiary. The executioner flipped the switch. Francis's lips puffed out; he jumped so that the chair wobbled. Officials demanded, "more juice" when they saw that Francis was not dying. After a few moments, Francis yelled, "Take it off! Let me breathe."[49] Prison officials stopped the execution and Francis was removed from the execution chamber. Francis went before the parole board, which quickly denied parole. Francis appealed all the way to the Supreme Court, which struggled with his claims of Constitutional violations. Four justices found that a second attempt at an execution was not a violation of the Eighth Amendment because the issue with the electric chair was an accident.[50] Justice Frankfurter sided with the majority, citing the long history of cases in support of the death penalty. But he expressed grave concerns about the situation involving Francis. In a harshly worded dissent, four justices condemned the situation. They called for a change in the approach for death penalty reviews. Francis was executed the day after the Supreme Court decision was published.

Ten years later, the court started to shift course for cruel and unusual punishment cases. *Trop v. Dulles*,[51] did not focus on the death penalty. The U.S. government refused to issue a passport for a native-born American. Trop was court-martialed for deserting during World War II. As a result of his desertion, the United States maintained that he lost his American citizenship. The Supreme Court disagreed, noting that the definition of "cruel and unusual" is not fixed: "the words of the Amendment are not precise, and that their scope is not static. The Amendment must draw its meaning from the evolving standards of decency that mark the progress of a maturing society."[52] Death penalty opponents seized on the sentiment, arguing that evolving standards mandated a fresh review for death penalty cases. Beginning in 1968, the court started to chip away at the century-old tradition of deference to state legislatures on death penalties. *US v. Jackson,*[53] and *Witherspoon v. Illinois*,[54] focused on the power of juries in death penalty cases. In *Furman v. Georgia*,[55] the court found death penalty cases arbitrary and capricious. The court found the Georgia death penalty provisions unconstitutional. In voiding Georgia's statute, the court also effectively voided every other death penalty statute in the country and commuted the sentences for more than 600 inmates on death row.

Three cases were consolidated in *Furman*; two rape convictions and one murder conviction. Each of the defendants was African-American. Each Justice assigned different written reasons. Five of the nine found that the application of the death penalty violated the Eighth and Fourteenth Amendments. Justice Douglas pointed to the English Bill of Rights, arguing that it was written to cure selective or irregular application of harsh penalties.

> "It would seem incontestable that the death penalty inflicted on one defendant is 'unusual' if it discriminates against him by reason of his race, religion, wealth, social position, or class, or if it is imposed under a procedure that gives room for the play of such prejudices."[56]

Citing a study of capital cases in Texas and conclusions from the President's Commission on Law Enforcement and Administration of Justice, Justice

Douglas found that the application of the death penalty was unequal. It was disproportionately imposed on the poor, African-Americans, and members of unpopular groups. While the law was theoretically impartial, juries unintentionally favor certain groups. This inherent defect in the death penalty meant that its application must be suspended until the defect could be cured. The moratorium was short-lived. By 1976, states were able to fix the constitutional deficiencies in death penalty statutes. Gary Gilmore of Utah was the first inmate to be executed after the moratorium. Oklahoma adopted lethal injection as a humane form of administering the death penalty in 1977.[57]

The court continues to struggle with the death penalty. In 1989, the court held that imposing the death penalty on minors was not cruel and unusual.[58] Sixteen years later, the court reversed course.[59] Executions of the mentally challenged were constitutional,[60] before they were considered cruel and unusual.[61] The Supreme Court continues to struggle with a clear definition in death penalty cases, which may be due to a reliance on the "evolving standards of decency" articulated in *Trop v. Dulles*.

Our Shifting Understanding of Cruel and Unusual

Perhaps the evolving standards of decency were exactly what the Founding Fathers intended. It is clear, however, that the application of the Eighth Amendment's cruel and unusual protections is radically different from its application in the early days of the Republic. Life sentences were exceedingly rare. Long prison sentences that deprived convicts of their livelihood and communities of their labor were sparingly used. The absence of the pillory, stock, and public executions would undoubtedly surprise eighteenth century Americans. On the other hand, there would be little public sympathy for a slow death caused by a firing squad's mistake. Delays caused by an ineffective lethal injection of cocktails would not create a public uproar. We have an amendment that grows from its roots in the English Bill of Rights to reflect a truly American criminal procedure.

Public Misunderstanding and Cruel and Unusual Myths

Myths are often perpetuated by misunderstandings passed along as truths. Children are socialized into believing that America is a nation of rights, defined by individual freedoms and the right to be left alone. The definition of cruel and unusual is different, less mythical than a set of poorly formed beliefs in constant revision as the historical background shifts, like a chameleon walking through backdrops of changing colors. This constant revision is true of all of the protections enumerated in the Bill of Rights but the definition of "cruel and unusual" is even more amorphous than freedom of speech, freedom of religion, or even the court defined right to privacy, perhaps because it is less central to who we are or how we define ourselves.

Public opinion about crime and punishment is largely uninformed and misinformed, based on a fear of crime that outpaces reality and a perception that the criminal justice system is more lenient than it really is.[62] In the abstract, the public typically favors harsh and punitive sentencing, though those attitudes often soften when the public takes into account the details of a specific case and the public is clearly open to alternative sentencing.[63] Curiously, over time, public support for incarceration has grown as have actual mass incarceration rates, though crime rates have gone down. In the 1960s, mass incarceration rates looked similar to other industrial democracies but by the 1980s U.S. incarceration rates were significantly higher, a gap that has continued to grow.[64]

The public, for the most part, considers the question of cruel and unusual punishment as secondary to the question of "justice," where perceptions of what is just is based more on the nature of the crime and the fairness of the verdict (and sentence) than on the actual punishment. Americans are not philosophically opposed to the death penalty but have practical reservations based on exonerations via DNA evidence and questions of systemic fairness.[65] Since 1972, a majority of Americans have favored "the death penalty for a person convicted of murder."[66] While support has declined from its peak in 1992 when 80 percent to 60 percent in 2013, this decline has little to do with a moral awakening or a more humane public. According to Gallup, 6 in 10 Americans believe that the death penalty is "morally acceptable." This number has remained relatively stable over time. Moreover, when asked if death penalty is imposed too often, the right amount or not enough, a plurality—44 percent—say that it is not imposed often enough while an additional 26 percent say it is imposed about the right amount. In the public mind, death is neither a cruel nor unusual punishment.

While support for specific punishments has shifted over time, the logic underlying that support has remained largely consistent. When asked why they supported the death penalty in a 2003 Gallup Poll, the most common response was that the death penalty was "an eye for eye" while the second most common response was because "they deserve it." Punishment, in the public eye, should be fair and proportional with cruelty in proportion to the cruelty of the crime. The most common reason for opposing the death penalty was that it is morally wrong to take a life, not that the death penalty is cruel or unusual.

If public opinion toward punishment is motivated by retribution, it is also motivated by ideas of rehabilitation.[67] Punishments should not simply be just, they should help to address the causes of crime, and reduce future criminal activity. As a result, public opinion is more open to alternative sentences than one might believe if simply reading the populist and punitive nature of opinion. Support for the death penalty, for example, declines when the alternative of "life without the possibility of parole" is added as an option. Locking up prisoners and throwing away the key provides a comparable and just outcome for much of the public, particularly if conditions are harsh and unpleasant.

Perhaps this is a more humane solution, but is also an option largely rejected by the Founding Fathers, many of whom would have preferred cutting off ears to imprisonment. Definitions of cruel and unusual, it is often argued, reflect *evolving standards of human decency*, evolving in this instance, however, should not necessarily be taken to mean more humane as humanity resides largely in the eyes of the beholder. Many of the Founding Fathers would have found our incarceration rates, the highest among advanced industrial democracies, far more disturbing and cruel than the death penalty.

Notes

1. Article 18, New Hampshire Constitution, 1784.
2. http://www.prisonstudies.org/highest-to-lowest/prison_population_rate?field_region_taxonomy_tid=All (accessed on December 4, 2014).
3. Robert K. Goidel, Craig Freeman, and Steven Procopio, "The Impact of Television Viewing on Perceptions of Juvenile Crime," *Journal of Broadcasting and Electronic Media* 50 (2006): 119–139.
4. 510 U.S. 1141 (1992).
5. The men Scalia referred to in the rape case were exonerated by DNA evidence. The two mentally challenged half-brothers spent 30 years behind bars for a crime they did not commit.
6. http://www.nola.com/crime/baton-rouge/index.ssf/2013/08/angola_warden_apologizes_for_v.html.
7. http://www.nydailynews.com/news/justice-story/anguish-angola-article-1.1754535.

8. http://www.nytimes.com/1994/09/17/us/making-hard-time-harder-states-cut-jail-tv-and-sports.html.

9. Carlos Berdejo and Noam Yuchtman, "Crime, Punishment, and Politics: An Analysis of Political Cycles in Criminal Sentencing," *Review of Economics and Statistics, Forthcoming; Loyola-LA Legal Studies Paper* No. 2012-50, December 28, 2012.

10. "Stride Toward Freedom: The Montgomery Story" [STF]: MLK 1958.

11. Later numbered Section 14.

12. *Origins of the Bill of Rights*, 232.

13. *Harmelin v. Michigan*, 501 U.S. 957, 968.

14. *Second Trial of Titus Oates*,10 How. St. Tr. 1227, 1314 (K.B. 1685).

15. *Furman v. Georgia*, 408 U.S. 238, 242 (1972).

16. English law distinguished between pre-trial actions and post-conviction punishment. English law allowed harsh punishment for accused wrongdoers who refused to defend themselves. What we may consider torture today was used to convince the accused to confess or provide a defense. Punishment strong and hard, or *peine forte et dure*, was used to punish mute prisoners. Under English law, silent prisoners were presumed guilty until 1827.

17. *Furman v. Jackson*, supra, 238.

18. Ibid., 244, fn 5 in case, 244. In 1791, five state constitutions prohibited "cruel or unusual punishments," see Del. Declaration of Rights, § 16 (1776); Md. Declaration of Rights, Art. XXII (1776); Mass. Declaration of Rights, Art. XXVI (1780); N.C. Declaration of Rights § X (1776); N.H. Bill of Rights, Art. XXXIII (1784), and two prohibited "cruel" punishments, Pa.Const., Art. IX, § 13 (1790); S.C.Const., Art. IX, § 4 (1790).

19. Ibid., 239.

20. Ibid., 244, fn 6.

21. Ibid., 244.

22. Ibid.

23. http://www.smithsonianmag.com/history/eastern-state-penitentiary-a-prison-with-a-past-14274660/?no-ist.

24. Cong. Globe 39th Cong. 1st Sess. 2542.

25. D. A. Blackmon, *Slavery by Another name: The Re-enslavement of Black People in America from the Civil War to World War II*, 1st ed. (Doubleday: Douglas A. Blackmon, 2008).

26. Ibid., 53.

27. 224 U.S. 616 (1912).

28. 445 U.S. 263 (1980).

29. 538 U.S. 11 (2003).

30. Ibid., 837.

31. *Estelle v. Gamble*, 429 U.S. 97, 103 (1976).

32. *Rhodes v. Chapman*, 452 U.S. 337, 349 (1981).

33. *Farmer v. Brennan*, 511 U.S. 825, 832 (1994).
34. *Hudson v. McMillian*, 503 U.S. 1 (1992).
35. *Hudson v. Palmer*, 468 U.S. 517, 526–527 (1984).
36. *In re Kemmler*, 136 U.S. 436.
37. *Weems v. United States*, 217 U.S. at 378.
38. *Trop v. Dulles*, 356 U.S. 86.
39. 99 U.S. 130 (1878).
40. Ibid., 132 "when any person shall be convicted of any crime the punishment of which is death,... he shall suffer death by being shot, hung, or beheaded, as the court may direct," or as the convicted person may choose. Sess. Laws Utah, 1852, p. 61; Comp. Laws Utah, 1876, 564.
41. http://www.nytimes.com/2008/04/23/opinion/23king.html?_r=0.
42. *In re Kemmler*, 136 U.S. 436, 447 (1890).
43. http://www.nytimes.com/2008/04/23/opinion/23king.html?_r=0.
44. 65 P. 169 (N.M. 1901).
45. Ibid., 170.
46. Ibid., 171.
47. *Weems v. United States*, 217 U.S. 349, 378 (1910).
48. Affidavit of official witness Ignace Doucet, dated May 30, 1946. State of Louisiana ex rel. *Francis v. Resweber*, 329 U.S. 459, 480 fn 2 (1947).
49. Ibid.
50. Affidavits obtained after the incident revealed that the guard and inmate assigned to prepare the electric chair were "so drunk it would have been impossible for them to have known what they were doing." http://www.nytimes.com/2008/04/23/opinion/23king.html?_r=0.
51. 356 U.S. 86 (1958).
52. Ibid., 100–101.
53. 390 U.S. 570 (1968).
54. 391 U.S. 510 (1968).
55. 408 U.S. 238 (1972).
56. Ibid., 242.
57. Though the first person to be executed by lethal injection was Charles Brooks of Texas in 1982.
58. *Stanford v. Kentucky*, 492 U.S. 361, 380 (1989).
59. *Roper v. Simmons*, 543 U.S. 551, 578 (2005).
60. *Penry v. Lynaugh*, 492 U.S. 302, 340 (1989).
61. *Atkins v. Virginia*, 536 U.S. 304, 321 (2002).
62. "Crime, Punishment and Public Opinion: A Summary of Recent Studies and their Implications for Sentencing Policy," *The Sentencing Project*, January 2000, available at http://www.sentencingproject.org/detail/publication.cfm?publication_id=146 (accessed on October 4, 2014); Kevin Wozniak, "American Public Opinion About Prisons," *Criminal Justice Review* 39 (2014): 305–314.

Wozniak finds that while Americans typically believe conditions are harsh, they would prefer conditions be "harsher still."

63. James Unnever and Francis Cullen, "The Social Sources of Americans' Punitiveness: A Test of Three Competing Models," *Criminology* 48 (2010): 91–101; Natasha Frost, "Beyond Public Opinion Polls: Punitive Public Sentiment & Criminal Justice Policy," *Sociology Compass* 4 (2010): 156–161.

64. Peter Enns, "Public Opinion and Mass Incarceration in the U.S. States," Paper presented at the *Annual Meeting of the American Political Science Association*, Chicago, IL, August 2013.

65. Frank Baumgartner, Suzanna De Boeuf, and Amber Boydstun, *The Decline of the Death Penalty and the Discovery of Innocence* (Cambridge: Cambridge University Press, 2008).

66. Unless noted otherwise, the data in this section are taken from Gallup, available at http://www.gallup.com/poll/1606/death-penalty.aspx (accessed on September 30, 2014).

67. Roger Matthews, "The Myth of Punitiveness," *Theoretical Criminology* 9 (2005): 175–201.

Conclusion

Bringing the Frog of Citizenship to a Slow Boil

Introduction

Our collective understanding of the Bill of Rights is clouded in misinformation and ignorance. We are unable to recall many of our most basic freedoms, like the right of people to peaceably assemble or petition government; and, we believe what is not true, convenient myths grounded in useful narratives and powerful metaphors. As a result, the protections enumerated in the Bill of Rights are less protective than they may at first appear. They are contingent upon historical context, institutional power, and the public's collective commitment to individual freedom.

The good news here is that the larger timeline of American political history reveals an expansion, albeit through jumps and starts rather than a simple linear progression, of individual rights and freedoms. We may fairly say that we are freer today than during most of American history. Individual freedom, however, is not a constant nor does it follow a predetermined path of expansion. There are no guarantees that tomorrow will be freer than today.

Any optimism about the longer historical view has to be tempered by the fact that Americans are more than willing to suppress dissent and limit freedom when faced with an external threat. The U.S. Patriot Act passed in the aftermath of the 9/11 terrorist attack, for example, allowed the indefinite detentions of immigrants and searches of homes and business without consent, and greatly expanded government surveillance capabilities of phone, email, and other online activities. In the wake of the attack, the Patriot Act was passed with little opposition. Those voices of dissent that did emerge were largely marginalized. More recent revelations that the

National Security Administration (NSA) monitored domestic telephone calls and online activities were largely met with a collective yawn, as most Americans seemed neither surprised nor outraged.

Throughout much of American history, individual freedom has been enhanced by our political geography. With the Atlantic and the Pacific Oceans as borders and no immediate enemy within easy reach, Americans could enjoy a relative security that promoted individual freedom. The shrinking of the world, however, brings the threat of terrorism closer to our living rooms and makes us all more vulnerable. The Islamic State (ISIS or ISIL), for example, uses online appeals to recruit American citizens to become homegrown terrorists, raising the risks of domestic terrorism supported and sponsored by foreign enemies.

Thomas Hobbes long ago outlined the implicit trade-off between security and freedom, arguing that, in all societies, individuals relinquish individual freedom to leave behind a state of nature where life was violent, brutal, and short. We have revisited these trade-offs throughout American history and we will revisit them in the future as new threats emerge and force us to reconsider how much individual freedom we are willing to sacrifice in order to be safe. The greater and more immediate threat, the more balance tilts away from freedom and toward security.

At the same time, the exponential growth of technology allows for greater monitoring of individual behavior, setting up the capacity for a more intrusive government and a collective loss of individual liberty. Cameras catch us speeding or running through red lights, they monitor us and watch us while we are shopping, and they capture our movements in public places. When a bomb exploded near the finish line of the Boston Marathon in April 2013, the FBI scanned through surveillance videos to identify Cechen brothers Dzhokhar and Tamarlan Tsarnaev as the suspects. The video proved invaluable in the subsequent investigation and the constitutionality of the surveillance is not in question. Yet, their use raises a question that goes to the core of individual freedom: Do American citizens have a right to *not* be under surveillance when in public places? Do they have a reasonable expectation of privacy when they are outside of their homes?

This is not simply a rhetorical question. In 2007, the Constitution Project issued "Guidelines for Public Video Surveillance," specifically raising the issue of when such surveillance equipment should (and should not) be acceptable.[1] The report notes that the use of surveillance equipment in local communities is most often rooted not in the threats posed by terrorists but by fears of local crime. Technology has allowed these video networks to grow increasingly intrusive via magnification, increased resolution, and motion detection. To return to the Boston Marathon bombing, federal authorities scanned over 13,000 videos to identify the suspects in just over 100 hours.[2] The suspects were identified when, unlike the rest of the crowd, they did not turn in the direction of the initial explosion.

Large scale video surveillances emerge as the hero in this particular investigation making it difficult to question its use. *"Are you saying, we shouldn't capture bombing suspects? Or that we should risk that they'll get away with it?"* It also fits within a larger theme of American public opinion toward surveillance, that is, if you aren't doing anything wrong, you have nothing to worry about; that is an open door for restricting individual freedoms. Heightened fear of terrorists or violent crime in combination with technologies that have capacity to grow ever more intrusive mean that individual freedom will be increasingly under threat.

Add in one last combustible element, the intrusions may not come from the government but from private companies, including our employers, who are under no obligation to respect a Bill of Rights that protects us from government but not from each other. Individuals can (and have) been fired for participating in protest activity, expressing their political opinion, and for online comments, posts, and blogs. Air Force Colonel Morris Davis was fired in 2009 from a research position at the Library of Congress for publishing a Wall Street Journal editorial criticizing the federal government for using military tribunals to try Guantanamo Bay detainees.[3] Notably, the op-ed had no bearing on his job responsibilities and was written outside of work. More recently, English Professor Steven Salaita had his faculty appointment at the University of Illinois withdrawn after posting "inflammatory" and "uncivil" criticisms of Israel on Twitter, and after the university received threats from donors that they would withdraw their financial support if his hiring was approved.[4] As with Morris Davis, Stephen Salaita's comments were made on his own time and had no bearing on his ability to perform his job at the university. Less than a decade ago, it is unlikely that Salaita's political comments would have been seen or heard beyond a small circle of friends. Social media, however, makes much of our private behavior public, often intentionally so. Even when we try to safeguard it using restrictive privacy settings or anonymous postings, what we thought was private and outside of work-related responsibilities can quickly be made public.

In contemporary politics, individual rights face challenges on multiple fronts. What we believe about these rights becomes important in determining how far they reach and what they protect. We are unlikely to call for an expansion of rights, for example, if we believe incorrectly that the Bill of Rights protects our right to speak freely against employers. Colonel Morris Davis and Professor Steven Salaita both believed they were well within the rights protected by the First Amendment when they lost their jobs. Our rights in these instances are more narrowly defined by the courts and legal precedent than our beliefs about when and how our rights protect us from retribution. Perhaps stated differently, we often believe we are freer than we are. Alternatively, misunderstandings about why specific rights were created may make us more willing to limit individual freedom. Due process rights are often linked to "criminal" rights protecting the accused but not the victims, but this is a misunderstanding of why these rights were protected in the Bill of Rights. They were not designed as criminal protections but as protections against authorities using criminal law as tool to repress political dissent. Because of this misunderstanding, we are more likely to shrug when these rights are violated. With this in mind, we turn now to revisit how each of these myths have helped to define our political beliefs and create our collective identity but at the considerable costs of defining and limiting debate and adding to our collective understanding.

The Myths that Define and Limit Us

Near the end of this exploration, we remain deeply agnostic about the role that myths play in our culture and in our collective understanding of the Bill of Rights. On the one hand, they help to define us and give us a collective identity as a nation of rights. While we have too often fallen short of our cultural commitments to individual freedom and equality before the law, the existence of this larger myth has been, and continues to be, employed to expand individual freedoms. The myths did not define the great social movements of American history but often empowered them with a language that resonated within the larger political culture. *Don't give us special protections, give us the natural rights promised to all Americans.* Yet, these myths are also limiting, giving us a false sense of security that our freedoms are cloaked in the protective coating of the Bill of Rights. Too often, our myths make us complacent. Convinced that rights are not only protected but they are applied equally and evenly throughout society, we see little reason to expand individual freedom or to protect groups and individuals who have been marginalized.

Our complacency, misinformation, and false sense of security make us, like a frog in slowly boiling water, susceptible to a gradual withering away of individual rights. The story has been told so often in so many contexts, it is now a cliché. But like myths, clichés hold power not because they are factually accurate but because they contain a truth that resonates. They are repeated because they are useful tools in how we think about and organize our world.

The boiling frog metaphor provides a simple cautionary tale. Slip a frog into a pot of boiling water and he will quickly jump out. Boiling water is a threat that even a frog can quickly recognize. Slip the frog into cool water and slowly heat it to a boil and the frog will never notice the gradual change. Scientists dispute the metaphor's accuracy. Boiling water would almost certain kill a frog before he could jump out and frogs typically don't sit still in cool water. Even if they did, they would likely jump out as the water warms rather than settle in for a slow boil.[5] The truth of the story, however, is not in its details but in the lessons it conveys. In the context of the Bill of Rights, the boiling frog serves as a warning about what can happen to our individual liberties when we slowly and gradually either give our rights away or let them be taken. Curiously, it has been used by both the left and the right in American politics to convey the same warning, though typically in defense of different individual rights, that is, the Second Amendment's right to bear arms versus the First Amendment's protection of artistic expression. Herein lies one additional threat to individual freedom: We most want to protect those rights that fit most easily into our ideological worldview or that affect us most directly.

(1) *A Parchment Barrier:* Perhaps our greatest myth is that individual rights require constitutional protection. As James Madison well understood when he first crafted the Bill of Rights, individual freedoms are best protected by carefully designed political institutions and a collective commitment to individual freedom. Enumerated rights are little more than a parchment barrier when institutions fail or our collective commitment waivers. Faith that the courts will be more protective of individual rights than legislatures or even democratic majorities is faith misplaced. Courts have, at times, been guardians of individual freedoms but they have also narrowly interpreted and selectively applied those same freedoms, often depending on how much they agree with the speaker. Like legislators and citizens more generally, justices (and judges) are products of a broader economic, political, and social

context, and their decisions largely reflect, and are constrained by, that context.

This is not to suggest that incorporating individual protections has no effect, it unquestionably adds a layer of protection by elevating rights to the level of constitutional law but it is misleading to believe that a simple act of incorporating rights ensures they will be protected. The best protection of individual rights has always been, and always will be, a tolerant, informed, and engaged citizenry. Alas, none of these conditions are met in contemporary democratic practice. Citizens are woefully uninformed, particularly about the structural components of government and the specific protections provided in the Bill of Rights. Public understanding of the First Amendment rarely extends beyond freedom of speech. Moreover, Americans are often intolerant of politically unpopular and least liked groups, thus recognizing freedom of speech as a fundamental freedom in the abstract but unwilling to extend it to unpopular groups or viewpoints.

The Bill of Rights does help to protect us from ourselves but it is a thin and uneven protection, providing no guarantee in the face of external threats or economic crisis. To paraphrase Thomas Jefferson's well-worn phrase about newspapers, were I forced to choose between constitutionally protected rights or an informed citizenry deeply committed to individual freedom, I would not hesitate to choose the latter.

(2) *Unequal Rights:* When we think of rights we think first of Thomas Jefferson's poetic assertion in the Declaration of Independence. "We hold these truths to be self-evident, that all men are created equal, that they are endowed by their Creator with certain unalienable Rights, that among these are Life, Liberty, and the Pursuit of Happiness." Despite Jefferson's soaring rhetoric, the application of the Bill of Rights has always been uneven, often because we have failed to acknowledge existing inequalities or, when acknowledged, we have argued that the inequalities are outside of the scope of constitutional protection. Equal rights for lesbians and gays, for example, are often derided as "special treatment."

Even today the Constitution and the level of protections we each enjoy from the Bill of Rights functions differently depending on where we live, who we are, and the quality of legal representation we can afford. African-Americans are treated very differently in our criminal justice system. When crimes are being investigated, African-Americans are more likely to be stopped and detained. Once detained, they are more likely to be arrested. Once arrested, they are more likely to be found guilty. And, once found guilty, they are more likely to receive longer sentences than Whites convicted of comparable crimes. These differences are widely recognized and acknowledged in the African-American community. It is not just an inside joke that African-Americans are often stopped for "driving while black" as the evidence suggests they are indeed stopped more often.[6] White Americans, in contrast, are more likely to believe the criminal justice system is colorblind and the results of the process fairly reflect individual misconduct.[7] When an unarmed African-American teen, such as Michael Brown, is subsequently shot by a White police officer, African-Americans see the incident as a confirmation of systemic inequalities. White Americans see it as an isolated and unfortunate incident but hardly reflective of larger societal inequalities or racial injustice.[8] Their sympathies often reside with the police officer, performing his job under difficult and trying circumstances.

Because the American public is too often unwilling to acknowledge inequities in the application of rights, such inequities persist. Disparities in criminal justice, for example, have grown despite the procedural protections established by the Warren Court and Civil Rights advances during the 1960s. This extends beyond criminal justice to the extension of free speech rights, religion, and other individual freedoms. The *Citizens United* decision, for example, extended the logic of *Buckley v. Valeo* and accepted the premise that free speech should be allocated on the basis of one's willingness and ability to pay. In fairness, some inequality is inevitable but too often we fail to see those inequalities because we believe equality already exist and that it is applied in equal measure and to everyone.

(3) *The Limits of Free Speech:* Nothing is more fundamental to democratic governance than the right to unfettered speech. Democracy falls apart in the absence of meaningful political opposition freely offering dissenting viewpoints. The democratic value of dissent only grows during times of crisis when dissenting voices are most likely to be suppressed but most needed to assure that the political system remains true to fundamental values. Freedom of speech is also the right Americans are most likely to recall and are most likely to cite as a source of pride about the U.S. political system. In the United States, citizens believe, we protect and honor freedom of speech.

Yet, the right to free speech is limited. Cases of libel and slander are obvious examples where rights to free speech are balanced against competing values. Equally important are the contractions of free speech rights during wartime and crisis.[9] "Loose lips sink ships" emerged as a piece of World War II propaganda but it also captures more general attitudes about First Amendment freedoms. When asked to make a trade-off between individual liberty and national security, Americans generally choose the latter. They are led (or follow) political elites who are willing to sacrifice individual freedom to assure a secure nation; thus shutting off debate when dissent is most needed.

The good news is that support for free speech typically rebounds fairly quickly once the crisis has passed, but there are moments when the window for free speech is tightly shuttered. And, it is not at all clear how free speech might fare if the crisis is extended or the threat fails to dissipate. James Madison's observation proves prescient:

Constant apprehension of War, has the same tendency to render the head too large for the body. A standing military force, with an overgrown Executive will not long be safe companions to liberty. The means of defence against foreign danger have been always the instruments of tyranny at home. Among the Romans it was a standing maxim to excite a war, whenever a revolt was apprehended.

    The contingent nature of free speech serves as helpful reminder of one of our more general themes: The definition of individual rights is heavily influenced by the broader economic, political, and social context. Free speech rights depend not just on the First Amendment but also the makeup of the Supreme Court, and the political pressures emanating from the president and congress.

(4) *The Dependent News Media:* Part and parcel to free speech is the belief in an independent news media capable of serving as watchdog over elected officials and alerting the public to the news and events that matter in their daily lives. This is the news media taught in journalism schools, the free press of the American Revolution, the free press deeply rooted in a muckraking tradition of investigative reporting, and the free press committed to facilitating democratic governance by producing and disseminating objective and nonpartisan information.

    Yet, it is also largely a myth. The independence of the news media, in theory, flows from its organization as a business operating in a capitalist economic system. This means the news media may be independent of government (though even this independence is overstated) but that it remains a profit-seeking business dependent on advertising revenue and audience ratings. The pressures created by these "independent" forces affect which stories become news and how these stories are told. Truly critical perspectives, for example, fundamentally questioning the American economic system as a cause of economic anxiety and dislocation, are unlikely to make it into the nightly news.

    Economics is not the only force limiting the news media as reporters are also dependent on government subsidies, favorable regulation, and access to government sources. The contemporary American media system would have been unthinkable in the absence of postal subsidies that encouraged the growth and extended the reach of daily newspapers, and major media organizations continue to benefit from favorable regulation. Practically speaking, this means the media are less independent than we typically believe and—despite criticisms of liberal bias—less critical of government than one might otherwise expect. First Amendment protections of a "free press" provide no guarantee that the news media that emerges will be capable of—or even interested in—providing the information necessary for effective democratic governance. If the audience demands the latest news on Miley Cyrus, public affairs will take a backseat. Similarly, the emergence of *Fox News* may have helped to fragment news audiences further but it also fits within a larger context of greater choice in news sources making a conservative alternative to traditional news channels more economically viable.

(5) *A Deist Nation:* In a country built on principles of religious toleration, it is perhaps surprising that Americans approach citizenship with such a religious fervor. Not far beneath the surface of the American political creed is the myth that the United States was formed as a Christian nation. Under this mythology, James Madison crafting the U.S. Constitution serves as a parallel to Moses bringing the Ten Commandments to the people of Israel. Throughout much of American history, religion has been favored first by the colonies and then by state governments. Yet, the federal government was founded primarily by deists, not Christians, who may have believed in a god but only loosely defined and not prone to interfering in the daily activities of governments or men. These founders were more influenced by the enlightenment than the Christian Bible. Religious toleration then was not simply intended for other Christian denominations but extended to those with very different beliefs about god and religion, including those who believed in a creator who largely left the world to its own devices and to those who didn't believe in god at all. This is not to say that our nation was, is, or ever will be atheistic, but rather that our history is rooted more firmly in a duality of religion and politics, of church and state. As such, we are no more a Christian nation than we are an atheist nation. Evidence suggests that we are a religious people, a spiritual people, but not a theocracy.

Dispelling the myth, however, tells only half the story. The myth of the Christian nation has served to help define the American political culture, and religion more broadly defined has been a key player in American historical development.

(6) *No Wall of Separation:* As much as religious conservatives get religion wrong, so too do secular liberals who insist on a strict wall of separation between church and state. While Thomas Jefferson famously used the metaphor of a wall of separation, it has never been close to a reality. Religion has inevitably been intertwined into public life. Arguably, much of our public religion involves generic "in God we trust" or "one nation under god" phrases less rooted in religious tradition than ceremonial use. Religion has occupied a larger and more invasive role in state governments. For example, taxes to support religious denominations were established in Massachusetts, Connecticut, and New Hampshire, a direct interference of the state in religious activity.

Throughout American history, religious movements and organizations have played a significant role in transforming American society, often with calls for greater social justice and fairness. The abolitionists, Civil Rights, and progressive movements, for example, were all deeply infused with religious influences and leadership. Religion continues to play an important role in contemporary politics though the most notable and controversial shift has been the politicization of more conservative religious groups, evangelicals and born again Christians, who used to focus on saving souls rather than political activism. Motivated to politics by the school prayer, bible reading, and abortion decisions, this group has become an important political constituency for Republican politicians. More generally, religious groups play an important role in political campaigns serving as key element in voting strategies, voter mobilization efforts, and messaging strategies. When Gallup (and other polling organizations) ask about candidate traits, voters say they are less willing to vote for an atheist for president than any other identification, including a Muslim, gay or lesbian candidate, or Mormon. And, studies in political psychology have found subtle religious cues, for example the presence of a cross in a television ad, can affect vote choice.[10]

Religion and politics are subsequently inevitably and intractably linked. Engagement in politics is often driven by religious beliefs and values, and religious groups play an important role in the political process. While this falls far short of "establishing" religion, it also falls short of a strict wall of separation, a useful myth for thinking about religious tolerance but hardly an accurate description of the realities of American politics.

(7) *No Standing Your Ground:* Over time the Second Amendment has become synonymous with an individual right to own a gun (or guns) for self-defense. The myth, that the Founding Fathers drafted the Second Amendment as a mechanism for personal protection, is well-rooted in English common law that defined the home as a castle and early American history where a wide open western frontier promised unlimited opportunity but also required self-reliance, particularly in terms of protecting life, liberty, and property. The timing of the Second Amendment, however, suggests that the Founding Fathers were much more concerned with the ability to establish and maintain militias for collective defense than with individual self-protection. Within this context, Shay's Rebellion frightened many political elites and created a sense of urgency behind the push for a new and stronger national government, and particularly a government capable of putting down armed rebellions. This context also helps shed light on the myth that the right to keep and bear arms was crafted to give the people a chance to rebel against an oppressive national government. While the constitution was crafted on the basis of a social contract between the people and their government, it was drafted to provide stability. Or perhaps stated differently, the right to keep and bear arms was crafted with an eye to putting down, and not to fomenting, rebellion.

Interpretations focusing on the connection between the Second

Amendment and state militias are undoubtedly correct but only capture half the truth. A state militia, after all, required armed citizens, capable of being called into duty. If gun control activists are correct that the focus was on state militias, they miss the importance of—and the right to—individual gun ownership. Militias were unthinkable in the absence of individual gun ownership. The Founding Fathers would have found both provisions important components for securing individual freedom. However, it is equally unlikely that the Founding Fathers would have thought the newly crafted federal government could not regulate gun ownership. Indeed, early militias laws carefully articulated the weaponry every male citizen needed to have at his disposal. This was not a right, it was a mandate. Moreover, as with the other rights protected by the Bill of Rights, the Second Amendment was thought to apply to the federal government but not to state governments that could regulate (or not) gun ownership. It is only recently that the right has been incorporated against state government action.

(8) *The Politics of Criminal Due Process:* Perhaps no rights are more important in protecting individual freedom than the protections embodied within procedural due process. Their importance relative to the public's recognition of their importance reflects one of the inherent shortcomings in political attitudes, that is, a lack of public knowledge of the historical context in which the Bill of Rights was developed. Due process rights were never designed to protect criminals but rather to protect individuals who might be targeted for political harassment. The principle is relatively straightforward: Individuals in a free society should not be subjected to routine and random searches from authorities or forced to make confessions. Such techniques have long been a tool of arbitrary and capricious authorities, not to control crime, but to limit opposition and dissent.

If one believes the use of criminal law for political retribution is a relic of bygone era, consider charges that the IRS targeted conservative political groups for investigation. While these charges are still being investigated at the time of this writing, there did appear to be a pattern of singling out conservative political organizations. Or consider the case of conservative author Dinesh D'Souza who pled guilty to charges that he violated federal campaign finance laws. While his guilty plea suggests he was indeed guilty of the charge, one can fairly question how often such charges are made, whether they result in a conviction, and the severity of the sentence imposed. More recently, Texas Governor Rick Perry (R) was indicted for abuse of power after vetoing funding for the Travis County District Attorney's Office. While one can fairly take issue with any of these examples, we do know that corruption investigations are subject to partisan biases—and that these biases extend across administrations.[11] In 2007, for example, the Bush Administration fired seven U.S. attorneys, allegedly for doing too much to investigate Republican officials and/or doing too little to investigate Democrats.

Criminal law can be a powerful tool for undermining political opposition and limiting political dissent. Unfortunately, because we too often see these protections as "criminal" rights we are often too willing to scale back on these protections, placing individual freedom at risk.

(9) *Surrendering Privacy:* In the classic novel *Catch 22*, the main character, Yossarian, struggles with a paradox. If you are deemed crazy, you are not allowed to fly any additional missions and may be released from your official duties. Indeed, if you are crazy, you need only ask. Asking to be released, however, is evidence you are not crazy. One of the more curious paradoxes of American political attitudes provides a similar catch. We jealously protect our private space but at the same time are more than willing to give it up upon requests, particular if the requests come from the police or some other authority figure. Indeed, we are so willing to give up this right that we are subsequently suspicious of anyone who does not yield to a physical search or electronic surveillance. Only people who have something to hide, after all, are unwilling to be searched or watched. We not only surrender our privacy, we expect others to do so as well.

Within the creation of the right to privacy, we also see a collective misunderstanding of context in which the Bill of Rights was drafted. The right to privacy was initially created as a penumbra from other rights included in the Bill of Rights. Subsequent rulings have shifted the foundation for a right to privacy to substantive due process. Regardless, nowhere in the U.S. Constitution or in the Bill of Rights is an explicit right to privacy mentioned or guaranteed. The creation of a new right, not explicitly protected in the Bill of Rights, raised concern that the courts had overstepped their constitutional authority. Yet, the logic ignores the Ninth Amendment and the historical context surrounding the drafting of the Bill of Rights. The Bill of Rights was never intended to set limits on the freedoms that would be protected by the U.S. Constitution.

First, the Ninth Amendment quite clearly opens the door for rights not explicitly enumerated in the Bill of Rights. Second, James Madison, Alexander Hamilton, and others argued against an enumerated set of rights specifically because it would give the appearance that only those rights specifically spelled out in the Bill of Rights would be protected. Thus, the Ninth Amendment provides that enumerating "certain rights, shall not be construed to deny or disparage others retained by the people." Nothing in American jurisprudence is static. Not only can the nature of existing rights change over time but so too can the rights that are protected.

(10) *The Cruelty of Imprisonment:* Context is critical to interpretation. Perhaps nowhere is this more apparent than in our understanding of cruel and unusual

punishment. Punishments that we would unquestionably consider cruel by contemporary standards were widely and regularly imposed in early American history. Today, most of the conversation around cruel and unusual punishment centers on the death penalty. While some controversy centers on methods of execution—is it better to shoot someone, hang them, electrocute them, or poison them—the central controversy is whether execution is itself morally acceptable. Perhaps ironically, the alternative—locking up criminals and throwing away the keys—might have been perceived as more cruel during the founding era where placing people in stocks, slitting their nostrils, or cutting off their ears was preferred to imprisonment. In determining what is "cruel and unusual" historical context plays an important, perhaps even a primary, role.

American public opinion on these matters seems less concerned with the penalty than with justice. For example, Americans are typically supportive of the death penalty, though support wanes when options for life without parole are provided or when the fairness of the death penalty is called into question. In the American public mind, cruelty is less of a concern than whether the punishment is proportionate and appropriate given the nature of the crime. The death penalty has subsequently had a longer stay in American jurisprudence than in comparable advanced democracies, principally because the American public supports its use.

The Amorphous Nature of Political Rights

Political rights are not static. They endure because they can be adapted to constantly evolving social, political, and economic norms. As the backdrop changes, so too does our interpretation of individual freedoms. The right to free speech, for example, is fundamentally different in 2014, an age of digital media and interactivity, than in 1800, the year Thomas Jefferson won election by campaigning against the Alien and Sedition Acts. None of the freedoms spelled out in the Bill of Rights mean what they did in 1791 when the first ten amendments to the Constitution were ratified.

Revolutions in technology, from the printing press to television to digital media, challenge existing definitions of free speech, privacy, unreasonable searches, and government surveillance. The noise of American politics has increased as the collective consequence of online communications is a virtual Tower of Babble in which voices compete to be heard above the endless chatter. At the same time, the ability of government to listen in on conversations, to track personal movements via GPS, or to watch public spaces via satellite or surveillance video has increased dramatically. All that we do or say can now be tracked at a level that was unthinkable not only in 1791 when the Founding Fathers were debating the Bill of Rights but just two decades ago. As the context for American politics shifts, so too must our definition of individual rights.

The enumeration of the Bill of Rights has meant that it is primarily the job of the courts, led by the Supreme Court, to interpret and reinterpret individual rights. This institutional arrangement is inherently undemocratic; rooted in a belief that legal knowledge—as opposed to democratic

Myth	How the Myth Defines Us	How the Myth Limits Us
We Need a Bill of Rights	We believe we are a nation of rights.	We are often too complacent in protecting individual rights believing they are static and already protected.
The Bill of Rights Applies Equally and to Everyone	We believe in equality as a principle and believe we have it in practice.	Too often, we fail to recognize inequalities in the application of rights, and incorrectly believe that rights protect us from employers, private businesses, and individuals.
No One Can Tell Me What to Say	We value the right to free expression and recognize its unique place in our constitutional system.	We are unwilling to extend these rights to disliked groups or unpopular individuals, and fail to connect the abstract idea of free speech to its specific application.
A Free Press is Independent from Government	We value the role of a free press in a democratic society, believing the news media should provide citizens with fair and objective information.	We fail to recognize the dependency of the news media on government (and vice versa), and we expect too much from the media. As a consequence, our trust in the media has fallen precipitously, and our current media system fuels polarization.
The United States is a Christian Nation	We connect deeply held religious identities to patriotism and citizenship.	We are willing to impose religious views on minority groups, often under the false pretense of Christian founding.
There is a Strict Wall of Separation	We recognize the role of religious toleration in society.	We fail to acknowledge the role that religion has played in American political development.

(Continued)

Myth	How the Myth Defines Us	How the Myth Limits Us
The Second Amendment Protects Us from Criminals	We believe in self-reliance and understand that government has limited role in protecting us in our homes.	We are often too quick to defensive postures, often justifying overreactions, particularly where there is a racial element. We are quick to downplay the role guns play in violent crime.
Too Many Criminals Get Off on Technicalities	We value security and justice, where justice is defined as guilty being punished for their crimes.	We fail to recognize the role of criminal law in suppressing political dissent, and make ourselves vulnerable to "law and order" candidates who whittle away at individual freedom.
We Believe in Privacy but let Government Search Our Home	We recognize the boundaries between the public and the private, and try to draw a line limiting government intrusion into our private lives.	Despite our belief in privacy, we believe that if you haven't done anything wrong, you shouldn't mind intrusions into private space.
Killing Isn't Cruel or Unusual	We believe that punishments should be proportionate to crimes, and that in general punishments should be humane.	We are generally supportive of the death penalty provided there is no torture involved, and don't mind locking up criminals and throwing away the key.

processes—is the best protector of individual liberty. There is some historical evidence to support the claim but the Supreme Court, like democratically elected legislatures, has been more than willing to narrowly define individual freedoms and limit the scope and applicability of the Bill of Rights. More to the point, as the composition of the court changes so too does the definition of individual freedom. Majorities change and the ideological fulcrum shifts and swings, as does the commitment to judicial activism relative to judicial restraint. As a result, the court cannot and does not speak with a single voice that transcends time and legal context, and their decisions are, like legislative policy decisions, the product of specific social, economic, and political context.

This means that rights are best protected not by a "parchment barrier" or even by an unelected panel of judges but by a public informed about why rights matter and deeply committed to protecting individual freedom. Yet, if we have learned anything from this investigation, it is that the public is uninformed, often lacking knowledge about the Bill of Rights specifically and politics more generally. The public is also misinformed, believing in much that is not true and resisting new information because it contradicts well-established and deeply rooted myths. In the context of an uninformed and misinformed public, our myths endure. They define us, rooting us in a larger narrative about who we are. Yet, they also limit us; and, in doing so, provide the potential for our freedoms to slowly and gradually slip away. Like the frog in slowly boiling water, we may not notice until it is too late.

Notes

1. "Guidelines for Public Video Surveillance: A Guide to Protecting Communities and Preserving Civil Liberties," *The Constitution Project*, 2007, available at http://www.constitutionproject.org/wp-content/uploads/2012/09/54.pdf (accessed on September 27, 2014).

2. "How the FBI Cracked the Boston Bombing Case," *CBS News*, April 15, 2014, available at http://www.cbsnews.com/videos/how-the-fbi-cracked-the-boston-bombing-case/ (accessed on September 27, 2014).

3. Peter Van Buren, "No Free Speech at Mr. Jefferson's Library," *Huffington Post*, November 28, 2011, available at http://www.huffingtonpost.com/peter-van-buren/no-free-speech-at-mr-jeff_b_1116884.html (accessed on September 27, 2014).

4. Mark Guarino, "Professor Fired for Israel Criticism Urges University of Illinois to Reinstate Him," *The Guardian*, September 9, 2014, available at http://www.theguardian.com/education/2014/sep/09/professor-israel-criticism-twitter-university-illinois (accessed on September 27, 2014).

5. "Next Time, What Say We Boil a Consultant," *Fast Company*, November 1995, available at http://www.fastcompany.com/26455/next-time-what-say-we-boil-consultant (accessed on September 20, 2014).

6. Christopher Ingraham, "You Really Can Get Pulled Over for Driving While Black, Federal Statistics Show," *Washington Post Wonkblog*, September 9, 2014, available at http://www.washingtonpost.com/blogs/wonkblog/wp/2014/09/09/you-really-can-get-pulled-over-for-driving-while-black-federal-statistics-show/ (accessed on September 20, 2014). The blog is based on the following report: Lynn Langston and Matthew Durose, "Police Behavior During Traffic and Street Stops, 2011," *Department of Justice: Bureau of Justice Statistics*, September 2013, available at http://www.bjs.gov/content/pub/pdf/pbtss11.pdf (accessed on September 20, 2014).

7. Mark Peffley and Jon Hurwitz, *Justice in America: The Separate Realities of Blacks and Whites* (Cambridge: Cambridge University Press, 2010).

8. "Stark Racial Divisions in Reactions to Ferguson Police Shooting," *Pew Center for the People & the Press*, August 18, 2014, available at http://www.people-press.org/2014/08/18/stark-racial-divisions-in-reactions-to-ferguson-police-shooting/ (accessed on September 21, 2014).

9. Geoffrey Stone, *Perilous Times: Free Speech in Wartime from the Sedition Act of 1798 to the War on Terrorism* (New York: W.W. Norton, 2005).

10. Christopher Weber and Matthew Thornton, "Courting Christians: How Political Candidates Prime Religious Considerations in Campaign Ads," *Journal of Politics* 74 (2012): 400–413.

11. Sanford Gordon, "Assessing Partisan Bias in Federal Public Corruption Prosecutions," *American Political Science Review* 103 (2009): 534–554.

Appendix

The Bill of Rights

1789 Joint Resolution of Congress Proposing 12 Amendments to the U.S. Constitution (from The National Archives)

On September 25, 1789, the First Congress of the United States proposed 12 amendments to the Constitution. The *1789 Joint Resolution of Congress* proposing the amendments is on display in the Rotunda in the National Archives Museum. Ten of the proposed 12 amendments were ratified by three-fourths of the state legislatures on December 15, 1791. The ratified Articles (Articles 3–12) constitute the first 10 amendments of the Constitution, or the *U.S. Bill of Rights*. In 1992, 203 years after it was proposed, Article 2 was ratified as the Twenty-Seventh Amendment to the Constitution. Article 1 was never ratified.

Transcription of the 1789 Joint Resolution of Congress Proposing 12 Amendments to the U.S. Constitution

Congress of the United States begun and held at the City of New-York, on Wednesday the fourth of March, one thousand seven hundred and eighty nine.

THE Conventions of a number of the States, having at the time of their adopting the Constitution, expressed a desire, in order to prevent misconstruction or abuse of its powers, that further declaratory and restrictive clauses should be added: And as extending the ground of public confidence in the Government, will best ensure the beneficent ends of its institution.

RESOLVED by the Senate and House of Representatives of the United States of America, in Congress assembled, two thirds of both Houses concurring, that the following Articles be proposed to the Legislatures of the several States, as amendments to the Constitution of the United States, all, or any of which Articles, when ratified by three fourths of the said

Legislatures, to be valid to all intents and purposes, as part of the said Constitution; viz.

ARTICLES in addition to, and Amendment of the Constitution of the United States of America, proposed by Congress, and ratified by the Legislatures of the several States, pursuant to the fifth Article of the original Constitution.

Article the first ... After the first enumeration required by the first article of the Constitution, there shall be one Representative for every thirty thousand, until the number shall amount to one hundred, after which the proportion shall be so regulated by Congress, that there shall be not less than one hundred Representatives, nor less than one Representative for every forty thousand persons, until the number of Representatives shall amount to two hundred; after which the proportion shall be so regulated by Congress, that there shall not be less than two hundred Representatives, nor more than one Representative for every fifty thousand persons.

Article the second ... No law, varying the compensation for the services of the Senators and Representatives, shall take effect, until an election of Representatives shall have intervened.

Article the third ... Congress shall make no law respecting an establishment of religion, or prohibiting the free exercise thereof; or abridging the freedom of speech, or of the press; or the right of the people peaceably to assemble, and to petition the Government for a redress of grievances.

Article the fourth ... A well regulated Militia, being necessary to the security of a free State, the right of the people to keep and bear Arms, shall not be infringed.

Article the fifth ... No Soldier shall, in time of peace be quartered in any house, without the consent of the Owner, nor in time of war, but in a manner to be prescribed by law.

Article the sixth ... The right of the people to be secure in their persons, houses, papers, and effects, against unreasonable searches and seizures, shall not be violated, and no Warrants shall issue, but upon probable cause, supported by Oath or affirmation, and particularly describing the place to be searched, and the persons or things to be seized.

Article the seventh ... No person shall be held to answer for a capital, or otherwise infamous crime, unless on a presentment or indictment of a Grand Jury, except in cases arising in the land or naval forces, or in the Militia, when in actual service in time of War or public danger; nor shall any person be subject for the same offence to be twice put in jeopardy of life or limb; nor shall be compelled in any criminal case to be a witness against himself, nor be deprived of life, liberty, or property, without due process of law; nor shall private property be taken for public use, without just compensation.

Article the eighth ... In all criminal prosecutions, the accused shall enjoy the right to a speedy and public trial, by an impartial jury of the State and district wherein the crime shall have been committed, which district shall have been previously ascertained by law, and to be informed of the nature and cause of the accusation; to be confronted with the witnesses against him; to have compulsory process for obtaining witnesses in his favor, and to have the Assistance of Counsel for his defence.

Article the ninth ... In suits at common law, where the value in controversy shall exceed twenty dollars, the right of trial by jury shall be preserved, and no fact tried by a jury, shall be otherwise re-examined in any Court of the United States, than according to the rules of the common law.

Article the tenth ... Excessive bail shall not be required, nor excessive fines imposed, nor cruel and unusual punishments inflicted.

Article the eleventh ... The enumeration in the Constitution, of certain rights, shall not be construed to deny or disparage others retained by the people.

Article the twelfth ... The powers not delegated to the United States by the Constitution, nor prohibited by it to the States, are reserved to the States respectively, or to the people.

ATTEST,

Frederick Augustus Muhlenberg, Speaker of the House of Representatives

John Adams, Vice-President of the United States, and President of the Senate

John Beckley, Clerk of the House of Representatives.

Sam. A Otis Secretary of the Senate

Amendments 11-27

Note: The capitalization and punctuation in this version is from the enrolled original of the Joint Resolution of Congress proposing the *Bill* *of Rights*, which is on *permanent display in the Rotunda of the National Archives Building*, Washington, D.C.

The Bill of Rights: A Transcription

The Preamble to The Bill of Rights

Congress of the United States begun and held at the City of New-York, on Wednesday the fourth of March, one thousand seven hundred and eighty nine.

THE Conventions of a number of the States, having at the time of their adopting the Constitution, expressed a desire, in order to prevent misconstruction or abuse of its powers, that further declaratory and restrictive clauses should be added: And as extending the ground of public confidence in the Government, will best ensure the beneficent ends of its institution.

RESOLVED by the Senate and House of Representatives of the United States of America, in Congress assembled, two thirds of both Houses concurring, that the following Articles be proposed to the Legislatures of the several States, as amendments to the Constitution of the United States, all, or any of which Articles, when ratified by three fourths of the said Legislatures, to be valid to all intents and purposes, as part of the said Constitution; viz.

ARTICLES in addition to, and Amendment of the Constitution of the United States of America, proposed by Congress, and ratified by the Legislatures of the several States, pursuant to the fifth Article of the original Constitution.

Note: The following text is a transcription of the first ten amendments to the Constitution in their original form. These amendments were ratified December 15, 1791, and form what is known as the "Bill of Rights."

Amendment I
Congress shall make no law respecting an establishment of religion, or prohibiting the free exercise thereof; or abridging the freedom of speech, or of the press; or the right of the people peaceably to assemble, and to petition the Government for a redress of grievances.

Amendment II
A well regulated Militia, being necessary to the security of a free State, the right of the people to keep and bear Arms, shall not be infringed.

Amendment III

No Soldier shall, in time of peace be quartered in any house, without the consent of the Owner, nor in time of war, but in a manner to be prescribed by law.

Amendment IV

The right of the people to be secure in their persons, houses, papers, and effects, against unreasonable searches and seizures, shall not be violated, and no Warrants shall issue, but upon probable cause, supported by Oath or affirmation, and particularly describing the place to be searched, and the persons or things to be seized.

Amendment V

No person shall be held to answer for a capital, or otherwise infamous crime, unless on a presentment or indictment of a Grand Jury, except in cases arising in the land or naval forces, or in the Militia, when in actual service in time of War or public danger; nor shall any person be subject for the same offence to be twice put in jeopardy of life or limb; nor shall be compelled in any criminal case to be a witness against himself, nor be deprived of life, liberty, or property, without due process of law; nor shall private property be taken for public use, without just compensation.

Amendment VI

In all criminal prosecutions, the accused shall enjoy the right to a speedy and public trial, by an impartial jury of the State and district wherein the crime shall have been committed, which district shall have been previously ascertained by law, and to be informed of the nature and cause of the accusation; to be confronted with the witnesses against him; to have compulsory process for obtaining witnesses in his favor, and to have the Assistance of Counsel for his defence.

Amendment VII

In Suits at common law, where the value in controversy shall exceed twenty dollars, the right of trial by jury shall be preserved, and no fact tried by a jury, shall be otherwise re-examined in any Court of the United States, than according to the rules of the common law.

Amendment VIII

Excessive bail shall not be required, nor excessive fines imposed, nor cruel and unusual punishments inflicted.

Amendment IX

The enumeration in the Constitution, of certain rights, shall not be construed to deny or disparage others retained by the people.

Amendment X

The powers not delegated to the United States by the Constitution, nor prohibited by it to the States, are reserved to the States respectively, or to the people.

Source: National Archives: http://www.archives.gov/exhibits/charters/bill_of_rights_transcript.html

List of Cases Cited

Abbington Township v. Schempp 374 U.S. 203 (1963)
Abrams v. United States (No. 316), 250 U.S. 616, November 10, 1919
Atkins v. Virginia 536 U.S. 304, 321 (2002)
Barron v. Baltimore 32 U.S. 243 (1833)
Benton v. Maryland 395 U.S. 784 (1969)
Board of Education v. Allen 392 U.S. 236 (1968)
Bradfield v. Roberts 175 U.S. 291 (1899)
Brown v. Board of Education 347 U.S. 483 (1954)
Board of Education v. Allen (1968) 392 U.S. 236 (1968)
Bowers v. Hardwick 478 U.S. 186
Buckley v. Valeo 424 U.S. 1 (1976)
Burwell v. Hobby Lobby Stores 573 U.S. ___ (2014)
Callins v. Collins 510 U.S. 1141 (1992).
Citizens United v. Federal Election Commission 558 U.S. ___ (2010)
City of Boerne v. Flores 521 U.S. 507 (1997)
City of Houston v. Hill 482 U.S. 451 (1987)
Chaplinsky v. New Hampshire 315 U.S. 568
Chicago, Burlington & Quincy Railroad Co. v. City of Chicago 166 U.S. 226 (1897)
Church of the Holy Trinity v. United States 143 U.S. 457 (1892)
Cohen v. California 403 U.S. 15 (1971)
Dist. of Columbia v. Heller 554 U.S. 570, 595 (2008)
Edwards v. Aguillard 482 U.S. 578 (1987)
Elk Grove Unified School District v. Newdow 542 U.S. 1 (2004)
Engel v. Vitale 370 U.S. 421 (1962)
Epperson v. Arkansas (1968) 393 U.S. 97 (1968)
Escobedo v. Illinois 378 U.S. 478 (1964)
Estelle v. Gamble 429 U.S. 97, 103 (1976)
Everson v. Board of Education 330 U.S. 1 (1947)
Ewing v. California 538 U.S. 11 (2003)
Farmer v. Brennan 511 U.S. 825, 832 (1994)
Francis v. Resweber 329 U.S. 459 ((1942) - case can be abbreviated to Chaplinsky v. New Hampshire 315 U.S. 568 (1942)1947)

214   List of Cases Cited

Furman v. Georgia 408 U.S. 238, 242 (1972)
Gideon v. Wainright 372 U.S. 335 (1963)
Gitlow v. New York 268 U.S. 652 (1925)
Good News Club v. Milford Central School (2001) 533 U.S. 98 (2001)
Gompers v. Buck's Stove and Range Co. 221 U.S. 418 (1911)
Graham v. West Virginia 224 U.S. 616 (1912)
Griswold v. Connecticut 381 U.S. 479 (1965)
Harmelin v Michigan 501 U.S. 957, 968 (1991)
Harris v. New York 401 U.S. 222 (1971)
Herring v. United States 555 U.S. 135 (2009)
Hudson v. McMillian 503 U.S. 1 (1992)
Hudson v. Michigan 547 U.S. 586 (2006)
Hudson v. Palmer 468 U.S. 517, 526-527 (1984)
Hustler Magazine, Inc. v. Falwell 485 U.S. 46 (1988)
Hurtado v. California 110 U.S. 516 (1884)
Illinois v. Perkins 496 U.S. 292 (1990)
Illinois v. Gates 462 U.S. 213 (1983)
In re Kemmler 136 U.S. 436 (1890)
Jacobellis v. Ohio 472 U.S. 38 (1985)
Jane Doe v. Action-Boxborough Regional School District 468 Mass. 64 (2014)
Katz v. United States 389 U.S. 347 (1967)
Kyllo v. United States 533 U.S. 27 (2001)
Lamb's Chapel v. Center Moriches Union Free School District 508 U.S. 384 (1993)
Lawrence v. Texas 539 U.S. 558 (2003)
Lee v. Weisemen 505 U.S. 577 (1992)
Lemon v. Kurtzman 403 U.S. 602 (1971)
Lewis v. U.S. 445 U.S. 55, 65 n. 8 (1980)
Mapp v. Ohio 367 U.S. 643 (1961)
Maxwell v. Dow 176 U.S. 581 (1900)
McCollum v. Board of Education 333 U.S. 203 (1948)
McDonald v. City of Chicago 130 S. Ct. 3020, 3030 (2010)
Meyer v. Nebraska 262 U.S. 390 (1923)
Miller v. California 413 U.S. 15 (1973)
Minersville School District v. Gobitis 310 U.S. 586 (1940)
Miranda v. Arizona 384 U.S. 436 (1966)
Missouri v. McNeely 133 S. Ct. 1552 (2013)
Moran v. Burbine 475 U.S. 412 (1986)
Mutual Film Corporation v. Industrial Commission of Ohio 236 U.S. 230 (1915)
New York v. Quarles 467 U.S. 649 (1984)
New York Times Co. v. Sullivan 376 U.S. 254 (1964)
Olmstead v. United States 277 U.S. 438 (1928)
Palko v. Connecticut 302 U.S. 319 (1937)

Penry v. Lynaugh 492 U.S. 302, 340 (1989)
Pierce v. Society of Sisters 68 U.S. 510 (1925)
Presser v. Illinois 116 U.S. 252 (1886)
Reynolds v. Simms 377 U.S. 533 (1964)
Reynolds v. United States (1879) 98 U.S. 145 (1879)
Rhodes v. Chapman 452 U.S. 337, 349 (1981)
Riley v. California 573 U.S. ___ (2014)
Roberson v. Rochester Folding Box Co 64 N.E. 442 (NY 1902)
Rosenberger v. University of Virginia 515 U.S. 819 (1995)
Roe v. Wade 410 U.S. 113 (1973)
Roper v. Simmons 543 U.S. 551, 578 (2005)
Rummel v. Estelle 445 U.S. 263 (1980)
Santa Fe Independent School District v. Doe 530 U.S. 290 (2000)
Schenck v. United States 249 U.S. 47 (1919)
Skinner v. Oklahoma 316 U.S. 535 (1942)
Snyder v. Phelps 562 U.S. ___ (2011)
Stanford v. Kentucky 492 U.S. 361, 380 (1989)
Stanley v. Georgia 394 U.S. 557 (1969)
Territory v. Ketchum 65 P. 169 (N.M. 1901)
Texas v. Johnson 491 U.S. 397 (1989)
Trop v. Dulles 356 U.S. 86 (1958)
Twining v. New Jersey 211 U.S. 78 (1908)
United States v. Cruikshank 92 U.S. 542, 544-545 (1875)
United States v. Jackson 390 U.S. 570 (1968)
United States v. Macintosh 283 U.S. 605 (1931)
United States v. Miller 307 U.S. 174 (1939)
United States v. Patane 542 U.S. 630 (2004)
Wallace v. Jaffree (1985) 472 U.S. 38 (1985)
Weems v. United States 217 U.S. at 378
Wilkerson v. Utah 99 U.S. 130 (1878)
Witherspoon v. Illinois 391 U.S. 510 (1968)
Zelman v. Simmons-Harris (2002) 536 U.S. 639 (2002)
Zorach v. Clausen 343 U.S. 306 (1952)

Bibliography

Abernathy, M. G. (1983). Should the United Kingdom Adopt a Bill of Rights? *The American Journal of Comparative Law, 31*(3), 431–479. doi: 10.2307/839986

Allan, J. (1996). Bills of Rights and Judicial Power: A Liberal's Quandary. *Oxford Journal of Legal Studies, 16*(2), 337–352. doi: 10.2307/764748

Amar, A. R. (1998). *The Bill of Rights: Creation and reconstruction.* New Haven: Yale University Press.

Amar, A. R. (2007). Creation, Reconstruction, and Interpretation of the Bill of Rights. In B. A. Shain (Ed.), *The nature of rights at the American founding and beyond* (pp. 163–180). Charlottesville: University of Virginia Press.

Balko, R. (2011). Myths of the Criminal Justice System: Part 2. *Huffington Post.* Retrieved September 3, 2014, from http://www.huffingtonpost.com/2011/06/22/myths-of-the-criminal-justice-system-part-two_n_881975.html

Battaglia, N. A. (2012). The Casey Anthony Trial and Wrongful Exonerations: How "Trial by Media" Diminishes Public Confidence in the Criminal Justice System. *Albany Law Review, 75*(3), 1579–1611.

Baumgartner, F. R., De Boef, S., & Boydstun, A. E. (2008). *The decline of the death penalty and the discovery of innocence.* Cambridge/New York: Cambridge University Press.

Beard, C. A. (1913). *An economic interpretation of the Constitution of the United States.* New York: The Macmillan Company.

Becker, M. E. (1992). The Politics of Women's Wrongs and the Bill of "Rights": A Bicentennial Perspective. *The University of Chicago Law Review, 59*(1), 453–517. doi: 10.2307/1599943

Bennett, L. (1990). Toward a Theory of Press-State Relations. *Journal of Communication, 40*, 103–125.

Berdejo, C., & Yuchtman, N. (2013). Crime, Punishment, and Politics: An Analysis of Political Cycles in Criminal Sentencing. *Review of Economics and Statistics, 95*, 741–756.

Birkland, T. A., & Lawrence, R. G. (2009). Media Framing and Policy Change after Columbine. *American Behavioral Scientist, 52*(10), 1405–1425.

Blackmon, D. A. (2008). *Slavery by another name: The re-enslavement of Black people in America from the Civil War to World War II* (1st ed.). New York: Doubleday.

Bork, R. (1971). Neutral Principles and Some First Amendment Problems. *Indiana Law Journal, 47,* 1–36.

Bosmajian, H. A. (1992). *Metaphor and reason in judicial opinions.* Carbondale: Southern Illinois University Press.

Brennan, W. J., Jr. (1989). Why Have a Bill of Rights? *Oxford Journal of Legal Studies, 9*(4), 425–440. doi: 10.2307/764241

Brewer, P. R. (2008). *Value war: Public opinion and the politics of gay rights.* Lanham: Rowman & Littlefield Publishers.

A Brief History of the NRA. *National Rifle Association.* Retrieved October 4, 2014, from https://www.nrahq.org/history.asp

Burstein, A., & Isenberg, N. (2013). *Madison and Jefferson* (2013 Random House Trade Paperback ed.). New York: Random House Trade Paperbacks.

Butler, P. D. (2013). Poor People Lose: Gideon and the Critique of Rights. *Yale Law Journal, 122,* 2176–2204.

Callaghan, K., & Schnell, F. (2001). Assessing the Democratic Debate: How the News Media Frame Elite Policy Discourse. *Political Communication, 18*(2), 183–213. doi: 10.1080/105846001750322970

Campbell, T., Goldsworthy, J. D., & Stone, A. (2006). *Protecting rights without a Bill of Rights: Institutional performance and reform in Australia.* Aldershot/Burlington: Ashgate.

Carey, G. (2011). Due Process. *First Principles.* Retrieved September 2, 2014, from http://www.firstprinciplesjournal.com/articles.aspx?article=867

Carr, D. (2013). Whistle-Blowers in Limbo, neither Hero Nor Traitor. *New York Times.* Retrieved August 31, 2014, from http://www.nytimes.com/2013/08/01/business/media/whistle-blowers-in-limbo-neither-hero-nor-traitor.html?_r=0

Carter, J. (1979). Crisis of Confidence. *American Experience.* Retrieved August 6, 2014, from http://www.pbs.org/wgbh/americanexperience/features/primary-resources/carter-crisis/

Chafetz, J. A. (2007). *Democracy's privileged few: Legislative privilege and democratic norms in the British and American constitutions.* New Haven: Yale University Press.

Chemerinsky, E. (2007). Rediscovering Brandeis' Right to Privacy. *Brandeis Law Journal, 45,* 643–657.

Chesterton, G. K. (1923). *What I saw in America.* London: Hodder and Stoughton, Limited.

Cole, D. (2003). Are Foreign Nationals Entitled to the Same Constitutional Rights as Citizens? *Thomas Jefferson Law Review, 25,* 367–388.

Conkle, D. (1988). Toward a General Theory of the Establishment Clause. *Northwestern University Law Review, 82,* 1113–1194.

Cornell, S. (2006). Mobs, Militias, and Magistrates: Popular Constitutionalism and the Whiskey Rebellion. *Chicago-Kent Law Review, 81*, 883–903.

Converse, P. (1964). The Nature of Belief Systems in Mass Publics. In D. Apter (Ed.), *Ideology and Discontent* (pp. 2012–2261). New York: Free Press.

Cook, T. E. (1998). *Governing with the news: The news media as a political institution.* Chicago: University of Chicago Press.

Craig, B. H., & O'Brien, D. M. (1993). *Abortion and American politics.* Chatham: Chatham House.

Critchlow, D. T. & Stachecki, C. L. (2008). The equal rights amendment reconsidered: Politics, Policy and social mobilization in a democracy. *Journal of Policy History* 20 (1): 157-176.

Cuddihy, W. J. (2009). *The Fourth Amendment: Origins and original meaning, 602–1791.* Oxford/New York: Oxford University Press.

Davis, D. (2010). *The Oxford handbook of church and state in the United States.* New York: Oxford University Press.

Davis, D. (2010). Religious Pluralism as the Essential Foundation of America's Quest for Unity and Order. In D. Davis (Ed.), *The Oxford handbook of church and state in the United States* (pp. 3–20). New York: Oxford University Press.

Davis, D. H. (1994, Spring). Religious Pluralism and the Quest for Unity in American Life, Editorial. *Journal of Church & State,* 245. Retrieved from http://lib-ezproxy.tamu.edu:2048/login?url=http://search.ebscohost.com/login.aspx?direct=true&db=a9h&AN=9502160135&site=ehost-live

Davis, D. W. (2007). *Negative liberty: Public opinion and the terrorist attacks on America.* New York: Russell Sage Foundation.

Davis, D. W., & Silver, B. D. (2004). Civil Liberties vs. Security: Public Opinion in the Context of the Terrorist Attacks on America. *American Journal of Political Science, 48*(1), 28–46. doi: 10.1111/j.0092-5853.2004.00054.x

Davis, J. (1975). Communism, Conformity, Cohorts, and Categories: American Tolerance in 1954 and 1972–3. *American Journal of Sociology, 81,* 491–513.

Debs, E. (1918). The Canton, Ohio, Anti-War Speech. Retrieved May 7, 2014, from https://www.marxists.org/archive/debs/works/1918/canton.htm

Dey, E., Ott, M., Antonaros, M., Barnhardt, C., & Holsapple, M. (2010). *Engaging diverse viewpoints: What is the campus climate for perspective taking?* Washington, DC: Association of American Colleges and Universities.

Dimock, M., Doherty, C., & Tyson, A. (2013). Amid Criticism, Support for Media's "Watchdog" Stands Out. *Pew Center for the People & the Press.* Retrieved July 17, 2014, from http://www.people-press.org/2013/08/08/amid-criticism-support-for-medias-watchdog-role-stands-out/

Drake, B. (2014). 5 Facts about the NRA and Guns in America. *FACTANK: News in the Numbers.* Retrieved September 19, 2014, from http://www.pewresearch.org/fact-tank/2014/04/24/5-facts-about-the-nra-and-guns-in-america/

D'Souza, D., & Campanella, J. (1991). *Illiberal education the politics of race and sex on campus* [sound recording]. Beverly Hills: Dove Audio.

Dunaway, J. (2008). Markets, Ownership, and the Quality of Campaign News Coverage. *The Journal of Politics, 70*(4), 1193–1202. doi: 10.2307/30219493

Dworkin, A. (1989). *Pornography: Men possessing women* (Pbk. ed.). New York: E.P. Dutton.

Foundation for Individual Rights in Education. "Spotlight on Speech Codes 2014: The State of Free Speech on Our Nation's Campuses" retrieved May 25, 2015. Available at http://issuu.com/thefireorg/docs/2014_speech_code_report_final

Ellsberg, D. (2013). Edward Snowden: Saving us from the United States of America. *The Guardian*. Retrieved August 29, 2014, from http://www.theguardian.com/commentisfree/2013/jun/10/edward-snowden-united-stasi-america

Ely, E. S. (1828). *The duty of Christian freemen to elect Christian rulers*. Philadelphia: W.F. Geddes. n. p.

Ely, J. H. (1980). *Democracy and distrust: A theory of judicial review*. Cambridge: Harvard University Press.

Ely, J. J. W. (1999). The Oxymoron Reconsidered: Myth and Reality in the Origins of Substantive Due Process. *Constitutional Commentary, 16*(2), 315.

Enns, P. (2013). *Public opinion and mass incarceration in the U.S. States*. Paper presented at the American Political Science Association, Chicago, IL.

Epp, C. R. (1996). Do Bills of Rights Matter? The Canadian Charter of Rights and Freedoms. *The American Political Science Review, 90*(4), 765–779. doi: 10.2307/2945841

Epp, C. R. (1998). *The rights revolution: Lawyers, activists, and supreme courts in comparative perspective*. Chicago: University of Chicago Press.

Epstein, L. (1995). *Contemplating courts*. Washington, DC: CQ Press.

Epstein, L., Parker, C., & Segal, J. (2013). *Do justices defend speech they hate? In-group bias, opportunism, and the first amendment*. Paper presented at the American Political Science Association, Chicago, IL.

Epstein, L., & Walker, T. G. (2010). *Constitutional law for a changing America. Rights, liberties, and justice* (7th ed.). Washington, DC: CQ Press.

Fahri, P. (2014). And Minder Makes Three: For White House Interviews, It's Never Just One-on-One. *Washington Post*. Retrieved July 23, 2014, from http://www.washingtonpost.com/lifestyle/style/and-minder-makes-three-for-white-house-interviews-its-never-just-one-on-one/2014/07/23/678b5e34-1084-11e4-98ee-daea85133bc9_story.html

Farkas, S., Johnson, J., & Duffett, A. (2002). Knowing it by Heart: The Constitution & its Meaning Survey. Retrieved February 2, 2014, from http://www.publicagenda.org/files/knowing_by_heart.pdf

Fassett, J. D., Pollock, E. E., Prettyman, E. B. J., Sander, F. E. A., & Barrett, J. Q. (2004). Supreme Court Law Clerks' Recollections of Brown v. Board of Education. *St. John's Law Review, 78*(3), 515–568.

Finkelman, P. (1990). James Madison and the Bill of Rights: A Reluctant Paternity. *The Supreme Court Review, 1990,* 301–347. doi: 10.2307/3109663

Finkelman, P. (1994). Thomas Jefferson and Antislavery: The Myth Goes On. *The Virginia Magazine of History and Biography, 102*(2), 193–228. doi: 10.2307/4249430

Franklin, C., & Kosaki, L. (1995). Media, Knowledge, and Public Evaluations of the Supreme Court. In L. Epstein (Ed.), *Contemplating courts* (pp. xix, 499). Washington, DC: CQ Press.

Franklin, D. (2014). Framing the Danger of Guns as a Public Health Risk Will Change the Debate Over Gun Control. *Washington Post.* Retrieved September 19, 2014, from http://www.washingtonpost.com/opinions/framing-the-danger-of-guns-as-a-public-health-risk-will-change-the-debate-over-gun-control/2014/05/02/e4a73490-cf27-11e3-a6b1-45c4dffb85a6_story.html

Friedman, B. (2009). *The will of the people: How public opinion has influenced the Supreme Court and shaped the meaning of the Constitution* (1st ed.). New York: Farrar, Straus and Giroux.

Friedman, T. L. (2005). *The world is flat: A brief history of the twenty-first century* (1st ed.). New York: Farrar, Straus and Giroux.

Frost, N. (2010). Beyond public opinion polls: Punitive sentiment & criminal justice policy. *Sociology Compass, 4,* 156–161.

Futrelle, D. (2012). Sex on the Internet: Sizing Up the Online Smut Economy. *Time.* Retrieved May 29, 2014, from http://business.time.com/2012/04/04/sex-on-the-internet-sizing-up-the-online-smut-economy/

Gerbner, G., & Gross, L. (1976). Living with Television: The Violence Profile. *Journal of Communication, 26,* 172–199.

Gilliam, F. D., Jr., & Iyengar, S. (2000). Prime Suspects: The Influence of Local Television News on the Viewing Public. *American Journal of Political Science, 44*(3), 560.

Glendon, M. A. (1991). *Rights talk: The impoverishment of political discourse.* New York/Toronto: Free Press/Collier Macmillan/Maxwell Macmillan.

Godin, S. (2011). *We are all weird the myth of mass and the end of compliance.* Brilliance Audio on compact disc [sound recording]. Grand Haven: Brilliance Audio.

Goidel, R. K., Freeman, C. M., & Procopio, S. T. (2006). The Impact of Television Viewing on Perceptions of Juvenile Crime. *Journal of Broadcasting & Electronic Media, 50*(1), 119–139. doi: 10.1207/s15506878jobem5001_7

Goldwin, R. (1997). *From parchment to power: How James Madison used the Bill of Rights to save the Constitution.* Washington, DC: AEI Press.

Gordon, S. C. (2009). Assessing Partisan Bias in Federal Public Corruption Prosecutions. *American Political Science Review, 103*(4), 534–554. doi: 10.1017/S0003055409990207

Green, S. K. (2012). The Second Disestablishment: The Evolution of Nineteenth-Century Understanding of Separation of Church and State. In T. J. Gunn &

J. Witte (Eds.), *No establishment of religion: America's original contribution to religious liberty* (pp. 280–306). New York: Oxford University Press.

Greene, J. (2012). Fourteenth Amendment Originalism. *Maryland Law Review, 71*, 978–1014.

Gross, K. (2008). Framing Persuasive Appeals: Episodic and Thematic Framing, Emotional Response, and Policy Opinion. *Political Psychology, 29*(2), 169–192. doi: 10.2307/20447111

Guarino, M. (2014). Professor Fired for Israel Criticism Urges University of Illinois to Reinstate Him. *The Guardian.* Retrieved September 27, 2014, from http://www.theguardian.com/education/2014/sep/09/professor-israel-criticism-twitter-university-illinois

Guliuzza, F. (1994). The Supreme Court, the Establishment Clause and Incoherence. In L. E. Lugo (Ed.), *Religion, public life, and the American polity* (pp. 115–144). Knoxville: University of Tennessee Press.

Gunn, T. J., & Witte, J. (2012). *No establishment of religion: America's original contribution to religious liberty.* New York: Oxford University Press.

Gunther, G. (1969). *John Marshall's defense of McCulloch v. Maryland.* Stanford: Stanford University Press.

Haider-Markel, D. P., Querze, A., & Lindaman, K. (2007). Lose, Win, or Draw? A Reexamination of Direct Democracy and Minority Rights. *Political Research Quarterly, 60*(2), 304–314. doi: 10.2307/4623831

Hamburger, P. (2002). *Separation of church and state.* Cambridge: Harvard University Press.

Hamilton, A., Madison, J., Jay, J., & Beeman, R. R. (2012). *The Federalist papers.* New York: Penguin Books.

Hamilton, J. (2004). *All the news that's fit to sell: How the market transforms information into news.* Princeton: Princeton University Press.

Haynes, C. (2012). 50 Years Later, how School-Prayer Ruling Changed America. *First Amendment Center.* Retrieved September 4, 2014, from http://www.firstamendmentcenter.org/50-years-later-how-school-prayer-ruling-changed-america

Herbst, S. (2010). *Rude democracy: Civility and incivility in American politics.* Philadelphia: Temple University Press.

Himberger, D., Gaylin, D., Thompson, T., Agiesta, J., & Kelly, J. (2011). Civil Liberties and Security 10 Years after 9/11. Retrieved April 27, 2014, from http://www.apnorc.org/projects/Pages/Civil-Liberties-and-Security.aspx

Hindman, M. S. (2009). *The myth of digital democracy.* Princeton: Princeton University Press.

Hirsch, P. (1980). The 'Scary World' of the Nonviewer and other Anomalies of Gerbner et al.'s Findings of Cultivation Analysis. *Communication Research, 7*, 403–456.

Hodel, G. (1997). Hung Out to Dry: 'Dark Alliance' Series Dies. *The Consortium.* Retrieved July 17, 2014, from http://www.consortiumnews.com/archive/crack9.html

Hoff-Wilson, J. (1987). The Unfinished Revolution: Changing Legal Status of U.S. Women. *Signs, 13*(1), 7–36. doi: 10.2307/3174025

Hoff-Wilson, J. (1989). Women in American Constitutional History at the Bicentennial. *The History Teacher, 22*(2), 145–176. doi: 10.2307/493969

Holcomb, J., Mitchell, A., & Rosentiel, T. (2012). Cable by the Numbers. *The State of the News Media 2012.* from http://stateofthemedia.org/2012/cable-cnn-ends-its-ratings-slide-fox-falls-again/cable-by-the-numbers/

Horowitz, D. (2006). *The professors: The 101 most dangerous academics in America.* Washington, DC/Lanham: Regnery Publishing/Distributed to the trade by National Book Network.

Hutson, J. H. (1999). Thomas Jefferson's Letter to the Danbury Baptists: A Controversy Rejoined. *The William and Mary Quarterly, 56*(4), 775–790. doi: 10.2307/2674235

Ingraham, C. (2014). You Really Can Get Pulled Over for Driving While Black, Federal Statistics Show. *Washington Post Wonkblog.* Retrieved September 20, 2014, from http://www.washingtonpost.com/blogs/wonkblog/wp/2014/09/09/you-really-can-get-pulled-over-for-driving-while-black-federal-statistics-show/

Iyengar, S., Norpoth, H., & Hahn, K. S. (2004). Consumer Demand for Election News: The Horserace Sells. *The Journal of Politics, 66*(1), 157–175. doi: 10.2307/3449777

Jäntti, M., Bratsberg, B., Røed, K., Raaum, O., Naylor, R., Österbacka, E., . . . Eriksson, T. (2006). American Exceptionalism in a New Light: A Comparison of Intergenerational Earnings Mobility in the Nordic Countries, the United Kingdom and the United States. Institute for the Study of Labor, IZA Discussion Paper No. 1938, retrieved December 6, 2014 from http://ftp.iza.org/dp1938.pdf.

Jefferson, T. (1801). First Inaugural Address in the Washington, D.C. Retrieved April 27, 2014, from http://www.bartleby.com/124/pres16.html

Jefferson, T. (1802). Jefferson's Letter to the Danbury Baptists. Retrieved August 6, 2014 from http://www.loc.gov/loc/lcib/9806/danpre.html..

Johnson, B. (2014). 7 Ways the World Went Crazy With 'As Nasty As They Wanna Be'. *Time.* Retrieved June 14, 2014, from http://www.rollingstone.com/music/news/7-ways-the-world-went-crazy-with-as-nasty-as-they-wanna-be-20140207

Jurow, K. (1975). Untimely Thoughts: A Reconsideration of the Origins of Due Process of Law. *The American Journal of Legal History, 19*(4), 265–279. doi: 10.2307/845053

Kates, D. B. (1986). The Second Amendment: A Dialogue. *Law and Contemporary Problems, 49*(1), 143–150. doi: 10.2307/1191614

Kim, Y., Chen, H.-T., & Zuniga, H. (2013). Stumbling upon News on the Internet: Effects of Incidental News Exposure and Relative Entertainment Use on Political Engagement. *Computers in Human Behavior, 29*, 2607–2614.

King, G. (2008). Cruel and Unusual History. *New York Times*. Retrieved September 19, 2014, from http://www.nytimes.com/2008/04/23/opinion/23king.html?_r=0

Kobylka, J. (1995). The Mysterious Case of Establishment Clause Litigation: How Organized Litigants Foiled Legal Change. In L. Epstein (Ed.), *Contemplating courts* (pp. 93–129). Washington, DC: CQ Press.

Kors, A. C., & Silverglate, H. A. (1998). *The shadow university: The betrayal of liberty on America's campuses.* New York: Free Press.

Kristol, I. (1971). Pornography, Obscenity, and the Case for Censorship. *New York Times Magazine*. Retrieved June 6, 2014, from http://www.rense.com/general87/obscenity.htm

Lambert, F. (2008). *Religion in American politics: A short history.* Princeton: Princeton University Press.

Langston, L., & Durose, M. (2013). *Police Behavior During Traffic and Street Stops, 2011.* Retrieved from http://www.bjs.gov/content/pub/pdf/pbtss11.pdf

Lawrence, L. (2013). School Prayer: 50 Years after the Ban, God and Faith more Present than Ever. *Christian Science Monitor*. Retrieved September 2, 2014, from http://www.csmonitor.com/The-Culture/Family/2013/0616/School-prayer-50-years-after-the-ban-God-and-faith-more-present-than-ever

Lepore, J. (2006). The Sharpened Quill. *The New Yorker*. Retrieved September 4, 2014 from http://www.newyorker.com/magazine/2006/10/16/the-sharpened-quill.

Lewis, A. (1964). *Gideon's trumpet.* New York: Random House.

Lewis, D. C. (2013). *Direct democracy and minority rights: A critical assessment of the tyranny of the majority in the American states.* New York: Routledge.

Lipka, M. (2013). South Carolina valedictorian Reignites Debate on Prayer in school. *Pew Research Center: Fact Tank*. Retrieved September 2, 2014, from http://www.pewresearch.org/fact-tank/2013/06/13/south-carolina-valedictorian-reignites-debate-on-prayer-in-school/

Lipset, S. M. (1996). *American exceptionalism: A double-edged sword.* New York: W.W. Norton.

Liptak, A. (2014). For Justices, Free Speech Often Means 'Speech I Agree With'. *New York Times*. Retrieved May 6, 2014, from http://www.nytimes.com/2014/05/06/us/politics/in-justices-votes-free-speech-often-means-speech-i-agree-with.html?_r=0

Liptak, A., & Schmidt, M. (2013). Judge Upholds N.S.A.'s Bulk Collection of Data on Calls. *New York Times*. Retrieved September 18, 2014, from http://www

.nytimes.com/2013/12/28/us/nsa-phone-surveillance-is-lawful-federal-judge-rules.html?ref=us&pagewanted=all&_r=0

Lock, S. (1999). *Crime, public opinion, and civil liberties: The tolerant public*. Westport: Praeger.

Lodge, M., McGraw, K., & Stroh, P. (1989). An Impression-Driven Model of Candidate Evaluation. *American Political Science Review, 83*, 399–419.

Lott, J. R. (2003). *The bias against guns: Why almost everything you've heard about gun control is wrong*. Washington/Lanham: Regnery Pub/Distributed to the trade by National Book Network.

Lott, J. R. (2010). *More guns, less crime: Understanding crime and gun-control laws* (3rd ed.). Chicago: The University of Chicago Press.

Lugo, L. E. (1994). *Religion, public life, and the American polity*. Knoxville: University of Tennessee Press.

Lukianoff, G. (2014). *Unlearning liberty: Campus censorship and the end of American debate* (Paperback edition. ed.). New York: Encounter Books.

Lyles, K. L. (1997). *The gatekeepers: Federal district courts in the political process*. Westport: Praeger.

Malcolm, J. L. (1983). The Right to Keep and Bear Arms: The Common Law Tradition. *Hastings Constitutional Law, 10*(2), 285–314.

Malcolm, J. L. (1994). *To keep and bear arms: The origins of an Anglo-American right*. Cambridge: Harvard University Press.

Marty, M. (2012). Getting Beyond the "Myth of a Christian America". In T. J. Gunn & J. Witte (Eds.), *No establishment of religion: America's original contribution to religious liberty* (pp. 364–378). New York: Oxford University Press.

Matthews, R. (2005). The Myth of Punitiveness. *Theoretical Criminology, 9*(2), 175–201. doi: 10.1177/1362480605051639

Matthews, R. K. (1984). *The radical politics of Thomas Jefferson: A revisionist view*. Lawrence: University Press of Kansas.

McChesney, R. W. (2013). *Digital disconnect: How capitalism is turning the Internet against democracy*. New York: The New Press.

McClosky, H. (1964). Consensus and Ideology in American Politics. *The American Political Science Review, 58*(2), 361–382. doi: 10.2307/1952868

McCluskey, J. H. (1987). *Law, justice, and democracy*. London: Sweet & Maxwell/BBC Books.

McGuire, K. T., & Stimson, J. A. (2004). The Least Dangerous Branch Revisited: New Evidence on Supreme Court Responsiveness to Public Preferences. *The Journal of Politics, 66*(4), 1018–1035. doi: 10.2307/3449527

Miller, J. C. (1951). *Crisis in freedom: The Alien and Sedition acts* (1st ed.). Boston: Little, Brown.

Moore, D. (2005). Public Favors Voluntary Prayer for Public Schools. *Gallup*. Retrieved August 21, 2014, from http://www.gallup.com/poll/18136/public-favors-voluntary-prayer-public-schools.aspx

Musgrove, W. (2008). Substantive Due Process: A History of Liberty in the Due Process Clause. *University of St. Thomas Journal of Law & Public Policy, 2*, 125–140.

Mustain, J. (2013). Sheriff's Office Sets Up Park Stakeouts to Ensare Gay Men. *The Baton Rouge Advocate*. Retrieved February 17, 2014, from http://the advocate.com/news/police/6580728-123/gays-in-baton-rouge-arrested

Mutz, D. C. (2007). Effects of "In-Your-Face" Television Discourse on Perceptions of a Legitimate Opposition. *The American Political Science Review, 101* (4), 621–635. doi: 10.2307/27644475

Nimmo, D. D., & Combs, J. E. (1980). *Subliminal politics: Myths & mythmakers in America*. Englewood Cliffs: Prentice-Hall.

Norpoth, H., & Segal, J. (1994). Popular Influence on Supreme Court Decisions. *The American Political Science Review, 88*(3), 711–724. doi: 10.2307/2944805

Nunn, C. Z., Crockett, H. J., & Williams, J. A. (1978). *Tolerance for nonconformity* (1st ed.). San Francisco: Jossey-Bass Publishers.

Nyhan, B., & Jason, R. (2010). When Corrections Fail: The Persistence of Political Misperceptions. *Political Behavior, 32*(2), 303–330. doi: 10.2307/40587320

Nyhan, B., Jason, R., & Ubel, P. A. (2013). The Hazards of Correcting Myths about Health Care Reform. *Medical Care, 51*(2), 127–132. doi: 10.2307/41714666

Obama's NSA Speech Has Little Impact on Skeptical Public. (2014). *Pew Center for the People & the Press*. Retrieved August 26, 2014, from http://www.people-press.org/2014/01/20/obamas-nsa-speech-has-little-impact-on-skeptical-public/

Opinion.Org, W. P. (2009). World Public Opinion: A Study of 24 Nations. Retrieved April 28, 2014, from http://www.ipu.org/idd-e/report09.pdf

O'Rourke, P. J. (2014). Who Actually Wants this Bill of Rights? *Daily Beast*. Retrieved August 6, 2014, from http://www.thedailybeast.com/articles/2014/04/12/p-j-o-rourke-who-really-actually-wants-this-bill-of-rights.html

Paine, T. (2004). *The age of reason: Being an investigation of true and fabulous theology (edited by Moncure Daniel Conway)*. Mineola: Dover Publications.

Paine, T., & Harry Houdini Collection (Library of Congress). (1891). *Age of reason: Being an investigation of true and fabulous theology*. New York: Peter Eckler, publisher.

Parry, R. (2006). Gary Webb's Death: American Tragedy. *Consortium News*. Retrieved June 19, 2014, from http://www.consortiumnews.com/2006/120906.html

Paterno, S. (2005). The Sad Saga of Gary Webb. *American Journalism Review*. Retrieved June 19, 2014, from http://ajrarchive.org/article.asp?id=3874

Patterson, T. E. (1993). *Out of order* (1st ed.). New York: A. Knopf.

Patterson, T. E. (2013). *Informing the news: The need for knowledge-based journalism*. New York: Vintage Books, A Division of Random House LLC.

Paulsen, M. S. (1997). Dirty Harry and the Real Constitution. *University of Chicago Law Review, 64*(4), 1457.

Paulson, K. (2013). America's Favorite Freedom. *State of the First Amendment Survey Report*. Retrieved December 6, 2013, from http://www.firstamendment center.org/sofa

Peffley, M., & Hurwitz, J. (2010). *Justice in America: The separate realities of blacks and whites*. Cambridge/New York: Cambridge University Press.

Popkin, S. L. (1994). *The reasoning voter: Communication and persuasion in presidential campaigns* (2nd ed.). Chicago: University of Chicago Press.

A Powerful Rebuke of Mass Surveillance. (2013). *New York Times*. Retrieved September 18, 2014, from http://www.nytimes.com/2013/12/17/opinion/a-powerful-rebuke-of-mass-surveillance.html?_r=1&

Primus, R. A. (1999). *The American language of rights*. Cambridge/New York: Cambridge University Press.

Prior, M. (2007). *Post-broadcast democracy: How media choice increases inequality in political involvement and polarizes elections*. New York: Cambridge University Press.

Prothro, J. W., & Grigg, C. M. (1960). Fundamental Principles of Democracy: Bases of Agreement and Disagreement. *The Journal of Politics, 22*(2), 276–294. doi: 10.2307/2127359

Rabban, D. M. (1981). The First Amendment in Its Forgotten Years. *The Yale Law Journal, 90*(3), 514–595. doi: 10.2307/795918

Rabban, D. M. (1997). *Free speech in its forgotten years*. Cambridge/New York: Cambridge University Press.

Rakove, J. (1988). James Madison and the Bill of Rights. *This Constitution: A Bicentennial Chronicle*. Retrieved August 6, 2014, from http://oldapsa.apsanet.org/imgtest/JamesMadison.pdf

The Right to Privacy in Nineteenth Century America. (1981). *Harvard Law Review, 94*(8), 1892–1910. doi: 10.2307/1340739

Rights, C. o. t. B. o. (2012). A UK Bill of Rights: The Choice before Us. Retrieved August 6, 2014, from https://www.justice.gov.uk/news/press-releases/cbr/the-commission-on-a-bill-of-rights-report-a-uk-bill-of-rights-the-choice-before-us

Roberts, J. (1992). Public opinion, crime, and criminal justice. *Crime and Justice, 16*, 99–180.

Rogers, D. (2007). Rights Consciousness in American History. In B. A. Shain (Ed.), *The nature of rights at the American founding and beyond* (pp. 163–180). Charlottesville: University of Virginia Press.

Romano, A. (2011). How Ignorant are Americans. *Newsweek*. Retrieved February 2, 2014 from http://www.newsweek.com/how-ignorant-are-americans-66053

Romer, D., Jamieson, K. H., & Aday, S. (2003). Television News and the Cultivation of Fear of Crime. *Journal of Communication, 53*(1), 88–104.

Rosenfeld, S. (2013). The NRA Once Supported Gun Control. *Salon*. Retrieved October 4, 2014, from http://www.salon.com/2013/01/14/the_nra_once_supported_gun_control/

Ross, T. (2013). BBC License Fee Should Be Cut or Scrapped, Poll Finds. *The Telegraph*. Retrieved July 15, 2014, from http://www.telegraph.co.uk/culture/tvandradio/bbc/10423117/BBC-licence-fee-should-be-cut-or-scrapped-poll-finds.html

Saad, L. (2011). Americans Express Mixed Confidence in Criminal Justice System. *Gallup Politics*. Retrieved September 8, 2014, from http://www.gallup.com/poll/148433/americans-express-mixed-confidence-criminal-justice-system.aspx

Saad, L. (2013). Americans Consider Individual Freedoms Nation's Top Virtue. *Gallup Politics*. Retrieved February 2, 2014, from http://www.gallup.com/poll/159716/americans-consider-individual-freedoms-nation-top-virtue.aspx

Scheingold, S. A. (2004). *The politics of rights: Lawyers, public policy, and political change* (2nd ed.). Ann Arbor: University of Michigan Press.

Schou, N. (2006). *Kill the messenger: How the CIA's crack-cocaine controversy destroyed journalist Gary Webb*. New York: Nation Books.

Sehat, D. (2011). *The myth of American religious freedom*. Oxford/New York: Oxford University Press.

Shain, B. A. (2007). *The nature of rights at the American founding and beyond*. Charlottesville: University of Virginia Press.

Shain, B. A. (2007). Rights Natural and Civil in the Declaration of Independence. In B. A. Shain (Ed.), *The nature of rights at the American founding and beyond* (pp. 116–162). Charlottesville: University of Virginia Press.

Shamir, M. (1991). Political Intolerance among Masses and Elites in Israel: A Reevaluation of the Elitist Theory of Democracy. *The Journal of Politics*, 53(4), 1018–1043. doi: 10.2307/2131865

Shirky, C. (2008). *Here comes everybody: The power of organizing without organizations*. New York: Penguin Press.

Siebert, F. S., Peterson, T., & Schramm, W. (1973). *Four theories of the press; the authoritarian, libertarian, social responsibility, and Soviet communist concepts of what the press should be and do*. Freeport: Books for Libraries Press.

Simon, S. (2014). Special Report: Taxpayers Fund Creationism in the Classroom. *Politico*. Retrieved September 4, 2014, from http://www.politico.com/story/2014/03/education-creationism-104934.html

Stark Racial Divisions in Reactions to Ferguson Police Shooting. (2014). *Pew Center for the People & the Press*. Retrieved September 21, 2014, from http://www.people-press.org/2014/08/18/stark-racial-divisions-in-reactions-to-ferguson-police-shooting/

Starr, P. (2004). *The creation of the media: Political origins of modern communications*. New York: Basic Books.

Stone, G. R. (2004). *Perilous times: Free speech in wartime from the Sedition Act of 1798 to the war on terrorism* (1st ed.). New York: W.W. Norton & Co.

Story, J. (1833). *Commentaries on the Constitution of the United States.* Boston/Cambridge Mass.: Hilliard Gray/Brown, Shattuck, and Co.

Stouffer, S. A. (1955). *Communism, conformity, and civil liberties; a cross-section of the Nation speaks its mind* (1st ed.). Garden City: Doubleday.

Stroud, N. J. (2011). *Niche news: The politics of news choice.* New York: Oxford University Press.

Sullivan, J. L., & Hendriks, H. (2009). Public Support for Civil Liberties Pre- and Post- 9/11. *American Review of Law and Social Science, 5,* 375–391.

Sullivan, J. L., Pierson, J., & Marcus, G. E. (1982). *Political tolerance and American democracy.* Chicago: University of Chicago Press.

Taibi, C. (2013). Journalists Protest Restrictions on Photographing of Obama, Compare White House to Soviet Union. *Huffington Post.* Retrieved July 24, 2014, from http://www.huffingtonpost.com/2013/11/21/white-house-photographers-protest-restrictions_n_4317284.html

Taylor, A. (2014). *The people's platform: Taking back power and culture in the digital age.* Toronto: Random House Canada.

Tebo, M. G. (2007). Who's a Citizen? Immigration reformists want to deny citizenship to 'anchor babies'. *ABA Journal, 93*(1), 30–33. doi: 10.2307/27846247

Unnever, J. D., & Cullen, F. T. (2010). The Social Sources of Americans' Punitiveness: A Test of Three Competing Models. *Criminology, 48*(1), 99–129. doi: 10.1111/j.1745-9125.2010.00181.x

Van Buren, P. (2011). No Free Speech at Mr. Jefferson's Library. *Huffington Post.* Retrieved September 27, 2014, from http://www.huffingtonpost.com/peter-van-buren/no-free-speech-at-mr-jeff_b_1116884.html

Warren, S. D., & Brandeis, L. D. (1890). The Right to Privacy. *Harvard Law Review, 4*(5), 193–220. doi: 10.2307/1321160

Webb, G. (1998). *Dark alliance: The CIA, the Contras, and the crack cocaine explosion* (Seven Stories Press 1st ed.). New York: Seven Stories Press.

Webb, G. (2005). Taking a Dive on Contra Crack: How the Mercury News Caved in to the Media Establishment. *Fairness and Accuracy in the Media.* Retrieved October 13, 2014, from http://fair.org/extra-online-articles/taking-a-dive-on-contra-crack/

Weber, C., & Thornton, M. (2012). Courting Christians: How Political Candidates Prime Religious Considerations in Campaign Ads. *Journal of Politics, 74*(2), 400–413. doi: 10.1017/S0022381611001617

Wiencek, H. (2012). The Darkside of Thomas Jefferson. *Smithsonian Magazine.* Retrieved December 6, 2014, from http://www.smithsonianmag.com/history/the-dark-side-of-thomas-jefferson-35976004/?no-ist

Will, G. (2012). The Constitutional Right to be Left Alone. *Washington Post.* Retrieved September 1, 2014, from http://www.washingtonpost.com/

opinions/the-constitutional-right-to-be-left-alone/2012/04/18/gIQA8YrlRT_story.html

Williams, J. A., Jr., Nunn, C. Z., & Peter, L. S. (1976). Origins of Tolerance: Findings from a Replication of Stouffer's Communism, Conformity, and Civil Liberties. *Social Forces, 55*(2), 394–408.

Wood, G. S. (2007). The History of Rights in America. In B. A. Shain (Ed.), *The nature of rights at the American founding and beyond* (pp. 233–257). Charlottesville: University of Virginia Press.

Woodham, C. (2008). Eastern State Penitentiary: A Prison with a Past. *Smithsonian Magazine*. from http://www.smithsonianmag.com/history/eastern-state-penitentiary-a-prison-with-a-past-14274660/?no-ist

Wozniak, K. (2014). American Public Opinion about Prisons. *Criminal Justice Review, 39*, 305–314.

Zakaria, F. (1997). The Rise of Illiberal Democracy. *Foreign Affairs, 76*(6), 22–43.

Zaller, J. (1992). *The nature and origins of mass opinion*. Cambridge England/New York: Cambridge University Press.

Index

Abernathy, Glenn, 7
Abortion and American Politics (Craig and O'Brien), 83
Abrams v. United States, 32
Accommodationists, 98–99
ACLU. *See* American Civil Liberties Union (ACLU)
Adams, John, 13–14
Advertisements
   financial information and, 163
   free press and, 49, 50
   revenues from, 53, 62, 163
Affordable Care Act, 85
African-Americans
   death penalty cases of, 181–82
   First Amendment and, xv
   punishments to, 175
   unequal rights and, 194–95
Age of Reason (Paine), 96
Alien and Sedition Act, xii, xvii, 52, 201
Alito, Samuel, 34, 123
All the News That Is Fit to Sell (Hamilton), 49
Amar, Akhil Reed, 13
Amazon, 60
American Civil Liberties Union (ACLU), 162
American democracy, 26–29
American equality, myths about, x
American exceptionalism, 72, 77
American jurisprudence, 107, 171
American political system
   based on ignorance and misperception, x
   freedom of expression in, 25–45
   freedom of speech in, 25–45
Annapolis Convention, 114
Anthony, Casey, 145–46
Anthony, Susan B., 17
Anti-Federalist, 1
   objections over bill of rights, 2–3
   suspicious of Madison's motives, 2
Anti-Islamic sentiment, 86
Articles of Confederation, 95, 114
Audiotaping, 164
Australia, 3
Authoritarian governments, xviii, 48, 133

Baltimore, city of, 13
Barron v. Baltimore, xvi, 13, 156
Beale, Robert, 172
Becker, Mary, 19
Benton v. Maryland, 139
Bible, 74, 108, 175
Bill of Rights, x, 207–212
   adoption of the Fourteenth Amendment and, 13
   after Civil War, 14
   applies equally and to everyone, xvi–xvii
   catalyst for, xi
   Commission on, 8
   criminal due process and, 199–200

cruelty of imprisonment, 201
deist nation and, 197
democracy without, 3–7
dependent news media and, 196–97
in email protection, 158
establishment clause and, 93
Fourteenth Amendment and, 14
Freedom House ratings and, 3–4
freedom of press and, xvii
freedom of religion and, xvii–xviii, 77
freedom of speech and expression, xvii, 25–45
gun ownership and, 198–99
LGBT populations and, 19–21
limited protection of, 13–17
limits of free speech and, 195–96
Madison and, 1–3
and myth of individual freedoms, xvi, 1–10
myths of, 98
myths play role in, 192–201
no wall of separation and, 197–98
political myth and, xi–xii
procedural due process and, 135–36
protected by Parliament, 8
to protect individual freedoms, xvi
protection against criminals, xviii
protection for criminals, xviii
public ignorance and, xii–xv
punishments and, 169
right of assembly, xix
right to privacy, xviii–xix, 151–67, 200
Second vs. First Amendment and, 193
to state action, 135
against state governments, 13
surveys towards, xiv–xv
technicality as, xviii
technical protections for, 133
unequal rights and, 194–95
U. S. Citizenship and, 21–23
women's protection by, 17–19
written, 5

Birth control
 health-care plans for, 16
 in workplace, 15
Blackmon, Douglas, 175
Blaine Amendment, 96
Board of Education v. Allen, 102
Boston Tea Party, 21
Bowers v. Hardwick, 20, 160
Bradfield v. Roberts, 98
Brandeis, Louis, 155
Brennan, William J., 8
Brewer, David, 78
Breyer, Stephen, 123
British Broadcasting Corporation (BBC), 58
Brown, Michael, 147
Brown v. Board of Education, 6, 102
Buckley v. Valeo, 40
Burwell v. Hobby Lobby Stores, 85

Cable television, 54, 58–59
Callins v. Collins, 170
Canadian Charter of Rights and Freedoms, 6
Carnal Knowledge (movie), 38
Carter, Jimmy, 84
CBS, 60
Cell phones, 153–54
 harassment and, 154
Censorship, 27. *See also* Free speech
Chaplinsky v. New Hampshire, 33
Chaplinsky, Walter, 33
Checks and balances, 12
Chicago, Burlington and Quincy Railroad v. Chicago, 136
Children
 citizenship, 21–22
 transportation reimbursement for, 99–100
China, news media and, 48
Christian heterodoxy, 75

Christian nation myth
  components of, 86
  constitutionalism and, 77–79
  early history of, 72–77
  established clause and, 74–76
  failure of Ely's movement, 75
  language of constitution and, 76–77
  one nation under God cases, 79–81
  people need of organized religion, 74
  RFRA Act and, 84–85
  on United States, 71–89
  variable of God and country, 79–81
The Christian Science Monitor, 108–109
Church
  creating national, 77
  establishment clause and, 94
  separating state and, 91
Church of the Holy Trinity v. United States, 78
Church of the Lukumi Babalu Aye v. City of Hialeah, 82
Citizens and citizenship
  Fourteenth Amendment and, 156–57
  freedom of expressions to, 27
  Magna Carta and, 172
  Miranda Rights and, 140–41
  rights to bear arms and, 115–16
  rule to become U. S., 21–23
  Supreme Court and, 21–23
Citizens United v. FEC, 41
City of Boerne v. Flores, 85
City of Houston v. Hill, 33
Civil Liberties, xii, 28, 133
Civil Rights Act of 1964, xv, 16, 198
Civil War, xvi, 13, 14
  Second Amendment and, 119–21
CNN, 54
Cohen v. California, 33
Comcast, 60
Commas, placement of, 116–17
Communism, 28
Community, defined, 38

Conestoga Wood Products v. Burwell, 85
Conformity, 28
Constitution, x. *See also* Bill of Rights
  deficiencies in death penalty, 182
  misreading of, 106
Constitutional law, mythological foundations of, 101–103
Contemporary politics
  Mary Ann Glendon and, xii
Context and right to privacy, 165–66
Corruption
  appearance of, 40
  in LGBT issues, 86
Craig, Barbara Hinkson, 83
Crime and punishment, 169–71
  public opinion about, 183–84. *See also* Punishments
Criminal justice system, 145–47
Criminal law, 133, 138, 199–200
"Crisis of Confidence" speech (Carter), 84
Cruel punishments, 171–78. *See also* Unusual punishments
Cultural commitment, 4, 7
Cultural resonance, 133

Davis, Derek H., 75
Davis, Morris, 191
Death penalty, 178–82
  constitutional deficiencies in, 182
Deaths, gun-related, 124
Declaration of Independence, x, 72
  implications of, 11–12
Declaration of Independence, 73
Deist nation, 197
Delau, Carl, 144
Democracy
  Madison distrust of, 2
  without Bill of Rights, 3–7
Democratic accountability, 55–57
Dirty Harry (film), 132, 133

Discrimination
  in housing, 21
  in schools, 21
  in workplace, 21
Disney, 60
District of Columbia v. Heller, 122
DNA evidence, 146
DNA testing, 132
Douglas, Stephen, 14

Economic rights, 15
Edwards v. Aguillard, 104
Eighth Amendment, 178
  cruel and unusual punishment in, 174
Elk Grove Unified School District v. Newdow, 80
Ellsberg, Daniel, 152
Employment Division v. Smith, 82
Engel v. Vitale, 101, 102
English Declaration of Rights of 1689, 173
Epp, Charles, 6
Equality
  lesbian, gay, bisexual, and transgender (LGBT), 19–21
Equal Rights Amendment (ERA), 18, 84
Escobedo v. Illinois, 140
Espionage Act, 31
Established religions, 74–75
Establishment clause, 91–112
  accommodationists and, 98–99
  Bill of Rights and, 93
  church-state debate and, 92–98
  defined, 94
  discrimination in violation of, 106
  implications of, 103–106
  jurisprudence, 99–100
  limits federal government powers, 94
  1962 and, 101–103
  perspectives on, 107
  protects state, 94
  religious liberty and, 92–93
  separationists and, 98–99
  Supreme Court and, 97–98
  violation, 80
Eugene v. Debs, 32
European Convention on Human Rights, 8
Everson v. Board of Education, 99
Ewing v. California, 178
External threat, 28

Facebook, 60, 61, 152, 163, 166
"Father of the Bill of Rights." *See* Madison, James
Federal government
  establishment clause limits the power of, 94
  Fifth Amendment and, 13
  protecting citizens against, 11–24, 135
  intellectual property and, 154
  restructuring, 114
Federalism, 12
Federalist administration, Adams's, 13
Fifth Amendment, xiv, 134
  federal government protection under, 13
Financial information
  advertisements and, 163
  right to privacy and, 162–64
Firearm ownership, 117. *See also* Gun ownership
Firearm Owners Protection Act of 1986, 122
First Amendment, xiii–xv, 192
  African-Americans and, xv
  application to citizens, 22
  establishment clause and, 94, 99
  freedom of religion and, 77
  free press and, 51
  Nazis protection and, 25, 26
  public understanding of, 194
  right to religion in, 156
  Supreme Court and, 31

First Amendment Survey, xiii
Fortune, 122
Fournier, Ron, 56
Fourteenth Amendment, xvi, 20, 21
    Bill of Rights and, 14
    due process clause, 95, 100
    Lincoln–Douglas debates and, 14
    right to privacy in, 156
Fourth Amendment, 135
    U.S. Constitution and, 141–45
Fox News, 52, 54, 56, 60
Franklin, Benjamin, 174
Freedom of expression, Jefferson's faith in, 27
Freedom of press/free press, xiv, 48–69
    as absence of prior restraint, 52
    cable television and, 58–59
    case study for, 63–66
    changing media and, 53–55
    China and, 48
    defined, 48–49
    democratic accountability and, 55–57
    democratic governance in, 49
    economic challenges in, 61–63
    economic forces influencing, 53–55
    government control over, 55–57
    government resources and, 51
    Internet and, 54, 58–59
    logics of, 51–53
    policy decisions create, 57–61
    political challenges in, 61–63
    role of digital media in, 56–63
    selling the news, 50
    social responsibility and, 49, 63
    transitioning, 53–55
Freedom of religion, xiv, 71–90
Free speech/freedom of speech, xiv
    campaign spending as, 40–41
    fighting words and, 33–35
    libel and, 39–40
    national security *versus,* 30–33
    9/11 terrorist attacks and, 28–29
    obscenity and, 37–39
    political correctness and, 35
    political tolerance and American democracy, 26–29
    speech code on campus, 35–37
    Supreme Court and, 29–30
    surveys for, 27–28
    World War I and, 31–32
    See also Freedom of expression
Furman v. Georgia, 181

Game Act, 118, 122
Garner, Eric, 147
Garner, Tyron, 160
Gender-neutral language, 19
Gideon v. Wainright, 102, 139
Gitlow v. New York, 139
Glendon, Mary Ann, xii
God
    Pledge of Allegiance under, 80–81
    variable of country and, 79–81
Godin, Seth, 59
Gompers v. Bucks Stove & Range Co., 31
Good News Club v. Milford Central School, 106
Google, 60, 152, 163
Government
    illiberal, 5
    procedural protections against, 133–34
    surveillance, 22, 151–68
    See also Federal Government
Graham, James H., 177
Graham v. West Virginia, 177
Gray, J. H. *See* Graham, James H.
Greene, Jamal, 14
Green, Steven, 96
Greenwald, Glen, 152
Griswold v. Connecticut, 77, 159
"Guidelines for Public Video Surveillance," 190
Gun control, 115
    public opinion on, 123–27

Gun Control Act of 1968, 121
Gun ownership, 113, 115, 126
  Bill of Rights and, 198–99
  UCSB shootings and, 123–24

Habitual Criminal Sterilization Act, 158
Hamilton, Alexander, 2
Hamilton, James, 49–50
Hand, Learned, 6–7
Hardwick, Michael, 160
Harvard Law Review, 155
Health data, 162–64
  right to privacy and, 162–64
Herring v. United States, 145
Hobbes, Thomas, 11, 190
Holmes, Oliver Wendell, 31
Horowitz, David, 37
Housing, discrimination in, 21
Hudson v. Michigan, 145
Human Rights Act of 1998, 8
Hurtado v. California, 136
Hustler v. Falwell, 40–41

"Illiberal" governments, 5
Illinois v. Gates, 143
Immigrants
  illegal, 22–23
  rights and protections to, 22
Immigration, foreign nations and, 21–23
Imprisonment, 172
Individual freedom, myths of
  Bill of Rights as weapon to protect, 8–9
  cultural commitment and, 5, 7
  democracy and, 3–7
  James Madison and, 1–3
  judicial protection of, 5
  Learned Hand speech about, 6–7
  Lochner era court rulings and, 14–15
  political resources and, 5
  in United Kingdom, 7–8
  value of constitutional protected rights, 7–9

Individual-level tolerance, 28
Individual liberties. *See* Individual freedom, myth of
Individual "right to bear arms," 116
Inequality, criminalization of sexual preference and, 20–21
Innocence Project, 132
Intellectual property, 154
Internet, 58
  digital democracy and, 58–59
  free speech and, 54
  See also Technology
Intolerance, of Muslims due to 9/11 terrorist attacks, 28–29
Israel, military threats in, 29

Jacobellis v. Ohio, 107
Jefferson, Thomas, x
  faith in freedom of expression, 27
  free press and, 52
  natural rights and, xi–xii
  view on slavery, 12
Jeffreys, George, 172
Johnson, Lyndon, 16
Journalists norms, 56–57
Judeo-Christian foundation, 84
Judeo-Christian traditions, xvii, 105
Judges
  individual liberty and, 5–6
  See also Supreme Court; Supreme Court cases

Katz v. United States, 77, 142, 158
Kemmler, William, 179
Ku Klux Klan, 35, 119
Kyllo v. United States, 142

Lamb's Chapel v. Center Moriches Union Free School District, 106
Language of constitution, 76–77. *See also* Free speech/freedom of speech
Lawrence, John Geddes, 160

Lawrence v. Kansas, 159
Lawrence v. Texas, 20
Legal support systems, 7
Legislative Affairs Division, 121
Lemon v. Kurtzman, 103
Leon, Richard, 162
Lesbian, gay, bisexual, and transgender (LGBT), 19–21
  equal protection for, 20
  public opinion and, 20
  speech codes on campus and, 35
Lewis v. US, 121
Limits of free speech, 195–96
Livermore, Samuel, 174
Lochner era court rulings, 14–15
Locke, John, 11

Madison, James, 1–3
  distrust of democracy, 2
  drafting Second Amendment, 118–19
  institutional framework, 12
  ten amendments as "parchment barrier," 1–2
Magna Carta, 171
Mapp, Dollree, 144
Mapp v. Ohio, 139, 143
Married Women's Property Act, 18
Mass intolerance, 28
Maxwell v. Dow, 137
McCollum, Henry, 147
McCollum v. Board of Education, 99
McDonald v. City of Chicago, 123
McReynolds, James, 121
Meyer v. Nebraska, 156–57
Microsoft, 152
Miller v. California, 38
Mill, John Stuart, 26
60 Minutes, 163
Miranda Rights, 139
Miranda v. Arizona, 102, 139

Modern communication system. *See* Internet; Newspaper; Radio; Telegraph; Television
Mormon Church, 82
Mutual Film Corp v. Industrial Commission of Ohio, 31
Myths
  of Christian nation, 71–89
  of criminal protection, 131–50
  of cruel and unusual punishment, 169–88
  defined, 71
  of dormancy, 97
  enlightenment, 72
  establishment clause, 91–112
  freedom of press, 47–70
  freedom of speech and expression, 25–46
  of government surveillance, 151–68
  of gun ownership, 131–50
  of individual freedom, 1–11
  about procedural due process, 145–47
  of technicalities and, 145–47

NAACP. *See* National Association for the Advancement of Colored People (NAACP)
National Association for the Advancement of Colored People (NAACP), 6
National Firearms Act of 1934, 121
National Journal, 56
National Prohibition Act, 142
National Rifle Association (NRA), 116
  gun control and, 121–22, 125
National security, free speech *versus*, 30–33
National Security Administration (NSA), xii, 152–53, 190
Nazi Party, 25, 26

NBC News, 147
News media
　American Founding and, 52
　political campaigns and, 60
　production from government resources, 51
　public opinion and, 146
　selling the, 50
　See also Internet; Newspaper; Radio; Television
Newspaper
　advertising revenues, 53
　credibility of, 53
　declining readership, 61–62
　quality and cost of, 53
Newsweek, xiii
New Testament, 74
New York Times, 52, 53, 55, 56, 62, 152
New York Times Co. v. Sullivan, 40
New Zealand, 3
9/11 terrorist attacks, xiv, 124
　government surveillance and Patriot Act after, 22
　individual-level tolerance and, 28–29
Nineteenth Amendment, 17
NRA. *See* National Rifle Association (NRA)
NSA. *See* National Security Administration (NSA)
Nude photographs, 37

Obama administration, 56
Obama, Barack, 55–56
O'Brien, David, 83
O'Connor, Sandra Day, 80
Old Testament, 74, 171
Olmstead v. United States, 141, 157
O'Rourke, P. J., xiv
Out of Order (Patterson), 56

Paine, Thomas, 96
Palko v. Connecticut, 139

Parchment Barrier, 1–2, 193–94, 203–204
Parliament, Bill of Rights protected by, 8
Patriot Act, xii, 22, 124, 161–62, 189
Patterson, Thomas, 56
Pauley, William III, 162
Pierce v. Society of Sisters, 157
Pledge of Allegiance, 80–81
Plessey v. Ferguson, 14
Political correctness, free speech and, 35
Political dissent, 26
Political myth
　Bill of Rights and, xi–xii
　defined, ix–xi
　See also Myths
Political resources, 4
Political rights, amorphous nature of, 201–204
Political tolerance, 26–29
Pornographic images, 37–38
Post–Civil War legislation, 117
Prayer at public school, 101–102, 105, 108
Privacy protection, public figures, 164
Procedural due process, 95
　case studies of, 136–41
　defined, 134–35
　myths about, 145–47
　origins of, 133–35
The Professors (Horowitz), 37
Public figures, privacy protection of, 164
Public ignorance
　Bill of Rights and, xii–xv
　myths and, xii–xv
Public misunderstandings, 182–84
Public opinion
　about crime and punishment, 183–84
　court decisions and, 30

in individual freedom, 7
myth of technicalities and, 145–47
research for free speech, 28
right to privacy and, 152–53
Public School Instruction Act, 104
Punishments, 169–84
   to African-Americans, 175
   criminal justice system and, 171
   cruel and unusual, 171–78
   death penalty as, 178–82
   English law and, 172–73
   imprisonment as, 170
   post–Civil War amendments for, 175
   prison isolation as, 175

Raban, David, 31
Racial discrimination, x
Radio, 53, 57, 58
Rational-basis test, 18
Ratliff, John H. *See* Graham, James H.
Reagan, Ronald, 105
Rehnquist, William, 80, 106, 107
Religion
   animal sacrifice in, 82
   establishment clause of, 74–75, 91–112
   Pledge of Allegiance and, 81–82
   and politics, 198
   See also Freedom of religion
Religious Freedom Restoration Act (RFRA), 84
Religious liberty, 72, 94, 107
   establishment clause and, 92–93
Religious pluralism, 75
Religious tolerance, 94, 197
Revenues, from advertisements, 61–62
Reynolds v. Simms, 102
Reynolds v. United States, 82, 92, 97–98
RFRA. *See* Religious Freedom Restoration Act (RFRA)
Right of assembly, xiv
Right to petition, xiv

Right to privacy, 151–67
   ambivalence about privacy, 165–66
   American beliefs about, 153
   context and, 165–66
   financial information and, 162–64
   government infringement of, 155–56
   health data and, 162–64
   Patriot Act and, 161–62
   sexual relations and, 159–61
   wiretapping and, 158–61
Right to worship, 96. *See also* Freedom of religion
Riley v. California, 142
Roberts, John, 34
Robertson, Phil, xv, 15
Roe v. Wade, 77, 83–84, 104, 159
Rogers, Daniel, 16–17
Romer v. Evans, 20
Roosevelt, Franklin, 15
Rummel v. Estelle, 177–78
Rummel, William James, 177–78

Salaita, Steven, 191
Same-sex marriages, 21
   opposition to, 86
Scalia, Antonin, 30, 81, 104, 116, 170
Schenck v. United States, 31
School District of Abbington Township v. Schempp, 102
Schools
   discrimination in, 21
   flag salute at, 79–80
   prayer laws, 101–102
Second Amendment, xviii, 113
   Civil War and, 119–21
   Game Act and, 118
   gun control and, 115
   importance of, 114
   individual "right to bear arms" and, 116
   Madison drafting, 118–19
   NRA, 121–22

placement of commas and, 116–17
post–Civil War history of, 120
Second Militia Act of 1792, 115
Second wave of disestablishment, 95–96
Sedition Act, 13, 31
Self-incrimination, xviii
Separationists, 98–99
Separation of powers, 12
Sexual relations, right to privacy and, 159–61
Shain, Barry Alan, 14
Sidis v. F-R Publishing Corp, 164
Simpson, O. J., 145–46
Sixth Amendment, xiv, 135
Skinner v. Oklahoma, 158
Slavery by Another Name: The Re-Enslavement of Black Americans from the Civil War to World War II (Blackmon), 175
Slaves and slavery
  debt, 176
  inequality of, 11
  individual's right to bear arms and, 117
  Jefferson view on, 12
Snowden, Edward, 152
Snowden leak case, 152
Social media. *See* Facebook; Twitter
Social responsibility of newspaper, 63
Social responsibility theory, 49
Speech code on campus
  political correctness and, 35
  trigger warnings and, 36
Speech, defined, 41. *See also* Free speech/freedom of speech
Stanley v. Georgia, 160
Stanton, Elizabeth Cady, 17
Starr, Paul, 57
Stewart, Potter, 107
Supernaturalism, 74
Supreme Court
  church-state debate and, 97–98
  citizenship according to, 22
  establishment clause and, 97–98
  exclusionary rule from, 132
  fighting words doctrine and, 34–35
  Fourteenth Amendment and, 15
  free speech and, 29–30
  incarceration rates, 132
  judicial ineffectiveness of, 6
  Miranda rights and, 132
  protected accused rights, 132
  protection against federal government, 13
  right to attorney and, 132
  right to privacy and, 20
  rulings protecting cell phones, 153–54
  treated First Amendment with pervasive hostility, 31
  upheld minimum-wage legislation, 15
Supreme Court cases
  Abrams v. United States, 32
  Barron v. Baltimore, 156
  Benton v. Maryland, 139
  Board of Education v. Allen, 102
  Bowers v. Hardwick, 20, 160
  Bradfield v. Roberts, 98
  Brown v. Board of Education, 102
  Buckley v. Valeo, 40
  Burwell v. Hobby Lobby Stores, 85
  Callins v. Collins, 170
  Chaplinsky v. New Hampshire, 33
  Chicago, Burlington and Quincy Railroad v. Chicago, 136
  Church of the Holy Trinity v. United States, 78
  Church of the Lukumi Babalu Aye v. City of Hialeah, 82
  Citizens United v. FEC, 41
  City of Boerne v. Flores, 85
  City of Houston v. Hill, 33
  Cohen v. California, 33
  Conestoga Wood Products v. Burwell, 85
  District of Columbia v. Heller, 122

Edwards v. Aguillard, 104
Elk Grove Unified School District v. Newdow, 80
Employment Division v. Smith, 82
Engel v. Vitale, 101, 102
Escobedo v. Illinois, 140
Eugene v. Debs, 32
Everson v. Board of Education, 99
Ewing v. California, 178
Furman v. Georgia, 181
Gideon v. Wainright, 102
Gitlow v. New York, 139
Gompers v. Bucks Stove & Range Co., 31
Good News Club v. Milford Central School, 106
Graham v. West Virginia, 177
Griswold v. Connecticut, 159
Herring v. United States, 145
Hudson v. Michigan, 145
Hurtado v. California, 136
Hustler v. Falwell, 40–41
Illinois v. Gates, 143
Jacobellis v. Ohio, 107
Katz v. United States, 77, 142, 158
Kyllo v. United States, 142
Lamb's Chapel v. Center Moriches Union Free School District, 106
Lawrence v. Kansas, 159
Lawrence v. Texas, 20
Lemon v. Kurtzman, 103
Lewis v. US, 121
Mapp v. Ohio, 139, 143
Maxwell v. Dow, 137
McCollum v. Board of Education, 99
McDonald v. City of Chicago, 123
Meyer v. Nebraska, 156–57
Miller v. California, 38
Miranda v. Arizona, 102, 139
Mutual Film Corp v. Industrial Commission of Ohio, 31
New York Times Co. v. Sullivan, 40
Olmstead v. United States, 141, 157
Palko v. Connecticut, 139
Pierce v. Society of Sisters, 157
Presser v. Illinois, 120
Reynolds v. Simms, 102
Reynolds v. United States, 82, 92, 97–98
Roe v. Wade, 77, 83–84, 104, 159
Romer v. Evans, 20
Rummel v. Estelle, 177–78
School District of Abbington Township v. Schempp, 102
Sidis v. F-R Publishing Corp, 164
Skinner v. Oklahoma, 158
Stanley v. Georgia, 160
Territory v. Ketchum, 180
Texas v. Johnson, 81
Trop v. Dulles, 181
Twining v. New Jersey, 138–39
United States v. Miller, 117
United States v. Macintosh, 78
United States v. Wong Kim Ark, 22
US v. Cruikshank, 120
US v. Jackson, 181
von Hannover v. Germany, 165–66
Wallace v. Jaffree, 108
West Virginia Board of Education v. Barnette, 79
Wilkerson v. Utah, 179
Wisconsin v. Yoder, 82
Witherspoon v. Illinois, 181
Zelman v. Simmons-Harris, 106
Zorach v. Clausen, 87, 100
Surveillance function, news media, 48
Surveys
　free speech, 27
　towards Bill of Rights, xiv–xv

Tea Party movement, 14
Technology
　public video surveillance and, 190–91
　revolutions in, 201–202
Telegraph, 57

Telegraph Agency of the Soviet Union (TASS), 56
Telephone, 57
Television, 53, 58
  crime news from, 133, 145–46
Territory v. Ketchum, 180
Terrorism
  criminal justice system and, 147
  9/11 terrorist attack, xiv, 189
Texas v. Johnson, 81
Thirteenth Amendment, 175, 176
Thomas, Clarence, 80
Time-Warner, 60
Traffic violation, 154
Trop v. Dulles, 181
Twining v. New Jersey, 138–39
Twitter, 60, 61, 166
Tyranny of absolutes, 107
"Tyranny of the majority," 5

United Kingdom, 3
  individual freedom in, 7–8
United States
  Christian nation myth on, 71–89
  Cold War tensions in, 80
  criminal justice system and, 147
  economic mobility in, x
  free press in, 49
  free speech surveys at, 27
  gun-related deaths in, 124
  news media and First Amendment, 51
  prison system in, 174
  rule to become citizen, 21–23
United States v. Macintosh, 78
United States v. Miller, 117
United States v. Wong Kim Ark, 22
Unusual punishments, 171–78
U.S. citizenship test, xiii
U.S. Constitution
  anti-federalist criticisms of, 1
  checks and balances, 12
  equality and, 12
  federalism, 12
  Fourth Amendment and, 141–45
  Madison's institutional framework and, 12
  separation of powers, 12
  value of protected rights of, 7–9
  See also specific Amendments; Bill of Rights
U.S. Postal Service, 153
US v. Cruikshank, 120
US v. Jackson, 181

Viacom, 60
Videotaping, 164
Violation
  convictions for Black Code, 176
  establishment clause, 80
  of personal privacy, 153
  right to privacy and, 155
  traffic, 154
Violence, gun-related, 121, 124
von Hannover, Caroline, 165–66
von Hannover v. Germany, 165–66
Voting
  for Blaine Amendment, 97
  property requirements for, 11
  rights to women, 17

Waite, Morrison R., 98
Wallace v. Jaffree, 108
Wall Street Journal, 62
Warrant, arrest, 144, 160
Warren, Samuel, 155
Washington, George, 114
Washington Post, 62
Watchdog function, news media, 48
Weapons, right to possess, 118–19
Web sites, porn sites, 37–38
West Coast Hotel Co. v. Parrish, 15

West Virginia Board of Education v. Barnette, 79
Whiskey Rebellion, 114
White, Bryon, 160
Wilkerson v. Utah, 179
Will, George, 159
Wiretapping, 158–61
Wisconsin v. Yoder, 82
Witherspoon v. Illinois, 181
Women
    equal protection of the laws for, 19
    legal discrimination against, 18
    patriarchal and sexist treatment of, 11
    protection by Bill of Rights, 17–19
    protection by gender-neutral language, 19
    racial discrimination against, 18
    rational-basis test and, 18
    sex-based inequality, 18
    voting rights to, 17
Wood, Gordon S., 12
Woods, William B., 120
Workplace
    birth control in, 15
    discrimination in, 21
World War I, 31–32
World War II, 25, 181

Yahoo, 60

Zelman v. Simmons-Harris, 106
Zorach v. Clausen, 87, 100

About the Authors

KIRBY GOIDEL is professor and fellow in the Department of Communication and the Public Policy Research Institute at Texas A&M University. Previously, he was the Scripps Howard Professor of Mass Communication and a professor in the Department of Political Science at Louisiana State University where he also served as director of the Public Policy Research Lab. Goidel is the author of *America's Failing Experiment: How We The People Have Become the Problem* and edited and contributed to *Political Polling in a Digital Age: The Challenge of Measuring and Understanding Public Opinion.*

CRAIG M. FREEMAN is professor of media law and entrepreneurial journalism at Oklahoma State University's School of Media and Strategic Communications. Previously, he taught at Louisiana State University where he won multiple teaching awards, served as an award winning host of Louisiana Public Square, was an elected member of the school board, and worked as an attorney specializing in media law and civil liberties. His research has been published in leading law reviews, and political science and communication journals.

BRIAN SMENTKOWSKI is the Associate Director of Faculty and Academic Development and research professor of government and justice studies at Appalachian State University. Previously, he was the co-director of the Center for Scholarship in Teaching and Learning, Professor of Political Science, and an Associate Dean of the College of Liberal Arts at Southeast Missouri State University. He has authored over 20 articles and book chapters on a broad range of topics including political parties, legislative elections, law and policy, and teaching and learning within and across the discipline.